POWER UP YOUR SMALL-MEDIUM BUSINESS: A GUIDE TO ENABLING NETWORK TECHNOLOGIES

Robyn Aber

Cisco Press

800 East 96th Street

Indianapolis, Indiana 46240 USA

Power Up Your Small-Medium Business: A Guide to Enabling Network Technologies

Robyn Aber
Copyright© 2004 Cisco Systems, Inc.
Published by:
Cisco Press
800 East 96th Street
Indianapolis, IN 46240 USA

Printed in the United States of America 1 2 3 4 5 6 7 8 9 0
First Printing March 2004
Library of Congress Cataloging-in-Publication Number: 2003100541
ISBN: 1-58705-135-4

Warning and Disclaimer

This book is designed to provide information about Internet technologies. Every effort has been made to make this book as complete and accurate as possible, but no warranty or fitness is implied.

The information is provided on an "as is" basis. The author, Cisco Press, and Cisco Systems, Inc. shall have neither liability nor responsibility to any person or entity with respect to any loss or damages arising from the information contained in this book or from the use of the discs or programs that may accompany it.

The opinions expressed in this book belong to the author and are not necessarily those of Cisco Systems, Inc.

Feedback Information

At Cisco Press, our goal is to create in-depth technical books of the highest quality and value. Each book is crafted with care and precision, undergoing rigorous development that involves the unique expertise of members of the professional technical community.

Reader feedback is a natural continuation of this process. If you have any comments regarding how we could improve the quality of this book, or otherwise alter it to better suit your needs, you can contact us through e-mail at feedback@ciscopress.com. Please be sure to include the book title and ISBN in your message.

We greatly appreciate your assistance.

Trademark Acknowledgments

All terms mentioned in this book that are known to be trademarks or service marks have been appropriately capitalized. Cisco Press or Cisco Systems, Inc. cannot attest to the accuracy of this information. Use of a term in this book should not be regarded as affecting the validity of any trademark or service mark.

Corporate and Government Sales

Publisher	**John Wait**
Editor-in-Chief	**John Kane**
Cisco Representative	**Anthony Wolfenden**
Cisco Press Program Manager	**Nannette M. Noble**
Production Manager	**Patrick Kanouse**
Development Editor	**Howard A. Jones**
Copy Editor	**Gayle Johnson**
Technical Editors	**Bob Klessig, Barbara Nolley, Saeed Sardar**
Team Coordinator	**Tammi Barnett**
Book and Cover Designer	**Louisa Adair**
Composition	**Mark Shirar**
Indexer	**Eric Schroeder**

CISCO SYSTEMS

Corporate Headquarters	European Headquarters	Americas Headquarters	Asia Pacific Headquarters
Cisco Systems, Inc.	Cisco Systems International BV	Cisco Systems, Inc.	Cisco Systems, Inc.
170 West Tasman Drive	Haarlerbergpark	170 West Tasman Drive	Capital Tower
San Jose, CA 95134-1706	Haarlerbergweg 13-19	San Jose, CA 95134-1706	168 Robinson Road
USA	1101 CH Amsterdam	USA	#22-01 to #29-01
www.cisco.com	The Netherlands	www.cisco.com	Singapore 068912
Tel: 408 526-4000	www-europe.cisco.com	Tel: 408 526-7660	www.cisco.com
800 553-NETS (6387)	Tel: 31 0 20 357 1000	Fax: 408 527-0883	Tel: +65 6317 7777
Fax: 408 526-4100	Fax: 31 0 20 357 1100		Fax: +65 6317 7799

Cisco Systems has more than 200 offices in the following countries and regions. Addresses, phone numbers, and fax numbers are listed on the
Cisco.com Web site at www.cisco.com/go/offices.

Argentina • Australia • Austria • Belgium • Brazil • Bulgaria • Canada • Chile • China PRC • Colombia • Costa Rica • Croatia • Czech Republic
Denmark • Dubai, UAE • Finland • France • Germany • Greece • Hong Kong SAR • Hungary • India • Indonesia • Ireland • Israel • Italy
Japan • Korea • Luxembourg • Malaysia • Mexico • The Netherlands • New Zealand • Norway • Peru • Philippines • Poland • Portugal
Puerto Rico • Romania • Russia • Saudi Arabia • Scotland • Singapore • Slovakia • Slovenia • South Africa • Spain • Sweden
Switzerland • Taiwan • Thailand • Turkey • Ukraine • United Kingdom • United States • Venezuela • Vietnam • Zimbabwe

About the Author

As technical marketing officer for the Commercial Segment at Cisco Systems, **Robyn Aber** defines thought leadership around the strategic and business uses of network technologies for small-medium business markets.

Before joining Cisco in May 2000, Ms. Aber had more than 25 years of IT, marketing, and strategic business development experience in pharmaceuticals/chemicals, retail, telecommunications, and data networking companies, including 3Com, Bellcore, OneWorld Systems, Sandoz, Inc. (now Novartis), and Halston. Her areas of expertise include venture development for emerging technologies, strategic alliances, and mergers and acquisitions. She also has an extensive background in broadband services.

Ms. Aber holds MBA and MS degrees from New York University and the University of Illinois, respectively, and has completed course work toward a JD degree. She has served on the boards of the SMDS Interest Group, the Corporation for Open Systems' ISDN Executive Council, and the VDSL Study Group of the DSL Forum. She also has been active in the Wi-Fi Alliance, ANSI T1E1.4, and ITU standards groups. Her more than 75 articles and white papers have been published in trade and business journals both in the U.S. and internationally. She is a frequent speaker at conferences on emerging technologies.

About the Technical Reviewers

Bob Klessig is director of engineering at Cisco Systems. Dr. Klessig leads the Metro Ethernet Services and Architecture division. He is also Vice President of the Metro Ethernet Forum where he is the co-chair of the Technical Committee, the chair of the Services Area of the Technical Committee, and a member of the board of directors.

Dr. Klessig was a founder of Telseon before joining Cisco. Telseon was the first competitive Metro Ethernet service provider to offer commercial service (February 2000) in North America.

Before joining Telseon, he was with 3Com where he developed and helped execute the corporate ATM strategy. Before joining 3Com, Dr. Klessig was at Bellcore and Bell Laboratories. While at Bellcore he led the conception, design, and specification of Switched Multi-megabit Data Service (SMDS), the first high-speed metropolitan area data service. His Bellcore responsibilities also included leading the RBOC participation and serving as Vice Chair in the IEEE 802.6 committee that wrote the IEEE standard for metropolitan area networks.

Dr. Klessig has a Ph.D. in electrical engineering and computer sciences from the University of California, Berkeley and is a co-author of the book *SMDS: Wide-Area Data Networking with Switched Multi-Megabit Data Service*.

Barb Nolley is the president and principal consultant for BJ Consulting, Inc., a small consulting firm that specializes in networking education. Since starting BJ Consulting, Barb has developed and taught training courses for Novell's Master CNE certification, as well as several courses for Cisco System's Engineering Education group and a CCNA track for the University of California-Riverside Extension. Certifications include the CCNA, CNE, and CNI. Barb lives and works out of an RV with her husband Joe. Recent ventures include working with RV Parks to set up broadband connections and Wi-Fi hotspots.

Saeed Sardar is a software development and testing engineer for Cisco Systems. Saeed works in the Cisco high-speed switching group and is responsible for all aspects of IOS services for the Catalyst 6000 family of products. His areas of specialty include Cisco multilayer switches, Cisco core routing software, intelligent super LAN cards, network protocols, and the Cisco Internetwork Operating System.

Dedications

To my husband, Bob, my soul mate and love.

And to my father, mother, and brother, Brian, a loving family and loyal boosters.

Acknowledgments

I would like to thank the following individuals for their respective contributions providing input into the book's technical solutions and underpinnings, for serving as sounding boards, and for sharing their marketing, strategic analysis, and public relations expertise: Robert Klessig, Ray Hadulco, Kathie Luedeke, Deepak Kini, Mohamed Babikir, Gautam Roy, Mauricio Perez, Lance Gallardo, Sean Beierly, Ed Kudey, Wesley Mukai, Alan Eng, Jim Christy, Albert Thong, Dan Nagel, Cory Tinkess, Michael Noonen, Julianne Whitelaw, and the Growing with Technology Awards applicants and winners, who serve as inspirations for their business visions and pursuit and achievement of success. Thanks also are due to my high school teachers Mrs. Darden and Alan Sponzilli and to professor Buzz McLaughlin for encouraging my interests in literature, the arts, and the theater, all of which I continue to draw upon in the business world as well as in my personal life.

Special thanks to John Kane, John Wait, Jim Schachterle, Howard Jones, and Doug Ingersoll of Cisco Press and Pearson Education for introducing me to the ins and outs of book publishing, and for their willingness to embrace a new and exciting target market: small-medium businesses.

Contents at a Glance

Contents

Icons Used in This Book

 Communication Server

PC

PC with Software

Sun Workstation

Macintosh

Access Server

Token Ring

Terminal

File Server

Web Server

Cisco Works Workstation

Modem

Printer

Laptop

IBM Mainframe

Front End Processor

Cluster Controller

Gateway

Router

Bridge

Hub

DSU/CSU

FDDI

Switch

Multilayer Switch

ATM Switch

ISDN/Frame Relay Switch

Network Cloud

Line: Ethernet

Line: Serial

Line: Switched Serial

Server

Content Engine

Content Switch

Introduction

To succeed and grow, small-medium businesses must identify and adopt the most effective means of operating. Essential to success are being tenacious, establishing competitive differentiation, adopting innovative (yet proven) tools to improve process efficiencies, stimulating workforce productivity, improving customer satisfaction, and boosting the company's bottom line. Internet technologies can help small-medium businesses do all this and more.

Typically, the challenge that most decision-makers face is figuring out which technologies to select and how to begin applying them. There are an overwhelming number of network technologies to choose from. Often they are described in technical jargon that is best suited for engineers, not potential business users. Most Internet technology discussions do not reflect value-creation relevance or near-term payback benefits to small-medium businesses.

This book is intended to fill the need for clear, jargon-free, business-aware Internet technology information. It is an educational guide written for business and technical decision-makers in small and midsize businesses (those with roughly 20 to 1000 computer users), across diverse vertical markets. This business value-focused technology primer does not assume that leaders possess in-depth technical expertise. It does, however, assume a familiarity with computers (desktop, laptop, and handheld) and business software, that you have outgrown the more consumer-class small office/home office (SOHO) networks designed for fewer than 20 users have outgrown, and the desire to invest in more-robust computer networking systems needed to grow an organization.

The network technologies profiled in this book, and the ways in which they are described, are targeted to CEOs, CFOs, CTOs, VPs of Operations, VPs/ Directors of IT, and CIOs who collaborate as decision-makers at growth-oriented, independent, small-midsized businesses. Those seeking to understand the business value of Internet technologies also would benefit from reading this book, because its intent is to provide an understanding of which core infrastructure, advanced, and emerging network technologies support small-midsized business goals, objectives, and applications. This book also helps prepare business leaders to develop strategic network plans and make more informed decisions about which technologies to invest in (in collaboration with advisors such as consultants, systems integrators, value-added resellers, service providers, network vendors, and so on). Furthermore, this book helps readers prepare business value-focused justifications for network technology investments. In other words, this book is designed to aid decision-makers in their understanding of networking technologies so that they can know which ones to invest in and what to ask their trusted advisors before making investments.

For every Internet technology profiled, the technology's business value is discussed. A high-level primer also discusses not only what the technology is and how it works (in plain, jargon-free language), but also the technology's business value. This book also provides examples of applications for which the technology is well-suited in small-medium businesses, its advantages and disadvantages (from business decision-maker and technical decision-maker perspectives), and key adoption criteria that decision-makers should consider.

This book is intended to be modular. It doesn't have to be read cover to cover. You can proceed directly to chapters on technologies that are of the most interest. If you are familiar with a particular technology, its business applications, and benefits, you can skip that chapter and go on to another without losing value. Alternatively, if you have a vertical market interest and you want to determine which technologies are relevant for that industry sector, you can start your reading in the vertical industry case studies chapter (Chapter 11) and get pointers to specific technologies you should read more about in the earlier chapters. Chapter 11, based on real customer implementations, is organized by industry and subindustry sectors. It showcases best practices that you can benchmark against and evolve toward as you build your own growth networks.

This book has four main parts. Part I, "The Value of Networking," highlights the evolution that is occurring from traditional business operations to electronically enabled business (e-Business) operations. It also discusses the business value of Internet technologies in general terms, provides strategic network planning considerations for small-medium business leaders, and identifies high-level factors to keep in mind when justifying Internet technology investments.

Part II, "Network Basics," which includes Chapters 2 through 6, sets the groundwork for establishing a flexible, integrated, intelligent business-class technology foundation for building a network-centric company. Topics in this part include what is a computer network, switching and routing, network security basics, intranets, extranets, and virtual private networks.

Part III, "Advanced Technologies," which includes Chapters 7 through 9, builds on the network basics. These are the technologies that are layered, along with business applications, upon a core network infrastructure. They also are the technologies that can provide competitive differentiation and enable value-added service capabilities to enhance a company's other product and service offerings and delivery methods.

Part IV, "Implementation Considerations," which includes Chapters 10 and 11, is intended to stimulate ideas about which Internet technology investments make sense in different market contexts. It also covers the alternative ways in which such technologies can be acquired and managed (insourced or outsourced), even in the limited-resource environments with which most small-medium business leaders grapple.

Powerful Internet technologies are available today that have been proven to stimulate small-medium business growth. Others continue to emerge. With this business-aware technology primer in hand, company decision-makers can play a more active role in planning, selecting, and investing in the network technologies that will support their unique visions of business success.

CHAPTER 1

PERFORMING WITH A NET: BECOMING A NETWORK-CENTRIC BUSINESS

Creating and sustaining a successful small-medium business is a formidable challenge. U.S. Census Bureau statistics highlight the fact that 10 percent or more of such businesses close their doors each year. Clearly there is no magic elixir for achieving success, or all business leaders would be quaffing it.

In spite of the challenges they face, growing companies can improve their odds of being one of the success stories. It just requires that they choose the right business focus, hire and retain talented employees, enlist competent advisors, engage reliable financial and business development partners, and adopt the right business technologies. The right technologies support growth, stimulate productivity, improve operational efficiencies, and enhance customer satisfaction. Simple, right?

Not exactly. Companies differ. There is no one formula for success. Each business must define its own targets and chart its own unique path to growth. In all the diversity and choices that can be made, there is one key given: technology. Technology is the common denominator that is needed across all businesses. Technology is essential to allow businesses to achieve more with less in tough times and to propel their momentum in good times. Internet technologies such as broadband, wireless, IP telephony, switching, and routing are vital resources to the opening and expanding of markets for small-medium companies. They allow smaller companies to be more adaptable and agile and to appear larger than they are. How Internet technologies can do this, and the unique business and investment value each technology can deliver, are discussed throughout this book.

Although Internet technologies can be powerful assets, business leaders must be committed to change if they plan to implement them and their associated applications. Workflows and processes, by necessity, must become more streamlined for these technologies to deliver on the promise of greater efficiency and cost-effectiveness. If executives are dead set against change and want to maintain the old ways of operating, there is no good reason to expend the fixed and recurring costs associated with making a company network-centric. Business technologies should be adopted only as a means to effect business process transformation, achieve a company's objectives more competitively, and deliver stakeholder value, not just to automate existing functional processes.

Along with process change comes organizational dynamics change. As small-medium businesses adopt Internet technologies for their asset value, they also tend to move away from relying on information technology (IT) as a pure support function to treating it as one that is more collaborative and integral in nature. Generally, business and technical decision-makers start working together more closely to chart the company's strategies and plan jointly how best to execute them. In fact, one of the key objectives of this book is to foster and promote closer collaboration between these decision-makers.

These new cross-functional collaborations are effective only if IT decision-makers understand how their business is measured for success and can justify technologies in business-relevant language. Conversely, business decision-makers must become more technically savvy—at least to the extent that they are familiar with the leading technologies and how they can help increase business value. By working together, rather than separately, business and technology executives can pool their knowledge and skills to generate tangible business value from all their investments, including Internet technologies.

Companies that are pursuing the transition to network enablement are often called electronic businesses (or e-businesses). Interestingly, virtually no executive at these companies, if asked, would say unprompted, "We are an e-business." Part of the reason for this is that companies using Internet technologies and associated business applications have adopted them incrementally and now take them for granted. As soon as a company has integrated technologies and applications into its core business operations, the "e" in e-business seems redundant; it is just assumed to be the new business as usual. At least, that is the ideal: for Internet technologies to become intrinsic to the conduct of successful business processes and practices (and therefore to be unobtrusive and invisible to end users). Technology for technology's sake is unacceptable.

The Business-to-E-Business Evolution

An e-business relies on the application of Internet and related technologies to the business and to the integration of a company's systems, processes, organizations, and value chains. Figure 1-1 shows the types of interactions that occur. E-business enablement is more than web commerce. It is about using technologies to improve productivity, efficiency, and profitability. Research shows that e-businesses, on average, tie together 39 percent of their customer, supplier, and partner value chain members. In doing so, their spending on e-business projects has risen every year since the burst of the Internet bubble in 2000, to the point where it now comprises 28 percent or more of all technical spending.

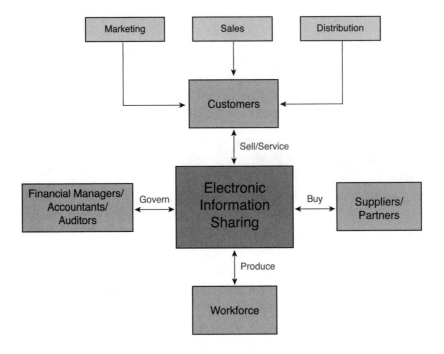

Figure 1-1   *E-Business Relationship Model*

E-Businesses Mirror Traditional Business Management

Actually, the underpinnings of being an e-business are not radically different from that of traditional, offline business management. The same principles apply. It is just the ways in which they are put into practice that differ. For that reason, e-business capabilities can be applied to all businesses. What most often drives the move to deploy e-business systems and applications is the desire to provide convenient customer service, to become more effective in dealing with partners, and to improve process efficiencies to achieve cost savings. Here are some reasons small-medium business executives give for their investigations into e-business enablement:

- Their customers expect increasingly faster service, self-service, and more extensive product and service selections.

- They want to attract new customers across broader geographic markets.

- They must start delivering goods and services more quickly, often in real-time, to remain competitive.

- They cannot handle the management of all company processes, at the quality levels desired, with their limited resources and current systems. They deal with this by keeping essential, mission-critical processes (those that contribute to the business's competitive advantage) in-house and streamline them using Internet technologies. If critical processes must be outsourced to service providers, e-business leaders maintain tight control over how they are operated and ensure that electronic linkages with the in-house processes are enabled. Functions and processes that represent no immediate risk to the business's sustainability are entrusted to others, with little concern about controlling their management.

E-Business Applications and Technologies

E-business applications, and the Internet technologies that enable them, are typically adopted progressively, in steps. Companies start with those that are more tactical and then gradually migrate to ones that are more strategic and collaborative in nature. The nine types of e-business systems described in this section are those that small-medium businesses most often implement. Their order corresponds to commonly followed deployment phases.

Table 1-1 summarizes the network technologies that small-medium businesses have installed to support such applications. The technologies highlighted in the table allow e-business applications to operate at high speeds (high performance) and with security, confidentiality, flexibility of location, and systems reliability. This usually results in a desirable level of customer satisfaction and workforce productivity, as well as cost savings for the company. Given the redundancy with which the same Internet technologies appear in the table, it should be evident that they are versatile. Company leaders therefore should ensure that their network technology investments are leveraged to their fullest extent. To help understand how best to do that, each Internet technology listed in the table is explained fully in subsequent chapters of this book.

Table 1-1   *E-Business Applications and Enabling Internet Technologies*

E-Business Application	Enabling Internet Technologies
Customer care	Broadband infrastructure, IP telephony, wireless LAN (WLAN), security, virtual private network (VPN), intranet, extranet, storage network
Web marketing	Broadband infrastructure, IP telephony, storage network, security
E-commerce	Broadband infrastructure, IP telephony, extranet, security
Web communications	Broadband infrastructure, WLAN, IP telephony, security
E-procurement	Broadband infrastructure, security, extranet, VPN, intranet, IP telephony, WLAN, storage network
Financial management	Broadband infrastructure, security, storage network, VPN, intranet
Workforce optimization	Broadband infrastructure, WLAN, VPN, intranet, security IP telephony, storage network
Manufacturing and distribution	Broadband infrastructure, security, extranet, VPN, intranet, IP telephony, WLAN, storage network
Sales force automation	Broadband infrastructure, WLAN, VPN, intranet, security, IP telephony

Application Categories

The nine e-business application categories described here are the ones most often implemented by small-medium businesses. These applications are used to improve internal and external communications, to extend brand awareness, to sell products online, to improve business process efficiencies, to boost workforce productivity, and more. Depending on its business priorities, a company will adopt some or all of these applications. There is no "right" mix and no "right" order of adopting them that can be generalized across all small-medium businesses. Each company must assess its business needs and invest in the applications and enabling technologies that are right for its own situation.

- **Customer care**—When businesses interact with customers, the more touch points (website, letters, e-mail, phone calls, sales calls, service visits, and so on), the better. Customer care e-business systems allow small-medium businesses to integrate communications and service channels into a cohesive knowledge base that can be tapped for more responsive, personalized, and profitable relationships. Because the cost of acquiring new customers greatly exceeds the cost of retaining existing customers, businesses should focus their resources on aggressively targeting and retaining their most attractive customers and on expanding their base of profitable customers. One of the best ways to achieve this is to implement a customer care system. This is the combination of hardware, software, and Internet capabilities needed to gather, manage, and share customer intelligence that can be used to create and deliver web-based marketing, sales, and customer service programs.

- **Web marketing**—Online direct marketing provides a channel for companies to expand their market reach, extend brand recognition, and contact customers with personalized messages. It can include promotional opt-in e-mailing (already used by more than 15 percent of small businesses and 35 percent of medium businesses), online advertising (banners placed on websites that targeted customers are likely to visit), electronic newsletters, and web-based loyalty programs. Web marketing is being used by an increasing number of small-medium businesses to integrate their traditional operations with online tools and services. They use it because it provides a flexible, customizable, and cost-effective means to reach and engage customers.

- **E-commerce**—Transactions can be performed anywhere along the continuum, from the display of a simple, static website (essentially an online brochure) to a fully interactive web-based ordering and e-marketplace portal for customers, agents, and trading partners (for online buying and selling). At the more sophisticated end of its spectrum, e-commerce allows companies to build one-on-one relationships with customers and to provide promotions and service features that are personalized to specific customers' purchase and product preference patterns. e-commerce can be employed to reduce sales costs, increase customer and market reach, boost revenues, improve inventory management, build stronger branding, and stimulate operational efficiencies for economic and competitive advantage.

- **Web communications**—Employees are as likely to receive an e-mail as a phone call to conduct business nowadays. Text-oriented e-mail is the most obvious form of web communication that companies can employ, but it is by no means the only one. Increasingly popular are multimedia e-mails (containing graphics and other streaming media), instant messaging, web-based videoconferencing, web-based fax (called fax over IP [FoIP]), and unified messaging capabilities that integrate data, voice, and video communications. Web-based communications are immediate and personal, they aid collaborative work processes, they have unlimited reach, and they can reduce travel costs. The information that is exchanged can be timely and rich in content as long as the network carrying the web exchanges is equipped with the performance characteristics to support such content at high speeds.

- **Web-based electronic procurement**—E-procurement, either through individual suppliers or online marketplaces and exchanges, gives employees access to approved materials and supplies, along with buying authority (up to preset thresholds). Product selections and payment terms are predetermined by the Purchasing Department. Distributed procurement gives all employees, but especially those at branch offices or remote sites, more flexibility to get what they need fast. It also allows Purchasing to focus on bigger issues, such as finding the best sources and prices for the goods that make the business thrive.

Additionally, e-procurement streamlines negotiation and contracting processes, automates purchasing for improved order fulfillment accuracy, and improves transaction reporting and tracking. It increases efficiency and speed by eliminating redundant tasks (improving productivity), helps manage suppliers, improves information flows, reduces paperwork, and lowers the overall cost of the purchasing process. With an e-procurement system in place, companies can locate suppliers with the best prices and quality and increase their buying power by qualifying for volume discounts when purchases are made through preferred vendors.

- **Financial management**—Finance departments produce the data that measures a company's financial health. The financial data guides the company's decisions about new opportunities and the strengthening of weaknesses. Some of the key roles of financial management are to monitor the business's financial performance, prepare forecasts and budgets, maintain records, oversee accounting and governance procedures, and ensure that there is enough cash to meet both current obligations and emerging prospects. It is critical that the Finance Department be able to provide decision-makers with current information. Business leaders and managers use this information to make decisions on the company's strategies, expansion or reduction plans, and so on. With web-based financial management systems and processes, companies can streamline needed management processes, provide real-time financial information (general ledger, fixed assets, accounts payable, accounts receivable, tax accounting, and so on), improve revenue management, and reduce administrative costs.

- **Workforce optimization**—A wide range of human resources functions can be moved onto the network to improve employee productivity, satisfaction, and retention. Workforce optimization systems let employees focus more on the core value and strategic aspects of their jobs and less on routine administrative processes. Typical systems are of two types: communications based (composed of news from management and other company reference information) and transaction based (mostly forms that employees complete and submit online rather than on paper). By using these systems, employees can view and modify benefits or payroll information, open requisitions to hire or reassign staff, create career development road maps, participate in training, submit expense reports, book travel, request and track vacation time, review company policies, check the employee directory, and so on. Self-service tools such as these help employees gather information easily and let them manage transactions on the web for faster responsiveness and improved productivity.

- **Manufacturing and distribution**—Manufacturing and distribution systems help minimize material and inventory costs, compress planning cycles for new products, and decrease lead times needed to help bring products to market faster. With the proper systems in place, companies can forecast better, improve cycle times, and change management. The impact is that production and delivery schedules can be managed to more closely correspond with changing market and customer needs. With improved communications, supplies can be located more quickly, and production bottlenecks can be identified and resolved efficiently. Internet-connected manufacturing systems also improve raw material control, inventory management, and information flows between production, assembly, subcontracting, and shipping processes.

- **Sales force automation (SFA)**—Sales teams thrive on accurate, up-to-the-minute information about customers, competitors, and company products. Sales force automation systems let salespeople find new prospects, check prices and inventories, place orders, and manage expenses through a single portal that is easily accessible 24/7/365 via PCs or handheld computers. By automating sales efforts, you can efficiently forecast, track, and fulfill orders, analyze sales and competitor trends, manage the sales pipeline, and reach sales representatives whether they are in the office or in the field. Such a system frees salespeople to spend more time on productive selling and less time on sales administration processes.

Implementing e-business systems and their enabling Internet technologies requires that the IT organization and business teams work closely and collaboratively. They must start by being aware of the key e-business applications in which technologies can be used. Analyst data show that 42 percent of companies' revenues have significantly increased as a result of implementing e-business systems. As well, 59 percent of companies surveyed report significant cost savings from their e-business applications and technologies.

The Business Value of Internet Technologies

Achieving business value with technology is about more than producing a quantifiable return on investment (ROI) for a piece of equipment. Technology-enabled business value encompasses the ability to increase customer satisfaction, stimulate revenue growth, increase profitability, improve workforce productivity, reduce risks, and optimize assets. The extent to which each is weighted, and ultimately achieved, varies from industry to industry and company to company. Generally, productivity improvement is viewed as a vital attribute for near-term small-medium business value creation. Partly that is so because productivity improvement is a means by which decision-makers can tangibly recognize and measure the positive impact of their technology investments on daily operations. Productivity is generally defined to include employee time savings, better overall resource utilization, streamlined efficiency, improved process effectiveness (including higher customer satisfaction), and lower costs.

A computer network infrastructure (or architecture), if properly aligned with a business's goals, can serve as a foundation and enabler for key applications, innovation that contributes to competitive advantage, and sustainable growth. Table 1-2 highlights the business transformation changes that small-medium business leaders can achieve by implementing appropriate Internet technologies (and by coupling them with solid business management). Other business value benefits that Internet technologies help deliver include the following:

- **Convenience**—For enabling self-services

- **Effectiveness**—Such as greater responsiveness to partners, suppliers, and customers

- **Efficiency**—Resulting from less redundancy of roles and data and easier integration across internal structures and functional operations

- **Closer working relationships**—As a result of information flowing easily across the company and to external value chain participants

Table 1-2 *Value Impact of Internet Technologies on a Business*

Less	More
Reactive	Preemptive
Tactical, activity-focused	Strategic, results-focused
Individual	Collaborative
Discrete	Integrated
Generalized	Personalized
Supply chain-oriented	Supply mesh-oriented
Organizational	Multiorganizational
Formulaic and restrictive	Innovative and enabling
Linear and hierarchical	Flexible
Slow	Real-time, interactive
Centralized	Decentralized
Location-specific	Location irrelevant, virtual, and mobile

By blending business goals and technology strategies for value creation, companies can build shareholder value and respond to organizational needs. Analyst research finds that almost 90 percent of business executives believe that IT investments enable the company's business strategies. What is needed is a formal method to bring business and technical experts and practices together to determine the business value benefits of Internet technologies to the company. That method is the creation of a strategic network plan.

Strategic Network Planning Considerations

With a strategic network systems plan, a company can significantly improve its chances of getting projects approved and funded. A network plan lets the company consciously and methodically review business and IT goals and combine them. It is the best way to achieve process efficiencies, cost savings, more responsive customer services, better collaboration with trading partners, and, ultimately, enhanced revenues and productivity.

A strategic network systems plan should tie together business objectives with networking technologies for both the short and long term. In other words, it should plainly state how technology can help a company reach its efficiency, productivity, and revenue goals.

Creating a Strategic Network Plan

At first, drafting a strategic systems plan might sound daunting, but it really is not. The plan can be created in a fairly short document, requiring just a brief time commitment from participants. In turn, it has the potential to deliver tremendous benefits to an organization for many years to come.

These are the steps to follow to get a strategic systems plan started:

Step 1 Get a copy of the company's strategic business plan to identify its overall business objectives and priorities. If no plan exists, the process of creating the network systems plan will help identify the company's strategic goals.

Step 2 Form a task team made up of business leaders, technical team leaders, and, in some cases, a trusted consultant or other outside advisor. Discuss the company's business priorities for the next 6 months, 12 months, and 18 months (at a minimum). This discussion should focus on what works well in the company, what doesn't, and what should be improved.

Step 3 Identify the kinds of network systems that support and enable the business issues and priorities just discussed.

Step 4 Conduct an IT and network audit to understand which business technologies are already in place and how they match the company's goals. It is important to determine the strengths and shortcomings of current systems and their relative importance to the business's objectives.

With these steps, a strategic network systems plan can be devised. This plan should spell out the following:

- **The company's business requirements paired with the corresponding technology (hardware, software, and services) systems that address them**—Analysts claim that more than 80 percent of those who have gone through the Internet technology for e-business application justification and investment process believe their implementation efforts resulted in IT's being more closely aligned with corporate strategy. Figure 1-2 highlights the perspectives that business decision-makers and technical decision-makers bring to the planning process and how they must come together in their thinking.

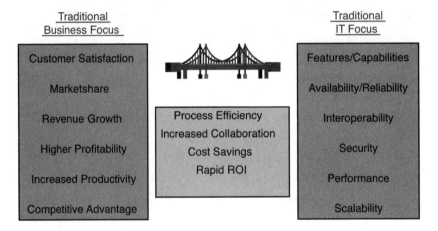

Traditional Business Focus		Traditional IT Focus
Customer Satisfaction		Features/Capabilities
Marketshare		Availability/Reliability
Revenue Growth	Process Efficiency Increased Collaboration Cost Savings Rapid ROI	Interoperability
Higher Profitability		Security
Increased Productivity		Performance
Competitive Advantage		Scalability

Figure 1-2   *Blending Priorities for Business Value Creation*

- **A timeline for investment and deployment that shows how the timeline tracks to the priorities in the overall company business plan**—Not every small-medium business needs every available computer networking technology—at least, not to start. Phasing, based on knowing what can and cannot be accomplished with each technology, should shape the investment plan.

- **A robust network architecture design**—Technology blueprints should be devised that include a network map of where the company is today technically and how the leadership team plans to build the network in an evolutionary way.

- **An anticipated budget**—The budget should include all costs (equipment, services, training, ongoing management, technical support, and so on).

- **Metrics to measure the success of Internet technology and associated investments**—This helps build credibility for future investments.

Today, all companies large and small, must justify their IT expenditures for business value. This strategic network plan is essential. It will guide the company's technology acquisitions for years to come, while delivering the greatest functionality and value.

Justifying Internet Technology Investments

The strategic network plan should serve as a business value framework that helps decision-makers evaluate and justify IT investment options. As part of the planning process, it is important for executive decision-makers to decide if they want to lead or follow IT trends that relate to their industry sector. Doing so will facilitate future justification processes. Small-medium businesses can take more rapid action to approve and adopt Internet technologies as soon as company strategy, technology support linkages, and investment priorities have been spelled out. With those issues resolved, the justification process becomes more focused on how to seize opportunities as they arise, and not how to react to competitors who have taken a market lead. Companies cannot afford to miss very many "first-in wins" opportunities and expect to succeed as a business.

Business investments (including those for Internet technologies) are most effective if they are justified as a part of a portfolio of assets rather than as discrete, independent projects (the traditional IT approach). The goal is to think of IT investments aligning with the company's balance sheet. This involves not only diversifying the new capital expenditures that are made, but also leveraging existing infrastructure investments to derive their full value. Figure 1-3 suggests three possible buckets for IT portfolio diversification and relative spending and payback objectives within each.

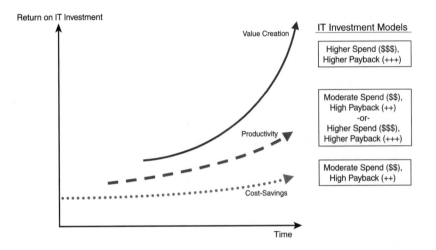

Figure 1-3   *Business Goals and Investment Strategies*

Asking the Right Questions

Deciding whether and how to justify a technology depends on a company's ability to deploy the technology and the potential benefits to be realized from adopting it. Company leaders must become skilled at evaluating and making sound investments in the technologies that will support their corporate strategies. Companies can achieve this by better understanding network technology options and asking questions such as the following:

- Which vertical industry trends or changes will the company address?

- Which e-business processes is the company currently using? Which one(s) is/are planned or under consideration?

- What strategic, operational, or process improvements (including effects on revenues, cost of goods sold, operating expenses, earnings, and so on) are anticipated?

- What are the new investment(s) goals? How important is direct payback?

- Do potential investments represent an innovative way to attract and retain customers?

- What are the risks to the company if an investment fails?

- What are the metrics for success (for example, eliminating redundant systems, expanded market coverage, increased market share, higher customer satisfaction, better resource utilization, improved cost savings or time savings, more on-time deliveries, greater service accuracy, and so on) and how will they be measured?

Competitive Advantage

Gaining competitive advantage is a key justification factor for enabling a small-medium business with Internet technologies. Building competitive advantage almost always involves technology. A number of elements comprise competitive advantage:

- **Time to market**—Timing is key. Getting and staying ahead of the competition is a must.

- **Customer focus**—All businesses need to be customer-centric. The popular battle cry is, "Hug a customer today!" Companies with successful e-business initiatives tend to be at or near the top of their industry sectors as a result of adopting such systems. Often the way they succeed at customer care is to let customers do more for themselves by providing self-service capabilities to speed up their business interactions.

- **Process improvements**—In some cases, processes might have to be redesigned or rearchitected to get the most out of them in the new e-business environment. A critical consideration for potential Internet technology acquirers is to consider the proposed system's adaptability to changing environments. When justifying Internet technologies, it is important to ensure that they are modular enough and their implementation capabilities flexible and scalable enough to be adapted as needed to new business models or market conditions throughout the defined payback period.

- **Cost savings**—Successfully taking costs out of current business processes via e-business enablement is another way for IT leaders to create credibility. If the network foundation that is established to support e-business applications and associated technologies flexibly can handle incremental software and hardware upgrades and enhancements, that system will deliver a lower total cost of ownership (TCO) than one that is nominally less expensive at initial purchase but also less flexible in its design.

Establishing and Maintaining Credibility

Credibility and business technology investments go hand in hand. It is important not only to tie technologies to business value, but also to know when to try to justify technologies using hard, quantifiable dollar figures and when not to. If the numbers presented are forced and inconsequential, the value of the proposed IT investment could lose its credibility (as would the person proposing it). ROI justifications cannot be made for every investment, especially those that address risks and negative impacts to an organization, because they cannot be directly linked to revenue gains. With some investments, it is better to accept that they will deliver soft versus hard benefits and to justify them accordingly.

To Lease or Not to Lease

A consideration worth weighing relatively early to midway through the justification process is whether to pursue lease financing to help reduce the overall cost of Internet technologies. Leases are usually available in short-term (less than one year payback) and long-term (more than one year payback) options. Technology vendors, value-added resellers (VARs), and financing companies provide a variety of lease types from which to choose. Here are some of the most common lease types:

- **Capital leases**—These work like a loan. Lessees build equity in their technology equipment as they make payments.

- **Operating leases**—These are considered "off the balance sheet." Monthly payments are expensed as budget items.

- **True leases**—These give lessees the option to purchase their technology equipment, at fair market value, at the end of the lease term.

One of the primary benefits of lease financing to small-medium businesses is that it helps them do the following:

- Manage growth by increasing their purchasing power.

- Prevent technology obsolescence with options for upgrades and equipment swaps possible throughout a lease term.

- Eliminate risk by allowing equipment to be returned at the end of the lease without regard for book value.

- Manage budgets because lease payments are predictable and fixed.

Companies that explore financing options should be prepared to provide lessors with information such as the following:

- Company's legal name and its location

- Credit application

- Several years' worth of financial statements (audited is usually preferred)

- Interim financial statements for the current year

- Company business plan (for newer-stage companies)

- Two to three years of company financial projections (for newer companies)

- Financing proposal

Monitoring Payback

After Internet technology investments have been justified and systems have been adopted, business leaders should monitor the benefits and payback they achieve with them to establish a track record for future proposals. Analyst research finds that more than 60 percent of IT executives say their companies closely analyze the value of their e-business efforts. In fact, small-medium businesses are more likely to do so than their larger counterparts. That same 60 percent significantly increase company revenues as a result of their e-business investments over a period of several years. And more than 70 percent realize measurable cost savings (costs such as transactions, customer acquisition and retention, non-IT staff, non-IT capital expenditures, travel, and logistics and warehousing).

Summary

Business decision-makers and technical decision-makers have a lot of choices to make in the running of their business. The one choice that is a given is the need for technology. Technology lets small-medium companies achieve more with fewer resources and to gain momentum in their drive toward sustainable success. By relying on the application of technologies to the integration of the company's systems, processes, organizations, and value chains, businesses assume the moniker of e-business.

Small-medium businesses typically adopt nine categories of e-business applications (customer care, web marketing, e-commerce, and so on). Internet technologies are used to support and enable these applications as a business operations foundation. The overall goal of combining software business applications with Internet and other technologies is to achieve business value. Business value is comprised of customer satisfaction, revenue growth, increased profitability, productivity improvements, lower risk, and asset optimization.

Companies can ensure that they remain focused on achieving desired value metrics by methodically developing a strategic network plan. This plan should be the result of collaborative efforts between a company's business and technical leaders. After they have jointly determined the best technologies to support company plans and objectives, the final essential step they must perform before adoption and implementation is to justify network technologies in business value terms. Knowing when to use hard and soft benefits, and considering creative options such as lease financing, are essential to this process. Growing companies can improve their odds of success by blending management know-how with Internet technologies to achieve desired elements of business value.

CHAPTER 2

WHAT IS A COMPUTER NETWORK?

A network is a group of two or more computers interconnected with various networking equipment. The computers can communicate with one another to share data (text, graphics, e-mail, spreadsheets, customer records, files, programs, sound, moving images, and so on). Each authorized user in a network can access shared files, distributed applications, and peripheral devices (printers, faxes, storage devices, and others) anywhere on the network. Networks are a cost-effective means to eliminate the purchasing of expensive devices for each employee or desktop.

Key Components of a Network

The basic equipment needed for a small-medium business network includes network interface cards (NICs), wired or wireless connection media, and networking software. Most networks also contain one or more hubs and/or switches to act as connection points for the computers and one or more routers to connect multiple networks within the company with networks outside the company. Each of these elements is illustrated in Figure 2-1 and described in the following sections. The figure shows how these components relate to each other and enable business services.

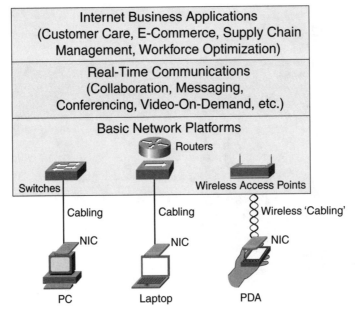

Figure 2-1   *Local Network Components*

NICs

Network interface cards (NICs or adapters) physically connect a computer to a network and allow the computer to talk to the network. They also provide the means for a network cable to connect to a computer. There must be a NIC on each computer or device in the network. NICs can be internal or external to the computer. On desktop computers, they usually are in a slot inside the computer. Laptop computers generally use external cards that fit into a PCMCIA (Personal Computer Memory Card International Association) slot. NICs play a vital role in determining a network's speed and performance. Often computers come with Ethernet interfaces built in. If that is the case, there is no need for a separate NIC.

Network Media

Network media options consist of twisted-pair cables, coaxial cables, single or multimode fiber-optic cables, and wireless. Each of these media are discussed in this section. Here are some important factors to keep in mind when considering network media:

- Desired transmission rate

- Distance over which the medium will operate

- Installation factors such as available space in conduits

- Environmental conditions in the office building and surrounding areas, such as electrical noise caused by heavy machinery

- Cost

Twisted-Pair Cable

Twisted-pair cable consists of two copper wires, each coated with plastic insulation, twisted together and enclosed in a protective outer sheath. The twists help improve signal transmissions and network communications reliability by making the cabling more resistant to electromagnetic interference (EMI). Typically, several pairs of wires are bundled into a cable. The most commonly used grades of twisted-pair cable are Category 3 (Cat 3) and Category 5 (Cat 5). Each type of twisted-pair cable offers different performance levels. It is important that the selected category support the performance level that is needed by business applications. Cat 3 is generally limited to supporting network traffic at speeds up to 10 megabits per second (Mbps) within an office, and Cat 5 runs up to 1000 Mbps for distances of up to 328 feet (100 meters). Furthermore, twisted-pair cabling can be either shielded (covered in an electrical conductor) or unshielded.

Twisted-pair cable used in Ethernet networks (the most common type of network) is usually unshielded twisted pair (UTP). Some of the advantages of twisted-pair cabling are that it is inexpensive, well understood, and easy to install and scale. Disadvantages are that it is sensitive to noise and interference, operates over only short distances (up to a few hundred feet), and has security vulnerabilities in that it can be tapped. In most office environments, sensitivity to interference is not a problem. However, it can be an issue in a factory, with its heavy electrical equipment, or in an elevator shaft.

Coaxial Cable

Coaxial cable (often called coax) is composed of one copper wire with another layer of conductor shielding it. Signals are encoded on coax in two ways: baseband and broadband. This broadband is different from the type of broadband that is used for wide area access systems and that is discussed in the "Bandwidth" section. The maximum distances that can be successfully achieved with coax (up to 1600 feet or 500 meters) are higher than that of UTP. Coax is potentially capable of very high data rates because its capacity in bits per second (bps) is proportional to the diameter of its inner conductor. It is also more immune to interference than UTP. However, as this medium gets thicker, it also becomes more difficult to work with and more expensive. Very few new small-medium business networks are being designed with coaxial cable because of these factors.

Fiber-Optic Cable

Fiber-optic cable (often called fiber) offers an alternative to coaxial cable for wired networks. Although a coaxial cable has 10,000 times the diameter of the glass fibers used for optical communications, it actually supports less bandwidth than fiber systems, which can support up to 100 gigabits per second (Gbps) or higher. The higher the frequency of the laser (or LED) light beam that sends the signal in a fiber system, the higher the bandwidth (the range of frequencies) delivered. A fiber-optic cable also can contain many more physical transmission strands than a coaxial cable because of the difference in size of each individual strand. When the bandwidth per strand and the number of strands are combined, the potential capacity of fiber becomes staggering.

Two types of fiber are available: single mode and multimode. Single mode can transmit data over longer distances (50 times farther, for up to 30 miles or 48 kilometers) and at higher rates than multimode. It is much smaller in diameter than multimode fiber. In fact, it is so small that only a single ray (mode or signal) of light can pass through it.

Multimode fiber, because it is larger, allows multiple light rays (or signals) to pass through it concurrently. As length increases, the modes begin to interfere with each other; thus, multimode transmission is used for shorter distances (up to 3000 feet or 914 meters). It is the main type of fiber used in Gigabit Ethernet networking.

Single-mode fiber is more expensive than multimode fiber, and because it is more difficult to splice on connectors, it also is more expensive to install. Given these factors, fiber cabling is often used for campus backbone connections that link the local networks in various buildings.

Some of the benefits of fiber-optic cable are that it delivers very high bandwidth, noise interference immunity (which is especially important in manufacturing environments), the ability to be deployed across long distances, high security (it cannot be tapped without notice), and a small deployment footprint. Its disadvantages are that it requires connections between segments when it is installed, and those connections must be spliced by experts to ensure reliable signal transmission. Fiber also is more expensive than coaxial cabling for short runs. It typically is most cost effective in runs that are greater than 3000 feet.

Wireless Connections

Another option for "cabling" is the air—the medium used for wireless connections from a computer, peripheral, or handheld device to the network. Wireless connections can be provided as an adjunct to physical cabling. In wireless, electromagnetic waves are transmitted through space to connect users in a network. The portions of the wireless spectrum that are usually deployed in such networks are infrared (also called IR or optical wireless), microwave, and radio waves or radio frequencies (RF). Infrared often is used by devices such as laptop and handheld computers for point-to-point communications where line of sight (LOS) transmission is assured.

Wireless is used in several different types of networks that operate over increasing distances:

- **Personal area networks (PANs)**—Devices worn or carried by an individual.

- **Local area networks (LANs)**—Span a building or campus.

- **Metropolitan area networks (MANs)**—A fixed last mile access alternative to digital subscriber line (DSL) and cable modems, used to connect multiple locations (even in wide area networks).

The benefits of using wireless are that it offers users the flexibility to be mobile and work in places where hard-wire cabling would be impractical or impossible to install. Wireless can also be combined with various types of access technologies for different parts of a network. Wireless enables faster setup time than fully wired networks and can extend the coverage of wired broadband access systems. The disadvantages of wireless as a network cabling medium are that it can suffer from various types of interference, often requires a clear line of sight to transmit signals, provides a limited amount of bandwidth compared to wired LANs, and is vulnerable to interception of data and other security breaches if it isn't secured properly.

Hubs, Switches, and Routers

Hubs are the devices to which cables connect from computers. For the most part, hubs have been replaced by LAN switches in business-class small-medium business (versus home-based business or consumer) networking environments.

Switches are used in a LAN to control the flow of data and handle the transfer of packets between network components. Typically, they are used to improve the performance of Ethernet networks by dividing (or segmenting) large, congested LANs into smaller LANs with fewer data collisions.

Routers are more intelligent devices than switches. In addition to linking networks and directing packets to the proper destination, they also can select the best transmission route from among various alternatives. This is useful whenever segments of a network are down. A router can redirect data traffic around a congested network segment to ensure that it reaches its destination in a timely manner. Routers also are used to connect LANs to WANs using DSL, Integrated Services Digital Network (ISDN), Frame Relay, or dedicated leased lines (T1/E1 or T3/E3 private lines).

Chapter 4, "Network Foundation Technologies—Switching and Routing," provides a more in-depth discussion of switching, routing, and hubs.

Types of Networks

A fundamental way to characterize a network is by size. Using this method, the most common types of data communications are local area networks (LANs), metropolitan area networks (MANs), and wide area networks (WANs). Figure 2-2 illustrates these network size differences.

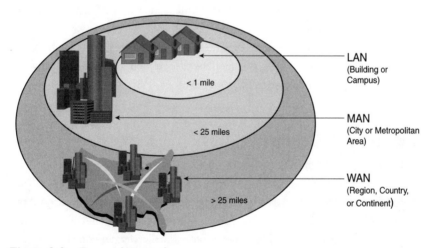

Figure 2-2   *Types of Networks*

Network Size

In a LAN, computers are connected across a short distance (such as within a room or building or across a campus). LANs are the smallest networks, essentially the foundation or building blocks of larger networks. Functional groups (marketing, finance, sales, engineering, and so on) often share information using a LAN that connects their PCs to a server (a bigger computer), which stores records relevant to the functional department. Each department might have its own LAN and might also connect to the LANs of other departments. Thus, someone in engineering can communicate with someone in marketing and manufacturing, and company-wide services such as e-mail can be supported. In general, LAN speeds are much greater than WAN speeds, sometimes by a factor of 75 or more. However, the technology that makes LANs work also limits the distances over which they operate. Switches and/or routers can connect LANs to one another to overcome such limitations.

MANs are the next networking size step. A MAN is a network of LANs spread out over a town, city, or metropolitan area. Different locations are connected by a communications link type such as leased lines from a telephone company or other service provider. The interconnection method depends on the application and the networked organization(s) frequency of use, as well as by what is available from service providers at the locations. A MAN can be used to connect a headquarters office with company branch offices or even with the networks of trading partners or customers.

In a WAN, computers are farther apart. They operate in regions, countries, and even across continents. WAN connections use telephone lines, microwave, satellite, or other long-distance telecommunications systems.

Intranets and Extranets

In addition to describing networks relative to size or geographic scope, they also can be classified according to function. Functional categories include intranets and extranets. They really just build on the Internet model, taking it one step further and making it even more valuable. An intranet is a private Transmission Control Protocol/Internet Protocol (TCP/IP) network that is open only to employees of a single organization. Intranets are internal communications vehicles and knowledge bases that serve as a company-wide information system. As such, they can vastly improve information flow and keep costs down within a company. An extranet extends a company's network beyond its boundaries to predetermined business partners, customers, suppliers, and others. Extranets let companies make selective information residing on their network available to these players.

Chapter 6, "Intranets, Extranets, and Virtual Private Networks," provides more details on intranets and extranets.

Network Configuration Types: Topologies

Networks also can be characterized by their basic shape or physical configuration, called their topology. A topology defines how devices are organized physically relative to one another in a LAN; their physical configuration doesn't necessarily reflect their logical connectivity. The three main types of network topologies are star, ring, and bus, as shown in Figure 2-3. The one most predominantly in use today is the star.

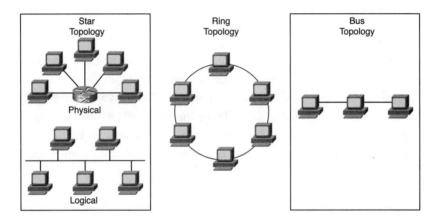

Figure 2-3   *Network Topologies*

Star Topology

In a star network topology, all endpoints or client devices (PCs, laptops, printers, and so on) are connected to a central device (typically a switch or hub). Transmissions received from any attached device (or node) are sent to other nodes as appropriate. Data is communicated by transmitting to, and receiving from, the central device. A star topology also is used with PBX systems for telephony interconnection. Ethernet (IEEE 802.3) 10/100/1000Base-T networks are the most widely used type of networks that use a star topology.

Ring Topology

With a ring topology, every node has exactly two links connected to it, usually forming a loop, with other nodes on the ring. Token Ring (IEEE 802.5) and Fiber Distributed Data Interface (FDDI) are examples of the types of networks that use this topology. Data is sent from one node to the next, around the ring in a single direction, until it ends up back where it started. Each node copies the data that is addressed to it as the data passes through the node.

Bus Topology

In a bus topology, all nodes (or endpoints) are connected linearly, one to another. With this physical topology, when one device transmits, the signal travels (propagates) down the cable in both directions, so all other devices on the cable "hear" it. A networking standard called Token Bus (IEEE 802.4) was implemented on LANs. Although Token Bus sometimes is used in manufacturing environments, the Ethernet standard has become most widely deployed in office environments.

Bandwidth

One of the key considerations in planning for, designing, and evaluating what type of network to invest in is how much traffic it can handle during peak times. It is important to ensure that the company network can deliver application services and support business processes at the performance levels required. If the network becomes congested, it can shut down a business or reduce its responsiveness. Bandwidth is a key factor in determining network performance. Two companies with the same number of network users require different amounts of bandwidth if the users are all on the network simultaneously versus accessing the network at different times of the day. A network with a relatively small volume of e-mail but lots of large file attachments (such as graphics files or streaming media) requires more bandwidth than a network with lots of e-mail traffic but few file attachments and no streaming media. Therefore, needed bandwidth is influenced partly by a company's size and also by the number of simultaneous users and the applications that will run on the network.

Bandwidth determines a network's information-carrying capacity. The higher the bandwidth, the more data that can be transported over a link in a given period of time. Bandwidth is technically defined as the range of frequencies that can be transmitted without interference or signal loss. The broader the range of frequencies that can be handled, the greater the information-carrying capacity. In other words, there is a direct relationship between bandwidth and capacity, generally expressed in bits per second (bps). In data communications, the term bandwidth is generally used interchangeably with capacity.

Narrowband and broadband are relative terms that refer to the data-carrying capacity of a network link. Generally, narrowband refers to one voice channel, consisting of 3 kHz (kilohertz) on an analog line or 64 kbps (kilobits per second, meaning 1000 bits per second) on a digital line. Broadband systems provide more bandwidth than narrowband. Generally broadband refers to rates of 1.54 Mbps and higher.

Cable modems and DSL are examples of high-bandwidth broadband systems that offer the potential for hundreds of channels, each carrying data, video, and audio signals. Cable offers rates of up to 10 Mbps. Users typically get considerably less than that (closer to 1 Mbps), however, because the total bandwidth is shared among all users. DSL services, such as ADSL (asymmetric digital subscriber line), can deliver download speeds of up to 8 Mbps and upload speeds of up to 1 Mbps over standard telephone lines. The typical DSL bandwidth delivered by service providers is on the order of 384Kbps. Because cable and DSL are "always-on" services, their bandwidth is readily available to users without the delay common to dialup systems.

A high-bandwidth connection is essential for productive Internet use. You can use 56 Kbps connections, but this is slow and inefficient, particularly when dealing with large file transfers or web page downloads. Broadband speeds of 1.54 Mbps or higher are becoming the minimum acceptable speed for business Internet users.

Both demand for and supply of network bandwidth have expanded dramatically in recent years. This is in line with the increased power and capabilities of computer systems and the move toward collaborative, real-time multimedia applications, which require the integration of data, voice, and video on networks. Much of the content that is transferred across the Internet has evolved from plain text to include graphics, animations, video, and sound. The bottom line is that multimedia content requires significantly more bandwidth than plain text. And the volume of this type of content used in businesses will continue to expand in the coming years.

Each application makes its own demands on a network, so it is important to know which ones a company will use so that you can determine the amount of bandwidth needed. Before trying to predict future bandwidth needs, it's a good idea to get a handle on applications used today and whether the company network has sufficient bandwidth to support them.

The Internet

The Internet is the largest internetwork in the world. It was developed more than 20 years ago by the U.S. Defense Department Advanced Research Projects Agency (ARPA). The network was originally called ARPAnet. Since then, the Internet has grown to include other networks located around the world and encompasses millions of computers. The Internet comprises networks that are attached to one another in a network of networks. A business that is connected to the Internet has access to these networks.

The World Wide Web (also called the web) is a global matrix of interconnected documents on the Internet. Clicking a cross-reference in one of these documents displays the referenced document, no matter where it is located in the world. This is possible because all systems that are part of the web use a common communications protocol, Hypertext Transfer Protocol (HTTP), to exchange documents and because all web documents use the same method, Hypertext Markup Language (HTML), to define document formatting.

Although the Internet has been around for a long time, the introduction of the web has catapulted the frequency and volume of its use. That is because searching the web for information became simple, and support for graphics, sound, and motion made the information that could be found there richer and more compelling. This richness contributed to the rise of e-commerce and the creation of electronic web storefronts. Encryption and other security features have made it possible to operate these online storefronts to buy and sell services and products securely. Increasingly, a presence on the web is as critical to doing business as being connected to the telephone network.

E-mail, file sharing between systems, and remote use of systems (Telnet) are examples of the kinds of Internet-based services that have been enabled for use by businesses (as well as by the original Internet users, the academic community). With Internet connections, business professionals gain access to needed information; collaborate with colleagues, customers, and partners; and work productively even while mobile.

A wealth of benefits are associated with incorporating the Internet and its technologies into small-medium business processes. A few are highlighted here. The Internet is an inexpensive and effective way for companies to distribute marketing information, financial reports, product and service details, and so on. Because the Internet and the web never shut down, this information is available 24 hours a day, allowing convenient, time-shifted business relationship opportunities. Information maintained on the Internet is also easy to keep up to date. Because customers, clients, and partners can download Internet-based information to their own computers, costs of printing, mailing, and distributing are reduced at the same time that service and response times are improved.

How Information Travels Across the Internet

Two key concepts are essential for understanding Internet information transfer—packet switching and the TCP/IP communications protocols. These core elements have remained fundamental throughout the evolutionary changes that have taken place with the Internet over the past several decades.

Packet Switching

Packet switching involves breaking digital messages from applications into chunks called packets, transferring those packets across communications channels, and reassembling them into their original order at their ultimate destination. This takes place in a series of steps:

Step 1 An application creates a message containing the data to be sent.

Step 2 Transmission Control Protocol (TCP) or User Datagram Protocol (UDP) breaks the information to be sent into units often called segments (inTCP) or datagrams (in UDP). A header, which contains information related to the packet, is appended to the front of the packet. This information helps with processing at the destination site.

Step 3 IP adds a source (sender) and destination (receiver) IP address as part of a digital "envelope."

Step 4 After being wrapped in this envelope, the packet is transmitted from a host computer through a series of routers until it reaches its final destination and is directed to the proper host computer there. Unless the sending and receiving destinations are located on the same LAN, packets typically are not sent directly from a source to a destination.

Step 5 As soon as a packet is received, the digital envelope and all headers are discarded, and the data inside can be recombined with the data from other packets that make up a complete piece of information.

Routers handle most of the work of directing and forwarding traffic on the Internet. They interconnect the thousands of different computer networks that make up the Internet. They also examine packets to see where the data is headed and then, based on the packet destination, determine the most efficient way to get it there. This is illustrated in Figure 2-4. IP packet-based network technologies are connectionless (that is, there is no dedicated circuit, as there is for a telephone call), and delivery of packets is not guaranteed. As a result, routers transfer packets without first making sure that the destination site is ready to receive them. When packets are received, that receipt is not acknowledged. The upside of this data-transfer approach of packet switching is that it does not require a dedicated circuit, and it can use any spare capacity on public network circuits.

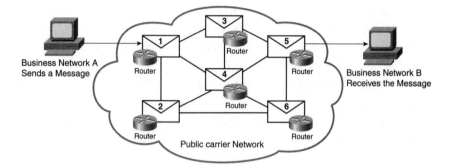

Figure 2-4   *Routers Direct Internet Traffic*

Addressing

Computers on IP networks need to know at least two things to communicate over the Internet—their own IP address and the IP address of a router that connects the LAN to a larger network and to the Internet. When one computer needs to send data to another, the IP protocol stack breaks the data into a series of packets and appends a packet header that contains addressing information for routing. It serves the same purpose as the From: and To: lines in an e-mail. IP routers then move packets from one computer to another by forwarding them based on a destination address (the IP number) in the header until the packet reaches a router connected to the destination LAN.

Because addressing is so essential to Internet communications, every computer on a network needs an address. The address uniquely identifies each computer and allows traffic on the network to be routed (or directed) from any computer to any other computer.

Networks that directly connect to the Internet must have an IP address assigned to them by the Network Information Center (InterNIC) or some other authority. Businesses usually get these addresses from their Internet Service Provider (ISP).

The current addressing scheme, IP version 4 (IPv4), uses an address with 32 bits, expressed as four decimal numbers between 0 and 255. For example, 24.2.3.33 is a typical IPv4 address. One part of the address identifies the network and subnetwork (a portion of the whole network) where a computer (or other network device) is located, and the other part identifies a specific device on that subnet. Concerns about addressing have led to the development of IP version 6 (IPv6). But IPv6 is not yet widely deployed. Chapter 9, "Emerging Technologies," discusses IPv6 in more detail, including market and technical drivers.

TCP/IP

Many protocols are required to support an end-user application across a network. Protocols define the rules that each computer must follow so that all systems in the network can exchange data. One of the most popular protocol families in use today is the TCP/IP protocol suite. The Internet runs over TCP/IP and also UDP.

TCP/IP and UDP

TCP/IP refers to a suite of protocols that includes Transmission Control Protocol (TCP), Internet Protocol (IP), and many others. TCP handles packet flow between systems, and IP handles the routing of packets. TCP/IP is a layered set of protocols. In fact, all modern networks are designed using a layered approach. Each layer takes responsibility for solving a part of the problem of transporting information across networking systems. By breaking the issues to be addressed into these layers, modular network designs can be adopted. This minimizes disruptions when new applications or user interfaces are added.

IP can be considered a library of routines that TCP calls on. Generally, TCP/IP is considered to have four layers, but other approaches also are used. The TCP/IP protocols were developed before the seven-layer International Organization for Standardization (ISO) Open Systems Interconnection (OSI) architecture, which is the usual reference model. Figure 2-5 presents a high-level comparison of the two models.

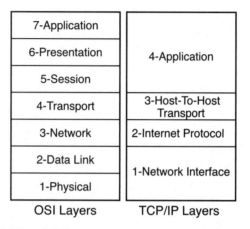

Figure 2-5   *TCP/IP and OSI*

The TCP/IP layers are as follows:

- **Application layer**—This layer has application protocols for supporting e-mail, file transfer, and other key business applications.

- **Host-to-host transport layer**—This layer provides end-to-end services needed by many applications shared between computers. TCP and UDP are the primary protocols at this layer.

- **Internet protocol layer**—At this layer, IP provides the basic service of getting data packets to their destinations.

- **Network interface layer**—This layer includes the protocols needed to manage a specific physical interface, such as Ethernet.

Remember that an IP message travels using either of two transport layer protocols: TCP or UDP. Transport layer protocols are responsible for the end-to-end delivery of traffic over a network. TCP includes an error-checking mechanism to ensure that all the data sent from one computer is received correctly at the receiver's end. UDP can be used in place of TCP for less-critical messages, because it does not offer the same reliability or error-correcting features. UDP does about as little as a transport protocol can. Aside from some light error checking, it adds nothing to IP. UDP typically is used to broadcast large amounts of data over the Internet.

Most ISPs (Internet Service Providers) use either TCP or UDP. Of these protocols, more use TCP than UDP, because it offers guaranteed, error-free, complete packet traffic delivery between computer systems.

Why isn't TCP always preferable to UDP if TCP provides a reliable data transfer service and UDP does not? There are a number of reasons:

- Some applications, such as IP telephony, are very time-sensitive. If an IP packet is lost, it is better to ignore it than to wait for TCP to retransmit it. For that reason, UDP is the preferred protocol with time-sensitive applications such as IP telephony.

- TCP requires a three-way handshake (or connection setup) before it can start transferring data, whereas UDP transfers without formal connection preliminaries. TCP therefore introduces delays when establishing a computer connection.

- TCP maintains a connection state in end systems that includes send and receive buffers, congestion control parameters, and sequence and acknowledgment parameters. This state information is needed to implement TCP's reliable data transfer. UDP does not maintain connection state and does not track those other parameters. As a result, a server for a particular application typically can support many more active clients (user devices or browsers) when the application runs over UDP rather than TCP.

- TCP segments have more overhead in their headers than UDP (20 bytes versus 8 bytes, respectively). The higher the overhead, the slower the network performance.

Some popular Internet applications and the transport protocols that they typically use are noted in Table 2-1.

Table 2-1 *TCP and UDP Protocol Usage by Application*

Application	Internet Transport Protocol
E-mail/Simple Mail Transfer Protocol (SMTP)	TCP
Remote terminal access (Telnet)	TCP
Web access/Hypertext Transfer Protocol (HTTP)	TCP
File Transfer Protocol (FTP)	TCP
Streaming multimedia/ Real-Time Transfer Protocol (RTP)	TCP
IP telephony (IPT)	UDP
Simple Remote File Transfer/Trivial File Transfer Protocol (TFTP)	UDP
Simple Network Management Protocol (SNMP)	UDP
Routing Information Protocol (RIP)	UDP
IP-to-name translation/ Domain Name Sevices (DNS)	UDP

OSI

Open Systems Interconnection (OSI) is another protocol model. It too is constructed of network protocols that are layered on top of one another. The OSI reference model was introduced in the 1990s to serve as a standard for data network design and product interoperability capabilities. It is made up of seven layers, each of which describes a specific aspect of the communications process. These layers define how signals and data are carried through networks. For the most part, the lower layers deal with hardware and connections, and the higher layers are application- and software-based.

The purpose of the OSI model is to allow networks to support any application and to simplify the development of network products by breaking their functions into elements called layers. Each layer communicates with the layer above it and below it. As data is transmitted from one user (or computer) to another user, the data moves down through the stack of layers and is modified so that it can be understood by the next layer. At the receiving user's end, the modified data moves in reverse through the layers until it ends up in its original format and can be understood.

The main differences between TCP/IP and OSI are as follows:

- The application layer in TCP/IP handles the responsibilities of Layers 5, 6, and 7 in the OSI model.

- The host-to-host transport layer in TCP/IP does not always guarantee as reliable a delivery of packets as the transport layer in the OSI model.

- The network interface layer in TCP/IP handles the responsibilities of Layers 1 and 2 in the OSI model.

Evolution of Networks in Businesses

In the business world, networks are evolving from a reliance on hard-wired connections between separate voice, data, and video networks into geographically dispersed, interconnected, and technologically converged information systems that use a mix of wired and wireless transmission media. Early business networks were set up as islands of information—mostly because of the limitations of technologies for interoperability. IT department infrastructures that were built to support these systems reflected them. There were separate information system (IS) (or data) and telecommunications (or voice) groups. Each of these departments operated autonomously and had little to do with the other group. It is not unusual to still see this type of legacy information technology (IT) organization in many businesses.

In that style of IT environment, it was difficult to combine information from a variety of sources (departments, customers, suppliers, and so on) to make business decisions rapidly. To conduct any kind of business analysis, an "aftermarket" of software and database systems evolved (called decision support systems) in which data could be extracted manually from separate databases and entered into rigidly programmed templates. Users could then generate reports on customer purchase patterns, inventory turns, financial status, responses to direct-mail campaigns, or whatever a company wanted to analyze. It was costly to invest in such decision support systems software and processors. Besides that, additional staff were needed to install and manage them. In spite of all the effort and expense they consumed, such systems were still unable to produce needed business information in real-time for rapid decision-making.

Originally, only high-end medium and large enterprises could afford the cost of networking hardware and software. However, in the past decade, prices have dropped with the introduction of new technologies. Affordable prices, coupled with the productivity and bottom-line benefits of using networks, have meant that networks, even those delivering enterprise-class capabilities, are becoming more commonplace in midsized and smaller businesses. Today's small-medium business communications networks consist of LANs, MANs, WANs, or, most often, some combination of them. The latest development has been the increasing convergence of data, voice, and video into unified systems. This trend will drive the need for more network bandwidth.

From a remote-access perspective, dialup systems relying on modems have been the norm for the last few decades. Today's V.90 (56 Kbps) modems are becoming dinosaurs that are increasingly limited in their ability to deliver services and applications over the Internet in the timeframes business users desire. The high performance delivered by broadband is becoming the norm. It is replacing slow narrowband systems for wide area networking that supports popular business applications such as customer relationship management, sales force automation, electronic storefronts, and others.

It is essential to understand the functions and components of networking systems to ensure that the network foundation upon which a small-medium business is built will be reliable and scalable (to grow with the business) and will support efficient business operations and competitive, differentiated service offerings.

Summary

Small-medium business decision-makers must remember that when they invest in computer networks, they are investing in a system. Devices should not be acquired piecemeal. Key components of a network, such as cabling media, adapters, switches, and routers, all must work together in harmony for a company to achieve optimal business efficiency and peak IT performance. These elements, when combined, create networks that vary in size (LAN, MAN, and WAN) and type (intranet and extranet). They are implemented to enable the business applications needed by each company. The most prevalent network topology in use today is the Ethernet-based star.

The amount of traffic is another critical consideration for decision-makers to keep in mind when planning, designing, and evaluating computer networks. The volume, frequency, and type of information to be exchanged influence network bandwidth requirements.

Company networks do not operate in isolation. The Internet has evolved as a pervasive means to access and share business information globally among employees, business partners, and customers. There are a wealth of business and technical benefits to incorporating its use into a small-medium business. Information is transmitted across the Internet using packet switching, IP addressing techniques, and a variety of protocols that govern the flow of data.

The sharing of converged data, voice, and video information among and within businesses is increasingly viewed as providing competitive differentiation and strategic advantage. Sophisticated systems, once affordable only to large enterprises, are now affordable to small and midsized companies as well. As these systems evolve, the role of IT in companies also is changing.

CHAPTER 3

LOCAL AREA, METROPOLITAN AREA, AND WIDE AREA NETWORKS

In office buildings and across campuses, local area networks (LANs) are used to connect computing devices, share software applications (accounting, customer relationship management, salesforce automation, and so on), exchange information among coworkers, and support shared access to the Internet. Metropolitan area networks and wide area networks (MANs and WANs) are similar to LANs but provide their services to users who are more geographically remote from one another. Regardless of the form of network used—LAN, MAN, or WAN—communications can be shared between individual users or broadcast for sharing between an individual and a specific group or groups of users. Connected groups can include functional departments within a small-medium business (marketing, finance, sales, engineering) or an entire value chain of business partners in complementary industry sectors (such as hospitals, clinics, physicians, medical labs, and pharmacies).

Given the connectivity services and coverage they deliver, LANs, MANs, and WANs together should be considered an enabling foundation by business managers for achieving such organizational goals as agility, personalized customer care, competitive differentiation, improved efficiencies and productivity, lowered costs, higher revenues, and guaranteed scalability for organizational growth. Local and wide area computer networks, if planned and designed to support company objectives, can become the strategic underpinnings for expanding a business and even entire value chains. However, it is important to keep in mind that before deploying a new network, some business process reengineering will likely be needed to improve workflows and to fully exploit the capabilities enabled by the new network. It is critical, when conducting network planning, to involve a trusted advisor who can anticipate and articulate what to expect in this regard. Only then can you gain the full benefit of and payback from chosen technologies. After all, there is no real benefit to simply automating existing business processes. The goal should be to change and improve the ways in which business is conducted.

Wired LAN Technologies: Ethernet Explained

LANs are the smallest form of business-class networks. Personal area or wearable network gadgets do not qualify because they cannot scale. LANs can be considered the foundation, or building blocks, of larger networks composed of multiple interconnected LAN segments and advanced technologies (such as IP telephony, security, wireless, storage networking, and others). Not only do LANs scale when combined, but they also have expanded in their own right. Data rates for business LANs have grown from 10 Mbps data speeds to 100 Mbps to 1000 Mbps (or 1 gigabit per second [Gbps]). Now 10 Gbps systems are emerging for use in business networks. Although the higher end of this data rate scale might be beyond the requirements and affordability of some small-medium businesses, the trend is unmistakably toward increasingly information-intensive applications that consume significant bandwidth and require very high-speed transport.

LAN Infrastructure

Because of its foundational potential, the quality and performance characteristics of a LAN infrastructure (hardware, cabling media, and software) can affect how and which applications a business can run, how effectively and reliably employees can communicate with one another, and consequently how responsive they can be to the company's customers, partners, suppliers, and other business associates. Consider this: If a LAN slows to a crawl as users are added to it or moved around, or if the network doesn't extend to where workers need to use it, strategic business applications cannot be supported. Such applications can let a company competitively differentiate itself or be efficient and productive in its business operations. Without this capability, the network's business value would be negligible, and the sunk capital costs to build it would indeed be sunk. It is important to choose a LAN infrastructure that operates in ways the organization needs it.

Ethernet

Ethernet is essentially the sole remaining LAN protocol from which to choose. But it comes in several bandwidth and implementation method flavors. Even IBM finally has abandoned the Token Ring LAN standard it advocated throughout the 1980s and '90s. Ethernet has thrived as a result of its scalability (from 10 to 1000 Mbps), low cost, proven reliability, and ease of deployment. It originated at Xerox in the 1970s and was designed to handle heavy, bursty (periodic) network traffic. Subsequently, the technology was internationally standardized with some refinements to the original design by the Institute for Electrical and Electronic Engineers (IEEE) 802.3 committee. The standard they produced spells out the various Ethernet components, how they interact with each other, and the rules for configuring an Ethernet network. It also provides for interoperability among various vendors' products, which has resulted in vendor competition and tremendous price/performance gains.

Although it is not necessary for business decision-makers to understand all the technical details of Ethernet standards, it is helpful to understand one basic architectural principle of Ethernet to gauge which type of Ethernet network to select for a small-medium business. Ethernet is based on the concept of contention. Contention occurs when two or more devices try to use a network at the same time even though only one can be supported. Because Ethernet is a shared-access medium, network devices (PCs, laptops, PDAs, printers, IP phones) must follow rules for sending data. Those rules include checking to see if other traffic is already being carried on the LAN. User devices listen for a signal. If a traffic signal is detected, another device cannot send information.

If two user devices transmit at the same time, their data collides, and both device transmitters must retransmit a short, random time later when the network is available (or idle) again. In technical language, this process is called carrier sense multiple access collision detect (CSMA/CD).

Essentially, what this boils down to is that Ethernet is a first-come, first-served approach to networking. The problem is that this collide-and-resend methodology creates additional overhead. It subtracts from Ethernet's stated high-speed performance levels because some bandwidth is lost to aborted transmissions. The impact is that the maximum Ethernet speeds (10, 100, 1000 Mbps) are mostly theoretical and rarely are achieved. For instance, with collision and contention overhead factored in, 10 Mbps Ethernet really only delivers speeds that are roughly 40 to 60 percent of its possible maximum, or 4 to 6 Mbps. Users can achieve speeds closer to the theoretical maximum with switched Ethernet more so than with shared (hub-based) Ethernet. It is important to keep these things in mind when selecting an Ethernet network infrastructure. Skimping on bandwidth to control initial network investment costs can add significantly to total costs of network ownership over time.

As alluded to, Ethernet LANs are composed of a family of implementations from which to choose:

- 10 Mbps Ethernet

- 100 Mbps Ethernet (also called Fast Ethernet)

- 1000 Mbps Ethernet (also called Gigabit Ethernet, GbE, or GigE)

Each of these Ethernet technologies is described in the following sections. Figure 3-1 shows a basic blueprint of potential uses for each of these technologies.

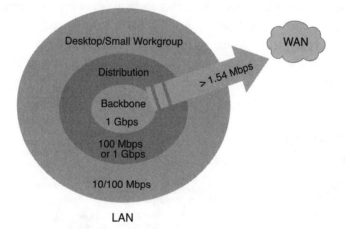

Figure 3-1 *Network Bandwidth Needs*

Because a company might be presented with a variety of Ethernet specifications as part of a network design proposal, it might help to understand some naming conventions before learning the characteristics of each option. Ethernet specifications start with a number that represents speed in Mbps. Next comes the type of transmission technology that is used (Base stands for baseband and Broad stands for broadband). The final component represents the physical cabling used. For example, 10Base-T stands for 10 Mbps Ethernet, delivered via baseband signaling over twisted-pair cabling.

10 Mbps Ethernet

The most basic form of Ethernet (10 Mbps Ethernet) sends and receives data at speeds of 10 million bits per second. Even though that might sound like a lot of bandwidth, it is important to determine what is suitable for every business's unique operating environment. Companies running multimedia (combined voice, video, and data) and real-time applications require at least 1.544 Mbps of committed, continuous bandwidth per user, per application. When Ethernet's overhead is taken into account, that 1.544 Mbps minimum bandwidth threshold per person is virtually impossible to achieve if 35 to 45 people are sharing a single 10 Mbps connection. It is important, therefore, when planning a first-time LAN installation or even a LAN upgrade to think about the number of potential network users and the types of applications they will operate concurrently. Then select a LAN that not only provides acceptable performance levels but also anticipates growth with some built-in bandwidth headroom. Figure 3-2 presents examples of applications commonly used by small-medium businesses and the bandwidths at which they usually operate.

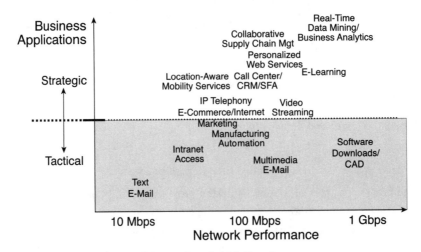

Figure 3-2   *Business Application Bandwidth Requirements*

The most likely 10 Mbps Ethernet transmission option a company will be offered is 10Base-T (10 Mbps Ethernet over unshielded twisted-pair [UTP] cabling). It is the best choice for affordable connections to the desktop. 10Base-T operates across 300-foot (91-meter) distances, which should be sufficient for smaller offices or single floors of medium-sized office buildings. 10Base-T has surpassed other 10 Mbps Ethernet options, such as 10Base2 and 10Base5, which were deployed using coaxial cabling and were prevalent in the 1970s and '80s.

When deciding whether to adopt a 10 Mbps LAN, consider that for a business of more than 20 to 25 employees, plain old Ethernet alone likely will be insufficient for the types of Internet access and collaborative applications that are popularly in use and continue to emerge. A 10Base-T Ethernet LAN is better suited for use in a home network or within a very small workgroup. In fact, basic Ethernet has lost ground to 100 Mbps Ethernet in most small-medium business networks.

One way to add to the efficiency of an existing 10 Mbps Ethernet workgroup LAN while migrating to a higher-speed company LAN is to partition (or segment) it. This involves connecting users to a switch instead of a hub. Each of these LAN segments is collision-free as a result of only a single user transmitting data on that segment. The impact is higher performance (faster speed), greater reliability, and better security. Networks are not that hard to segment, but they do require a professional network analysis to ensure that traffic loads are not increased rather than decreased. Chapter 4, "Network Foundation Technologies—Switching and Routing," provides more detail on switches and routers and how they can be used cost-effectively in a LAN.

100 Mbps Ethernet

The next Ethernet bandwidth step, 100 Mbps Ethernet, is typically called Fast Ethernet. It also is an IEEE standard and carries the designation 802.3u. Fast Ethernet is an order of magnitude faster than basic Ethernet. Yet it is backward-compatible with basic Ethernet, so the two technologies can coexist in a single network. One of the key drivers for Fast Ethernet has been the continued emergence of information-rich business applications that require faster and faster data transmissions. In addition, the difference in price between 100 Mbps Ethernet devices and 10 Mbps devices has become very small.

Here are some of the advantages of adopting Fast Ethernet versus basic Ethernet:

- Fast Ethernet is relatively easy and inexpensive to implement.

- It can carry converged data, voice, and video traffic at a rate that is ten times faster than basic Ethernet.

- It is based on the same technology as basic Ethernet, and it integrates smoothly with existing 10 Mbps Ethernet networks.

- It operates over the same cabling as 10 Mbps Ethernet. This allows companies to benefit from not having to consume more conduit or ceiling space for cabling (a considerable factor when an office building has space limitations), and the cost of stringing new cable is eliminated.

- It enables gradual network migration rather than a forklift upgrade. This is particularly useful for networks that are not yet amortized.

For companies that have a basic Ethernet network installed and that want to upgrade, one step to take in moving toward Fast Ethernet is to replace users' Ethernet network interface cards (NICs) with Fast Ethernet NICs designed to support 10 Mbps and 100 Mbps speeds, or to use autosensing, known as combination Ethernet/Fast Ethernet (10/100) NICs. The Fast Ethernet NICs that support 10/100 Mbps are a better choice than the autosensing alternative. It is virtually impossible to even find NICs and PCs that operate only at 10 Mbps anymore. Additionally, business-class Ethernet switches are available that include both 10 Mbps and 100 Mbps ports. This lets 10Base-T and 100Base-T LAN segments be connected to the same switch as a transition step.

100Base-T supports dual speeds of 10 and 100 Mbps. The most popular approach for deploying it is to use Category 5 UTP cable for transmission distances up to 300 feet (91 meters). Other Fast Ethernet implementation options can be considered as well, such as those that use multimode fiber.

A consultant, systems integrator, value-added reseller (VAR), or equipment vendor can help with the more-complex aspects of upgrading a LAN or planning a new LAN installation. This includes things such as evaluating a company's cabling needs, specifying cost/performance trade-off choices, deciding how to blend different network types, determining whether company computer systems will support the desired level of network performance, and other such design issues. Given the relative costs of basic Ethernet and Fast Ethernet, faster is the way to go for all but the very smallest businesses (those with fewer than 15 to 20 employees).

1000 Mbps Ethernet

Gigabit Ethernet (sometimes called GigE or GbE) is yet another order of magnitude faster than Fast Ethernet. It operates at speeds of 1000 Mbps (which is equal to 1 gigabit per second [Gbps]) and is backward-compatible with its lower-speed counterparts Fast Ethernet and basic Ethernet when transmitted over twisted-pair copper cable. Two separate IEEE task forces focus on standardizing Gigabit Ethernet. The IEEE 802.3ab Task Force focuses on specifications for GigE over copper cabling (called 1000Base-T), and the IEEE 802.3z Task Force defines GigE over fiber. Additionally, the Gigabit Ethernet Alliance was formed as an industry association to ensure that interoperability between 10/100/1000 Mbps Ethernet systems is addressed.

The benefits of deploying Gigabit Ethernet over copper cabling (Category 5, 5e, or 6 options) include the following:

- Gigabit Ethernet over copper helps users be more productive by taking advantage of more-powerful, bandwidth-intensive applications and spending less time doing so.

- It improves server throughput and performance, and it costs less to implement and maintain than fiber.

- It reduces backbone bottlenecks for distances up to 300 feet (91 meters).

- It leverages data administrators' expertise with Fast Ethernet installations.

The advantages of deploying Gigabit Ethernet over fiber include the following:

- Gigabit Ethernet over fiber provides greater security, because it is almost impossible to tap into fiber without detection.

- It offers noise immunity from electromagnetic interference (EMI).

- It enables more extended reach than copper networks (greater than 300 feet or 91 meters).

As companies adopt intranet and extranet network models that are used by workers for real-time, high-performance applications (such as software downloads, multimedia web access, data backup, and so on), network traffic patterns change, and higher bandwidth is required to deliver desired response times. With companies reporting network traffic growth of 500 to 600 percent per year, networking systems must scale to keep up. One of the worst things that could happen is for network congestion to lessen worker productivity or shut it down entirely.

Addressing the issue of congestion on Ethernet backbones was a key driver for the development of Gigabit Ethernet. It has become so popular for doing so, in fact, that GigE has displaced other technologies such as asynchronous transfer mode (ATM) and fiber distributed data interface (FDDI) in the LAN. In its role as a backbone technology, GigE can be used by smaller businesses to connect a number of 10/100 switches to a 100/1000 switch and also to connect application servers to the 100/1000 switch. Figure 3-3 shows these device connections.

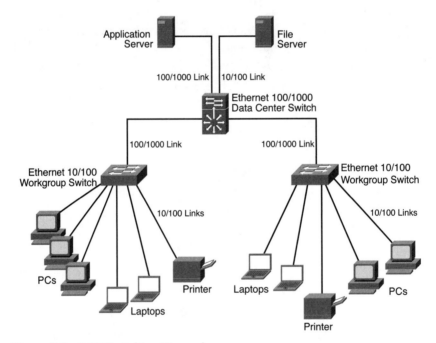

Figure 3-3   *LAN Switching Hierarchy*

In medium-sized businesses, IT staff might even choose to deliver GigE to the desktop to improve data-intensive business application responsiveness and overall performance of the company network. Strategic business applications such as multimedia e-mail (e-mail with graphical attachments), real-time video, software distribution, customer relationship management (CRM), supply chain management (SCM), and enterprise resource planning (ERP) are putting unprecedented demands on business networks. Gigabit Ethernet can help answer these demands.

A key question to resolve, however, is whether Gigabit Ethernet systems are overkill for particular small-medium businesses. Do they pay back in business value what they cost to implement? Do they deliver more power than could possibly be tapped? The answer is: It varies. There is no simple formula to apply. Factors to consider, among others, are the number of simultaneous network users, the types of applications being run, the potential business opportunity costs, and the competitive environment of the relevant market sector. These are the types of questions that should be addressed on a case-by-case basis, by technical and business decision-makers and their network systems advisors. What should be emphasized is that the questions that should be asked and answered first are the business-related ones. The technology solution decisions follow as enablers of the business factors and priorities, not vice versa.

WAN Access and Technologies

Although sharing information among colleagues on a LAN is critical to conducting business efficiently, most businesses cannot afford to work in a vacuum. Workers want and need to be able to share knowledge and communicate with customers, partners, and suppliers. In general, they need to be able to access information that supports the business in a variety of locations. A LAN alone cannot achieve that, nor can it address the need for unfettered external communications. Wide area communications links must be added.

LANs and WANs as End-to-End Systems

By enabling internetworking between LANs and WANs, you can support communications that involve remote LAN-to-LAN (for instance, headquarters to branch office), user-to-LAN (remote teleworking), and user-to-WAN or LAN-to-WAN connections (including Internet access). Think of the information-sharing flexibility this affords a small-medium business. In essence, what is created is a networked virtual office or a boundary-free organization, in which employees can conduct business anywhere and at any time. In many cases, the productive workday can be extended by 2 hours or more.

It is important to think of the LAN and WAN as integrated in an end-to-end communications system. For this system to work smoothly, you must avoid bottlenecks at all costs. When planning a network (new or upgrade), you must ensure that if a high-performance LAN is supporting key business processes and applications, the WAN it connects to has enough bandwidth so as not to slow performance significantly. This translates to broadband end to end.

The Last Mile

Bandwidth is not an issue for businesses to be concerned about in the core infrastructure of public carrier networks. Rather, they must focus on the last mile (also called the first mile, the local loop, and the access network). The last mile also is sometimes called a MAN link. In other words, it is the part of the telecommunications network that links a company's LAN with access services to the WAN and to a service provider's local switching office (or central office), as shown in Figure 3-4.

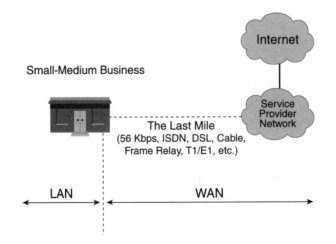

Figure 3-4 *The Last Mile*

Achieving an integrated, high-speed, end-to-end network can create design and management challenges for a company, especially when network components are acquired by IT staff piecemeal from different vendors and service providers. Sometimes when data administrators acquire what they consider "best of breed" products from multiple suppliers, those products don't work as effectively as expected when combined to create whole solutions. This might result in ongoing and significant network management costs as the IT staff learns about, monitors, and adjusts various devices for optimum performance. Products designed to work together as a whole system tend to do so at peak performance.

Last-mile WAN access services are offered by a variety of service providers (SPs), such as Internet Service Providers (ISPs), incumbent local exchange carriers (ILECs—mostly the former Bell Telephone companies), interexchange carriers (IXCs—the long-distance telephone companies), cable TV companies (multiple service operators [MSOs]), competitive local exchange carriers (CLECs), application service providers (ASPs), managed service providers (MSPs), and so on.

Available access service options include the following:

- **Circuit-switched services**—These dialup connections are used to establish a dedicated, but temporary, communications path that lasts only for the duration of a call. When the call is completed, the carrier's switch ports and other resources are freed up for other customers to use. Examples of circuit-switched services include analog dialup modem connections (usually at 56 Kbps speeds) and Integrated Services Digital Network (ISDN) connections. Analog dialup is a narrowband service; ISDN is sometimes considered narrowband and other times broadband. One problem with using analog circuit-switched services is that the quality of transmission depends on the switches and trunk lines used. Quality therefore can vary from call to call. Another drawback includes the limited connection speeds available to both. For these reasons, circuit-switched services are typically used as affordable backup solutions in case a leased line or other link becomes unavailable. Because they are considerably less costly than dedicated leased lines, they also are used in low-traffic WAN environments in which a continuous connection is unnecessary.

- **Packet-switched services**—Packet switching does not use dedicated end-to-end physical connections. Data is transmitted in packets across a public data network owned by a carrier. Packet-switched services offer the affordability that comes with using public network facilities. Unlike dialup access, however, packet services provide broadband speeds, service quality, and always-on access that is similar to that of a private, dedicated network service. Examples of packet-switched services most used by small-medium businesses include the various flavors of digital subscriber line (DSL), cable modems, and Frame Relay.

- **Dedicated leased lines**—These are essentially connections that are set up (or nailed up) as a permanent, private, point-to-point network link between two or more locations. They are reserved to be always-on and are available to carry network traffic at any time. Leased lines are typically fairly expensive, because service provider facilities must be dedicated to a single customer, even when they are not being used. Examples of leased-line service options include the various types of T-carrier, such as T1 (1.544 Mbps), fractional T1 (bandwidth in 64 Kbps increments up to 1.544 Mbps) and T3 (45 Mbps). In Europe, the equivalent services are E1 (2.048 Mbps) and E3 (34 Mbps). Dedicated leased lines are most popular with higher-end medium businesses and larger enterprises that need reliable, high-bandwidth WAN links between branch offices.

- **Cell-switched services**—These are similar to packet switching but use small, fixed-size cells rather than variable-length packets. Asynchronous Transfer Mode (ATM) is the most popular cell-switching technology.

Broadband WAN Access

Broadband access services are essential to enhancing productivity for small-medium businesses that operate any or all of the following critical applications:

- Sending or receiving e-mails with large attachments
- Connecting with customers, suppliers, or other locations to exchange time-sensitive information

- Conducting online research via the web

- Handling company procurements online

- Running promotions using online permission marketing of products or services

- Collaborating with remote colleagues or partners on electronic documents, software development, and so on

- Participating in web-based e-learning programs

- Hosting company meetings via videoconferencing

The Business Value of Broadband

Recent Yankee Group research studies have found that 78 to 80 percent of small businesses and 87 to 89 percent of medium businesses in the U.S. that are online use some form of broadband access instead of dialup. The same study showed definitively that the use of dialup access services in small-medium businesses is shrinking by a compound annual growth rate of 8.4 percent.

The business value realized by these small-medium organizations that adopted broadband included the following:

- 82 percent thought broadband communications had improved their internal business process efficiencies.

- These businesses generated more revenues than businesses without broadband by a factor of approximately 2 times for small businesses and 5 times for medium businesses. The revenue increases were predominantly the result of greater productivity per employee.

- More than 78 percent claimed that the Internet helped them deliver better customer service.

- More than 70 percent reported that the Internet had become so vital to their company that business could not be conducted without it.

- 64 percent had improved the ways they work with external partners.

- 50 percent thought broadband had improved their customer-focusing processes.

- Of those using broadband in their companies, 100 percent either already have broadband at home or plan to get it within the next 12 months.

The main point is that most small-medium companies need broadband bandwidth to support the kinds of applications they generally use. The most popular broadband WAN access options include DSL, Frame Relay, T1/E1, and fractional T1 dedicated leased lines. Cable modems also are used, but to a lesser extent in businesses than in residences. Metropolitan Ethernet (Metro Ethernet), another broadband access technology option for these users, is discussed in Chapter 9, "Emerging Technologies."

High-Speed WAN Access Services

As noted, small-medium businesses can consider a number of WAN access options, ranging from narrowband (low-speed) to broadband (high-speed). Table 3-1 compares the pros and cons of selected high-speed wide-area services. These options are described in more detail in the following sections.

Table 3-1   *Broadband WAN Access Service Options*

Service	Description	Pros	Cons
ADSL	Up to 8 Mbps to a business; up to 2 Mbps to the Internet	High-speed; low cost; popular business option	Limited availability; security vulnerability
SDSL	1.54 Mbps in both directions—to business and to the Internet	High-speed; low cost; popular business option	Limited availability; security vulnerability
Frame Relay	56 Kbps to 1.54 Mbps packet-switched service	Multiple speeds; added bandwidth available when needed	Less reliable than dedicated leased lines (such as T1)
Fractional T1	128 Kbps to 1.54 Mbps dedicated service	Dependable; guaranteed speed; less costly than T1; pay for what is used	Priced for low usage; usage over 256 Kbps is more costly
T1/E1	Dedicated point-to-point 1.54 Mbps (T1)/ 2.048 Mbps (E1) leased line	Dependable; guaranteed speed; set monthly price	Setup and monthly fees are costly
T3/E3	Dedicated point-to-point 45 Mbps (T3)/34 Mbps (E3) leased line	Dependable; guaranteed speed; set monthly price	Setup and monthly fees are costly

56-Kbps WAN Access

The most common type of legacy Internet connection is the analog dialup connection using an asynchronous modem. Modems deliver speeds of up to 56 Kbps (56,000 bits of information per second). 56 Kbps is not fast enough for videoconferencing, multimedia, large file transfers, and so on. Although this narrowband connection might be fine for home users (at least those who do not engage in online gaming), businesses typically want greater speed and broadband connectivity. The plus side of 56 Kbps dialup is that it is inexpensive and universally available. Its major drawback is that it is the slowest type of connection available. This is an instance of a WAN access technology that could slow business productivity to a standstill.

ISDN WAN Access

Integrated services Digital Network (ISDN) is a system of telephone networks that has been around since the 1980s. It allows data, images, voice, and video to be transmitted simultaneously on a single digital channel. It can operate through the standard telephone jacks in offices (and homes) using existing copper telephone wiring (usually without special conditioning). Because ISDN is an entirely digital service, there is no analog-to-digital conversion, and users can gain the benefit of the full bandwidth of each channel. Furthermore, ISDN eliminates the requirement that a separate line be used for each additional device (such as another computer, fax, or telephone), because it can combine separate data signals into a single channel. This cuts down on access lines and costs. Depending on the source, ISDN is classified as either narrowband or broadband. The definition that is used depends on the context.

ISDN is available in two options for last-mile access—basic rate interface (BRI) and primary rate interface (PRI). BRI offers three digital channels—two at 64 Kbps and one at 16 Kbps—for a total bandwidth of 144 Kbps. The speed is symmetrical; send and receive bandwidth are equal. Usually it is possible to bond (join or combine) the two 64 Kbps channels and use them as a single 128 Kbps channel. PRI is for users with greater capacity requirements. It allows for a total bandwidth equivalent to a dedicated T1 (1.544 Mbps) or E1 (2.048 Mbps) link.

Unlike a dedicated, point-to-point T1/E1 line, however, ISDN is a switched service that relies on an intelligent switching infrastructure.

Although ISDN BRI is faster than analog modems, widely available in most metropolitan areas, and globally standardized, its main problem is that it is not significantly faster than a good 56 Kbps modem with one channel. When both 64 Kbps channels are used, the connection is twice as fast, but both channels accrue usage charges. Like analog dialup, ISDN is limited in its ability to support bandwidth-intensive business applications.

DSL WAN Access

Digital Subscriber Line (DSL) is designed to carry data and voice traffic simultaneously. It uses standard, ubiquitously installed copper-pair telephone wires but makes better use of the bandwidth than plain old telephone service (POTS). DSL provides improved speed and performance over analog dialup and ISDN. It's like getting access to about 24 modems on one telephone line.

DSL comes in a variety of flavors, the most common of which are asymmetric digital subscriber line (ADSL) and symmetric digital subscriber line (SDSL). SDSL is sometimes also called g.SHDSL, using the International Telecommunication Union (ITU) standards designation.

Asymmetric refers to the fact that data is sent downstream from the wide area network to a company network faster than it is sent upstream from the company back to the public WAN. For instance, ADSL delivers a theoretical 7 to 8 Mbps downstream to subscribers but only a 2 Mbps connection upstream to the Internet or public network. Most often, service providers throttle back the top speed of DSL lines so that they do not cannibalize sales revenues of their dedicated T1 line services. The result is that business subscribers are likely to get performance that is closer to 2 Mbps downstream and less than 1 Mbps upstream to the public network.

Symmetric DSL delivers data at the same speed both downstream from the WAN to the organizational LAN and back upstream. SDSL typically delivers up to 2 Mbps transmission rates and therefore mimics the performance of a dedicated T1 line, but at a lower cost to the subscriber.

The key advantage of DSL versus analog dialup modems and ISDN is speed. A complex web page that could take several minutes to load using these lower-speed services can appear in seconds over DSL. In addition to connection speed, reliability, and always-on connectivity are the main reasons for its popularity. DSL technology usually operates over a distance of about 3 miles (4-8 kilometers) from the telephone central office (exchange) or remote terminal. However, some service providers won't deliver service beyond 12,000 feet (3.7 kilometers) from their central office to ensure higher-quality performance. With DSL, maximum speed is a direct function of the distance over which the service is delivered, the type of cabling that is used, and the type of DSL (ADSL, SDSL, and so on). The longer the distance a DSL signal travels, the lower the achievable speed. So distance is what affects performance the most with DSL.

Besides speed and always-on connectivity, other advantages of using DSL include the following:

- The same line can be used for voice calls as well as data transmission.

- Typically, no new wiring is needed. DSL uses the phone line that's already installed.

- Customer premises equipment (CPE) is typically included as part of the subscription from service providers.

- DSL is an effective and affordable high-speed remote-access option for teleworkers who connect to the office LAN (and company intranet) while working at home.

- Good price/performance. Generally speaking, users pay at least twice as much for a dedicated T1 line than for DSL. For the cost of a single 1.544 Mbps T1 connection, a small-medium business could have three or four DSL lines. Beyond recurring service fee savings, the initial installation costs for a T1 are usually more than for a DSL line.

DSL technology continues to evolve and be upgraded. ADSL-2 lengthens the loop distance over which the service operates. As a result, DSL can now reach an additional 5 to 10 percent of potential subscribers. Because service availability in the U.S. has sometimes been an issue with DSL, this raises customer coverage from 80 percent to about 90 percent of the accessible market. ADSL-2 also increases achievable data rates to 25 Mbps under ideal circumstances.

Cable Modem WAN Access

Cable modems offer a relatively inexpensive way to connect very small businesses (fewer than 20 employees—called SoHo (or small office, home office) to the Internet. For the most part, cable plant passes through more residential than commercial areas in the U.S. It is therefore used less frequently than DSL for small-medium business WAN access.

Cable modems operate differently than conventional modems. An analog modem is connected to a telephone line that runs to the phone company switching office. A cable modem uses a cable TV company's RF (radio frequency) system, which runs through the neighborhood to a cable headend at the cable provider's location. Whereas a telephone line has a dedicated path to the service provider location, a cable modem connection uses a shared network, in which all users of the system in a neighborhood contend for the available bandwidth. The maximum number of simultaneous users supported varies with each service provider. All the devices connected to this cable network system can talk and listen to each other. This shared network access approach is important to keep in mind when considering WAN service options. It is important from an information security and privacy perspective, as well as with regard to system performance.

Cable modem speeds vary widely, depending on the type of network architecture employed and the number of simultaneous users on the network. Implementation options include one-way and two-way systems. In a one-way system, the cable plant transmits downstream to users, and a dialup analog line serves as the return path. With a two-way system, the cable plant is used in both directions. In the downstream direction (from the network to a user's computer or LAN), cable networks are engineered to deliver up to 27 Mbps. This is the total amount of available bandwidth, which is shared among all users of the system. It is not reserved for a single company or residential user. Few computers can connect at such high speeds anyway. A realistic transmission rate for cable modem systems is 1 to 3 Mbps. When sending information to the Internet in the upstream direction, the theoretical maximum speed is 10 Mbps. Again, most cable modem users experience lesser speeds of between 500 Kbps and 2.5 Mbps.

Here are some advantages of cable modem systems for business use:

- Cable modem systems can carry large amounts of computer data downstream.

- If the cable plant is well maintained by the cable company, cable modems are typically faster for downloads than most DSL lines.

- Cable modem connections are only slightly more expensive than dialup services, yet they provide broadband, always-on WAN access.

The downsides of using cable modems include the following:

- U.S. industrial and commercial business areas have limited cable modem service availability.

- There is much variability in speed. As more users are added to this shared WAN technology, lower speeds will be realized on a per-user basis.

- The potential for RF interference exists. Because cable is an RF network system, it is vulnerable to interference from other RF systems.

- Security vulnerabilities exist. As a result of its shared-architecture design, business information transmitted across a cable modem system could be at risk for interception or corruption if not properly secured.

Frame Relay WAN Access

Frame Relay is a high-speed WAN communications technology used in thousands of small-medium business networks throughout the world. The service (sometimes called just Frame) originated in the 1990s as an affordable private-line replacement technology for the transmission of data. Now it regularly transmits not only data, but also voice and video information. Frame is widely used to provide both intracompany and intercompany LAN-to-LAN connectivity. As such, it has been widely adopted as a WAN solution for businesses to share information with their remote branch offices and even business partner locations.

A number of Frame Relay advantages have been mentioned in this chapter. Others include the following:

- Frame Relay is more economical than a leased line. In other words, it offers a lower total cost of ownership (TCO). Because it is a packet-switching technology, Frame Relay is also more efficient than dedicated leased lines. A Frame Relay network is a common point of connection for multiple LAN-to-LAN connections. Each site needs only a single last-mile connection to the Frame Relay network. This feature can offer considerable savings to businesses on both last mile access charges and network access equipment capital expenditures.

- Frame Relay offers low overhead and high reliability.

- It is standardized, widely available, and proven as a WAN technology.

- It interworks with other WAN technologies such as ATM.

Its name essentially describes what Frame Relay does: It relays frames (or packets) across public networks between two or more sites. It offers the predictable, guaranteed bandwidth necessary for client/server communications. Frame Relay also supports more unpredictable, heavier than usual, bursty traffic when that need arises. This high-speed packet-switching service usually operates at 1.544 Mbps rates, but Frame Relay also offers its users bandwidth scalability. It is possible to bond two Frame Relay circuits to provide 3 Mbps or higher throughput, up to a maximum 45 Mbps rate.

To connect locations using Frame Relay, subscribers ask their service provider to register the specific LAN endpoints between which they will exchange information. They also must reserve and pay for sufficient bandwidth to support the business applications to be run. This reserved bandwidth (called committed information rate [CIR]) is what a service provider promises to deliver as the service level for a subscribing company's use. If a company wants to change either the designated endpoints or the amount of bandwidth, it must place another service order with the service provider. Connections in Frame Relay are purchased as permanent virtual circuits (PVCs). PVCs essentially provide the same kind of continuous connection as a private leased line, but without the high cost or dedicated resources. With a virtual circuit, no bandwidth is reserved or used unless data is being sent. Frame Relay customers are charged only for their level of usage on the public network, not for the privilege of reserving switched ports and bandwidth for potential use.

The lower the committed information rate (or bandwidth service level) subscribed to, the lower the cost of Frame Relay to a customer. But it is important to understand and keep in mind the company's needs when choosing services to ensure that productive communications are not being sacrificed to achieve short-term operating expense savings. The right price/performance balance must be struck. Lost business resulting from slow customer responsiveness or downtime from an overloaded network can cost a company significantly more than the next-higher speed increment of a Frame Relay service. A consultant, VAR, network integrator, or network equipment vendor can help a small-medium business assess its communications requirements and recommend the proper service option and appropriate service level.

ATM WAN Access

Asynchronous Transfer Mode (ATM) is a high-speed technology based on the transmission of small, fixed-size cells. This cell-switching approach makes ATM more predictable and allows more efficient and rapid switching of voice, data, and video traffic. ATM can provide greater service level guarantees than packet services such as DSL, cable modems, or Frame Relay.

ATM was designed to run over fiber-optic cable and deliver scalable bandwidth from 52 Mbps to 2 Gbps. As such, it has proven ideal in network backbones for long-haul Internet links. It supports real-time multimedia applications (such as videoconferencing, e-learning, and video multicasting) without difficulty and can be used equally effectively in LAN, MAN, and WAN environments. As a result of the emergence of gigabit Ethernet in the LAN, however, ATM has mostly been relegated to MANs and WANs (from which it originated in the 1980s). This shift is partly because ATM is one of the most complex communications technologies to operate in public or private network infrastructures. The bottom line is that as a connectivity technology, ATM is seldom used by small-medium businesses. It is most widely implemented in the core network infrastructures of public telecommunications carriers.

Private, Dedicated Leased-Line WAN Access

Service providers such as local exchange carriers, long-distance carriers, and ISPs offer T1, fractional T1, and T3 dedicated lines. In Europe, the equivalents are E1 and E3 lines. These private-line services involve leasing a communications channel that is reserved for the use of that business. Private lines such as these are not shared with or accessible to other companies on the public switched telephone network (PSTN).

Advantages of dedicated, digital private lines include the following:

- **Digital service end-to-end**—This ensures high-quality, low-error transmissions.

- **Continuous, reliable availability with low delay**—This means that there is never a delay for setting up a connection. Consistent and low delay is good for voice, data, and video communications.

- **Guaranteed consistency of WAN performance**—The same amount of bandwidth is always available.

- **Security**—Private digital lines are harder to tap than dialup lines.

- **Scalable bandwidth**—This is important for demanding business applications.

- **Flexibility**—Leased lines support point-to-point and multipoint communications between headquarters, branch offices, and partner or supplier locations.

The major drawback is cost. Typically, users pay a flat monthly fee no matter how much the service is used. This gives customers the right to unfettered access to secure network resources. Prices vary regionally and by service provider, but they are usually based on a combination of end-to-end distance of the private line and its bandwidth capacity. As a ballpark figure, dedicated lines can run 12 to 25 times or more the price of a public network DSL access service on a monthly basis.

As mentioned earlier, private lines can be purchased in various bandwidth increments that deliver symmetrical bandwidth. That is, information travels at the same speed in both the sending and receiving directions. These increments include T1/E1 or multiple T1s/E1s (at 1.544 or 2.048 Mbps per line), fractional T1 (increments of 64 Kbps, often starting at 384 Kbps and going up to 1.544/2.048 Mbps), and T3/E3 (45/34 Mbps).

T1s and E1s are the most widely adopted dedicated line options. Each T1/E1 (1.544/2.048 Mbps) line is composed of 24 64 Kbps channels. These lines are implemented as either channelized or unchannelized. Channelized leased lines are typically used for voice communications. Each 64 Kbps channel carries its own traffic, making it the T1 equivalent of having 24 modems on a single line. An unchannelized leased line is essentially just one big transmission pipe used for high-speed data traffic. As a point of capacity comparison, a T1 or E1 line carries roughly 60 times more data than a 56 Kbps analog modem. Service providers can also bond multiple T1s/E1s to provide a company with more bandwidth as the number of applications and users on its networks grows.

Even though leased-line prices have dropped considerably, T1 lines can still be expensive for some smaller and even midsized companies. Some businesses just don't generate enough traffic to justify a full T1 or E1. Those that can use less than a full T1 can contract to use fractions of the total T1 line, called a fractional T1 (abbreviated as F-T1). When ordering an F-T1 from a service provider, a company actually receives a full T1 circuit, but the ISP limits the transmission. The subscriber pays for only the channel capacity it orders—256 Kbps, 384 Kbps, 524 Kbps, and so on.

On the other hand, there are some companies for which a T1 (or E1) or multiple T1s/E1s are insufficient to support their applications. In those rare instances, a T3, or 45-Mbps (or E3 [34 Mbps]), circuit is the next dedicated, leased-line increment. For most small-medium businesses, a T1 or multiple T1s should be sufficient to handle required peak information traffic loads.

Virtual Private Networks (VPNs) represent another potential wide-area access method. They demonstrate that there are inexpensive alternatives to expensive dedicated private-line, packet, and cell services. Using affordable VPN solutions is another way for small-medium businesses to achieve secure remote access. VPNs, and the role they play in remote access, are discussed in Chapter 6, "Intranets, Extranets, and Virtual Private Networks (VPNs)."

Summary

LANs, MANs, and WANs allow businesses to connect employees, strategic partners, and customers across distributed geographies. Distance is irrelevant when companies are linked with networks. The ease and flexibility of communications that are achieved with LANs, MANs, and WANs make all connected parties appear as if they are in close proximity.

The leading technology used in LANs is Ethernet. It is available in bandwidths that range from 10 Mbps to 1000 Mbps. 10 Gbps varieties of Ethernet are also emerging. Ethernet LANs are used by small-medium businesses for applications including multimedia e-mail, IP telephony, customer relationship management, e-commerce, and more.

LANs connect to WANs and form end-to-end information systems. A variety of access technologies are used to deliver these last-mile connections. LAN-to-WAN link options include circuit switched services, packet switched services, dedicated leased lines, and cell switched services. Broadband WAN services provide small-medium businesses with the highest business value for their IT investment. The most popularly adopted broadband WAN services for business users are ISDN PRI, DSL, Frame Relay, and T1/E1 or T3/E3 private, leased lines.

CHAPTER 4

NETWORK FOUNDATION TECHNOLOGIES— SWITCHING AND ROUTING

A solid network foundation is the key to business agility, process efficiency, productivity, and competitiveness. It provides intelligent services such as security, availability, reliability, and quality of service (QoS). This makes it possible for small-medium companies to run desired business applications and advanced technologies, establish competitive advantage, extend or streamline their operations, improve responsiveness to customers and partners, and reduce the costs of ongoing network management.

Routers and switches are the keys to a strong network foundation. Together they enable the intelligent, end-to-end movement of converged data, voice, and video information within or outside the business.

Switches and routers provide the following network functions:

- Switches connect users directly to the network and serve as the primary path for traffic moving within local networks. As more-sophisticated business applications, higher volumes of traffic, and tighter security measures have put greater demands on the network, switches have evolved to give companies greater intelligence and control.

- Routers deliver information from a source to its intended destination via the most efficient route across different types of networks. As networks have developed, the line between the roles of switches and routers has continued to blur. The clear trend is toward switches prevailing in the LAN, while routers dominate in the WAN and at the company perimeter (or LAN edge) for WAN access.

Small-medium businesses are becoming increasingly dependent on networks to operate efficiently, serve customers effectively, and work with partners and suppliers more collaboratively. Faced with all the challenges and opportunities of competing in a fast-paced environment, growing companies must be especially confident that their networks can support business evolution. Building an effective network foundation is integral to, and an operational insurance policy for, achieving e-business transformation. You can think of this foundation as equivalent to a person's skeletal structure. It is the support system. The stronger, healthier, and more flexible is, the greater the range of movement, carrying capacity, and longevity or stamina. A network foundation serves that same skeletal role for a business.

It is vital that small-medium businesses focus their attention on the critical success factors that drive growth in their particular market. They cannot afford to expend precious time rearchitecting, relearning, and managing networks. Network infrastructures should be the invisible plumbing that enables the transport of company information and communications and enables efficient processes. When the invisible becomes visible and companies run up against infrastructure limitations, this can lead to revenue losses, information privacy breaches, and customer dissatisfaction. This is because network problems can result in poor responsiveness and/or the dissemination of faulty data. Such occurrences can seriously undermine a company's competitiveness and credibility.

The way to avoid such problems is to ensure that the foundation or core infrastructure is well constructed, adaptable to changing environments, intelligent, and operable with minimal administrative intervention. The network should not be so time-consuming to set up and manage that it detracts from the business's primary focus.

The Value of a Business-Class Network

As noted previously, the key elements of an intelligent network foundation are switches and routers that deliver security, availability, reliability, and quality of service. A business-class network should provide the following capabilities:

- **Protection from security breaches**—Budget-conscious small-medium companies might feel particularly conflicted as they weigh the costs associated with implementing comprehensive network security against the cost of potential breaches. When security features are integral to a network's foundation, they simplify management while they protect business operations, improve business resiliency, prevent damage to intellectual property assets, mitigate business disruptions, and reduce the network's total cost of ownership (TCO).

- **Continuous availability and network reliability**—As business information systems become ever more strategic to a company's success, so does the importance of keeping them *always online*—able to recover from failure—and accessible anywhere. The proliferation of powerful desktops and servers running bandwidth-intensive applications has some networks straining to keep up. With each new user, device, or application, the underlying infrastructure comes under that much more stress. The network foundation must be prepared to support increasing numbers of users with 24/7 uptime; run new services and applications; extend its reach to new offices, customers, and partners; and support a more mobile workforce. The bottom-line business impact of an available network is increased productivity.

- **Quality of service**—QoS lets small-medium businesses use the network infrastructure, including LAN and WAN connections, more efficiently. As networks continue to converge (integrate voice, data, and video into a single network), it becomes increasingly important to ensure the efficient coexistence of high-priority and low-priority information transfer. Incorporating QoS into the network foundation lets you assign higher priority to business-critical applications and delay-sensitive traffic such as voice, video, and real-time transactions.

Network Foundation Relevance

When thinking about the business value of a solid network foundation, you cannot help but ask, "Does this apply to my business?" or "Do I really need this?" A business-class, intelligent network foundation is suitable for use by any small-medium business to which the following criteria apply:

- The business depends on a network to handle mission-critical operations.

- It runs e-commerce and web applications that exchange real-time information online with customers, partners, and employees.

- It is concerned about adding new business applications while maintaining the performance level of existing applications.

- It is poised for growth or is experiencing growth that is straining the limits of the existing network infrastructure.

- It wants to implement advanced technologies such as IP telephony, storage networks, wireless mobility, and security or a VPN (virtual private network).

- It wants to compete or partner with larger businesses—in terms of geographic reach, types of customers served, or hours of operation.

The critical network foundation elements (switches and routers), along with their value propositions and related investment decision criteria, are covered in this chapter.

LAN Switching

Switches are a fundamental part of most networks. They let multiple users communicate directly with each other. As such, they offer the potential for collision-free, high-speed networking. In essence, switches create a system of simultaneous, parallel, point-to-point connections between pairs of devices.

Here are some benefits that can be realized by using LAN switches:

- **Increased network scalability**—The network can expand easily as the business grows.

- **Improved bandwidth performance for each network user**—This is important in environments where users operate multimedia applications or conduct frequent client/server database interactions.

- **Multiple simultaneous connections**—Many simultaneous data transfers can take place between pairs of devices connected to switch ports. This is not possible with hub-based networks.

- **Reduced congestion and information transmission delay**—This translates to more efficient business application access. Remember that network segmentation is used to minimize the number of users contending for LAN bandwidth on each segment (switch port).

- **No single point of failure**—With proper network design, there are fewer chances for network failure.

- **Improved manageability and security through the use of virtual LANs (VLANs)** — VLANs group individual users into logical workgroups with common interests or business functions. Data broadcasts are restricted to designated members of the group (also called the *broadcast domain*). This functionality gives companies the flexibility to move employees around physically yet still maintain their functional ties via the VLAN without network reconfiguration. VLANs are discussed in more depth later in this chapter.

A small-medium business can choose from a variety of switch types. The most popular options are the following:

- **Layer 2 switches** — Also called desktop or workgroup switches.

- **Layer 3 switches** — Also called routing switches or multilayer switches.

Layer 2 Switching

Conventional Ethernet switches are data link layer (Layer 2 or L2) devices. This means that they operate at Layer 2 of the OSI (Open Systems Interconnection) reference model. In general, Layer 2 services enable the transfer of data across physical connections. Figure 4-1 shows how end-user network devices (nodes) connect to L2 switch ports. Like bridges, which also operate at Layer 2, the L2 switch dynamically learns the MAC addresses (Ethernet addresses) of devices on each of its ports. It then switches traffic to the intended ports as needed.

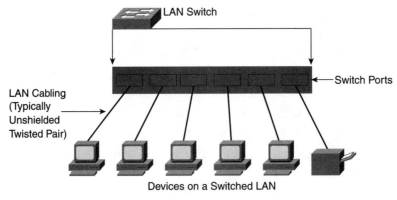

Figure 4-1   *Layer 2 Switched LAN Connections*

Switches operating at Layer 2 are very fast because they directly switch data from port to port based on the physical hardware addresses (MAC addresses) that are assigned to network devices during manufacturing. The trade-off for their speed is that they usually are not as intelligent as routers. That is, they do not look at the data packets being transferred to learn anything about where they are going or make any filtering or traffic direction decisions about them. Such decisions require end-to-end knowledge of the network. Switches know only about their locally connected devices.

LAN Switches Replace Hubs

Layer 2 desktop switches are designed to replace hubs and to provide each network device with dedicated bandwidth for higher performance. A hub represents the most basic kind of network. It operates at Layer 1, which means that it physically connects nodes (including computers, servers, printers, and so on). When data comes into a hub, the hub broadcasts it to all other network nodes (attached devices). Although hub-based LANs are still implemented in many very small businesses (including home-based businesses), they cannot effectively support the business applications that most companies are deploying today. Besides its lack of advanced functionality, a hub-based network has other shortcomings, including the following:

- **Value**—The cost of switches is essentially the same as hubs. Users get significantly more price/performance value from switches than they do from hubs.

- **Scalability**—The limited, shared bandwidth of a hub network restricts its growth. As users and applications are added, network performance and availability often drop dramatically.

- **Latency**—Latency (or delay) can become unacceptable as the network expands, again compromising performance.

- **Failure**—Hub-based networks are notorious for failing, because just one faulty device can cause problems for other devices attached to the hub.

An analogy to consider when thinking about the differences between a switched network and a hub network is that of a highway. With a hub, the network is like a single-lane highway, with data traffic often sluggish or backed up because of a problem or even a crash along the road. A switch-based LAN, however, is more like a multilane highway with traffic flowing in both directions. Users communicate at much higher speeds and with far greater reliability on the switch. They can add traffic to the network without slowing one another down and simply bypass any problem.

Most companies find the migration from hubs to intelligent switches to be simple, nondisruptive, and highly cost-effective. Upgrading to a switch from a hub is relatively painless, because the switch accepts the same cabling and connections as the hub it is replacing. For small-medium businesses that are installing a first-time LAN, a switched network approach is clearly the way to go to protect network investments and build in growth headroom.

Layer 2 switched networks, although more robust than hubs and less costly than Layer 3 switches or routers, also have their shortcomings:

- **End-to-end visibility**—Switches have no indication of the location of particular devices in a distributed network. They know only about devices that are directly connected.

- **Scalability**—Switches use flat addressing (that is, they provide a single level of addressing). In an L2 switched network, data messages are sent to all network-attached devices. There is no hierarchy of message delivery, as there is when using routers. This limits transmissions to a single connected workgroup (domain).

- **Broadcast storms**—*Broadcast storms* saturate a network and create overhead that throttles bandwidth and slows performance. Broadcasts grow with network size and travel throughout switched networks. When growing a Layer 2 switched network from 100 to 1000 users, decision-makers should keep in mind that broadcast volume will grow at least tenfold.

VLANs

Software-based virtual LANs (VLANs) organize network devices into logical workgroups (or broadcast domains) independent of physical location. VLANs can offer some relief from Layer 2 switching drawbacks and can help manage broadcasts. Many medium-sized companies have adopted VLANs to deal with the limitations of Layer 2 switching. These companies use VLANs to structure a network for growth.

Any device anywhere on an L2 switched network can be a member of a VLAN, regardless of where other VLAN members are located. However, it is essential that these devices be connected to switches that support VLAN functionality. This is usually designated as IEEE 802.1Q-compliant. Each VLAN acts as a separate network. In fact, for members of different VLANs to communicate, a router (or a Layer 3 switch) must be used—even if they are connected to the same switch. Every VLAN node (and only those nodes) "hears" the broadcast traffic sent by other VLAN members sharing the same VLAN.

Membership in a VLAN is determined by business preferences called *policies*. Policy criteria can include IP address (listing specific addresses in a domain), port number (assigning physical switch ports to a logical workgroup), or application (such as customer relationship management, sales force automation, call center, and so on). Using business functions as a policy example, the marketing staff might be spread throughout a building, yet if they are all assigned to a single VLAN, they can share resources and bandwidth as if they were connected to the same physical LAN segment or subnet (portion of a network). The resources of other departments, such as finance and engineering, can be invisible to the marketing VLAN members, accessible to all VLANs, or accessible to only certain individuals based on specified IT policy parameters. Figure 4-2 shows VLANs being used to subdivide functional workgroups.

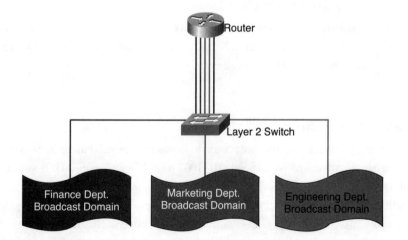

Figure 4-2 *Logical VLAN Workgroups*

VLAN Benefits

User productivity and adaptability are key drivers for business growth and success. Implementing VLAN technology is becoming a popular means to enable a network to more flexibly support business goals. The primary benefits of using VLANs are as follows:

- **Security**—Groups that have sensitive data are separated from the rest of the network, decreasing the chances of confidential information breaches.

- **Cost reduction**—Cost savings result from less need for expensive network upgrades and more efficient use of existing bandwidth and uplinks. Some of the savings are reduced by administrative costs needed for IT staff to configure VLANs into switches.

- **Higher performance**—Dividing flat Layer 2 networks into multiple logical workgroups (broadcast domains) reduces overall network utilization and boosts performance.

- **Broadcast storm mitigation**—Dividing a network into smaller logical networks results in lower susceptibility to broadcast storms.

- **Simpler project or application management**—VLANs bring together all required players in a way that makes managing a project or working with a specialized application easier.

- **Improved IT staff efficiency**—Moves, adds, and changes are easier and less expensive to perform. Network administrators' time is freed up for proactive network management.

Layer 3 Switching

Routing used to be the only way to connect internal business networks. However, the advent of wire speed (10, 100, 1000 Mbps) Layer 3 (L3) switches with virtually no delay now lets LAN traffic be connected without the use of traditional routers in the backbone. Standalone routers mostly have been relegated to handle LAN/WAN edge access and WAN connectivity. This is similar to how high-performance Fast Ethernet and Gigabit Ethernet have nudged ATM from the LAN to the WAN. Figure 4-3 shows how Layer 2/Layer 3 switches dominate in the LAN backbone and in the distribution network and how routers dominate at the network edge for WAN access.

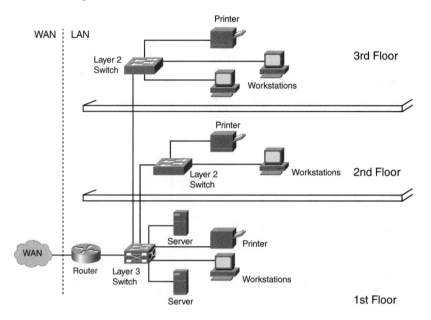

Figure 4-3 *Complementary Roles of Switches and Routers*

In spite of the benefits they deliver, L3 switches are essentially marketing, rather than technological, innovations. For all practical purposes, an L3 switch is a high-performance router (that is, a hardware-based IP router) that is optimized for use in a company's LAN or intranet. Performance is the key factor that distinguishes an L3 switch from a traditional router. An L3 switch can forward packets many times faster than most routers because it does not have the overhead of supporting multiprotocol functionality or the comprehensive filtering functions of a router. L3 switches are lean, mean machines.

L3 switches do the following:

- They route IP packets and sometimes IPX protocol packets. Traditional routers are needed if other protocols need to be routed.

- They switch nonroutable traffic at Layer 2 (by MAC address). This helps blur the line between L2 and L3 switches.

- They forward frames at wire speed rates with latencies of typically a few microseconds.

- They support only LAN-based routing.

- Switches are less expensive than traditional routers that have similar performance.

Benefits of L3 switches include the following:

- **High performance**—They deliver wire speed to the desktop, which helps mitigate network bottlenecks.

- **Ease of use**—They are easy to install and configure, and they offer unified management.

- **Scalability**—They can grow from small to very large networks.

- **Compatibility**—They work seamlessly with L2 switches and traditional routers.

In converged networking environments that carry multimedia traffic, L3 switching is becoming the *de facto* foundation for meaningful QoS. QoS is needed to support such applications as videoconferencing and IP telephony; it can also provide fast access to centralized servers.

Intelligent LAN Switch Adoption Considerations

When implementing advanced networking technologies (IP telephony, wireless mobility, security, storage networking, and others) and Internet-based business applications, it is vital to deploy intelligent LAN switches as part of a core network foundation. These switches should feature functionality such as the following:

- **High availability and quick response time**—Ensures the reliable delivery of time-critical information.

- **Integrated security**—Protects sensitive areas of the network and its data.

- **Quality of service (QoS)**—Network administrators can assign priorities to business-critical traffic for consistent, predictable delivery.

- **Web-based management and friendly graphical user interfaces (GUIs)**—Save network administrators time and ensure management efficiency.

Consider a number of criteria and features when choosing an intelligent LAN switch. Select a switch that:

- Doesn't drop frames under heavy loads
- Delivers low latency (delay measured in microseconds)
- Provides local and remote network management options
- Offers plug and play installation for quick setup
- Offers load balancing for traffic management
- Ensures ease of adding bandwidth as the network grows or more-demanding applications are added
- Provides redundancy of the switch and its power supplies for backup and network resilience
- Offers hot-swappable modules for easy maintenance and uninterrupted network uptime
- Offers lower cost per port than traditional routers
- Includes or can enable VLAN support to reduce network management costs in growing networks

Factors to Discuss with a Trusted Advisor

Small-medium business decision-makers should ensure that their consultant, reseller, or equipment vendor, as well as their in-house IT staff, take into account the following factors to determine the most appropriate intelligent switches to deploy. There is an array of LAN switch types from which to choose. It is important to select the proper switch to support the business's current and evolving requirements and network budget. Here are some factors to consider in gauging which switch is most suitable:

- **Current network traffic patterns**—Ideally, traffic patterns should be baselined for a few weeks to identify which users or groups require higher bandwidth and whether user-generated information flows are one-to-one (peer-to-peer) or many-to-one (client/server). Putting the right number of users on a switch can balance traffic loads and guarantee higher performance.

- **Company expansion plans**—Switches must be able to handle current and future users. Consider the number of employees to be added (or reduced), new buildings on a campus, new functional groups to be formed, company acquisitions that might bring diversified network infrastructures, and so on.

- **Business software adoption plans**—Bandwidth must be sufficient for the applications to be run. Both current and future media must be considered.

- **LAN upgrade plans**—If the LAN will be upgraded from Ethernet to Fast Ethernet to Gigabit Ethernet, the switch must be able to support that.

- **Advanced network technology adoption plans**—Bandwidth must be sufficient for any new advanced technologies to be deployed, such as IP telephony to replace PBX systems, storage networking, wireless LANs, network security, and others.

For business-critical and growing networks, a foundation built on intelligent switching offers high performance, availability, scalability, security, and improved manageability for a reasonable cost.

The Role of Routing in Computer Networks

The primary business drivers for routing are to provide ubiquitous, secure, and ready application availability and web access for employees. This must be done with a total cost of ownership (TCO) that is affordable and justifiable in light of the company's objectives and initiatives. When properly used as part of a network foundation, routers can help optimize application availability, improve employee productivity, boost customer responsiveness and loyalty, and spur company competitiveness and time to market. Routers also can help overcome the limitations of geography between small-medium businesses and their customers, partners, and suppliers. They can mitigate business conduct restraints that are tied to physical office locations.

Routers carry out two basic functions—they select a path between networks, and they securely transmit information packets across that path toward an intended destination. In so doing, they draw on routing protocols and algorithms. These algorithms are designed to plot routes using such criteria as throughput, delay, simplicity, low overhead, reliability/stability, and flexibility. Tables of available routes and their conditions are created so that routers can use the most efficient paths possible for each transmission. This process is similar to maps created by auto clubs that show drivers where roadwork is under way so that they can avoid potential areas of congestion. When a packet is received at a router, the router opens it, looks at the network destination address, and then calculates the *next hop* in the best, or lowest-cost, route to the destination. A hop is measured by the passage of a packet through a router. For example, if a packet passes through three routers, it uses three hops to reach its destination. Achieving low cost with routing is especially important, because WAN bandwidth is expensive.

Routers can be hardware- or software-based. They are different from Layer 3 switches in that they support multiple protocols besides IP. They can connect different kinds of networks to form internetworks (and therefore are said to be *medium-independent*). Routers also differ from Layer 2 switches because they enable the building of very large networks, such as the Internet. This is in sharp contrast to the limited scalability of Layer 2 networks using L2 switches. Internetworking is about linking computing devices and workers through a maze of telecommunications lines. This ability to provide communications route diversity across various links is what ensures that business applications sustain an uptime level that is satisfactory to business executives.

To small-medium business end users, routers are merely connectivity devices or intermediaries. The simplest router configuration possible has only two interconnected networks, or interfaces—an Ethernet LAN connection and a WAN connection. With the exception of the IT staff that manages them, most network users communicate through routers rather than with routers. In fact, hackers sometimes try to direct traffic to routers to shut down a business. That is the principle behind denial of service (DoS) attacks. Security precautions must be taken to protect against this. Chapter 5, "Network Security Basics," discusses the appropriate precautions.

As mentioned previously, L2/L3 switches now dominate the LAN. Routers work with switches in a complementary manner to provide WAN access. Switches hand off traffic to routers at the *network edge* to access the Internet or send information across a WAN. The network edge is the demarcation between the company LAN and the WAN, or between a teleworker's home LAN and the WAN. When employees send e-mails or access the web, they are typically sending their messages and information requests locally using switches and across the Internet via a number of routers.

Access Routing Adoption Decision Criteria

Like their switching counterparts, routers that are employed in small-medium businesses should deliver high performance, flexibility, and intelligent business-class services such as the following:

- Availability in the form of various types of redundancy and survivability for network resilience.

- Security such as VPN support, intrusion detection, integrated firewall, and access control lists (ACLs). Chapter 5 provides more details.

- QoS for traffic scheduling, queuing, and policing.

- Hot-swappable modules for easy maintenance and uninterrupted network uptime.

- Scalable manageability for all sizes of businesses.

Consumer-class routers, although they offer attractive commodity prices, might fail when exposed to the rigors of a growing business's applications. This could bring a business to its knees. Such products also could lead to higher TCO over time and result in a patchwork of networking devices that are difficult to manage. The right router can establish a solid foundation for business networking and growth.

Measuring the Success of a Network Foundation

It is critical that the success of a network foundation deployment be measurable. Here are some metrics that can be established for tracking purposes before an installation:

- Increased employee productivity
- Improved responsiveness to clients, customers, suppliers, and partners
- Reduced network downtime
- Improved confidence in adding new software applications
- More-dependable and far-reaching application availability
- Greater business resilience and agility
- Lower administrative and support costs

Summary

Small-medium businesses are becoming increasingly dependent on computer networks for efficient operations, responsive customer service, and collaboration with partners. Switches and routers are the keys to a strong network foundation. Together they enable the end-to-end movement of data, voice, and video information.

A network foundation can be considered equivalent to a person's skeletal structure. It is the support system. Like the human skeleton, a network foundation should handle its role invisibly but efficiently. If the network becomes visible, it can become intrusive. If that happens, the network detracts from a company's focus on its core business practices.

Foundational network elements should protect a company from security breaches, ensure continuous operations, and deliver quality of service. The core elements of a network foundation include switches and routers. Switches are a fundamental part of most networks. They let multiple users communicate with each other. Small-medium businesses can choose from a variety of switch types, including Layer 2 and Layer 3. Routers provide scalability, security, ready application availability, and web access for employees. They involve two basic functions—selecting paths between networks and securely transmitting information.

Keep in mind a number of factors when evaluating network switch and router investments. The first criterion is always to ask what a company's business objectives are. The answers will drive the technical criteria for level of availability, type of security, quality of service guarantees, network management, and so on.

CHAPTER 5

NETWORK SECURITY BASICS

Security becomes a critical concern as small-medium businesses shift more of their core operations to the network. The stakes are now higher. Security attacks have moved beyond the realm of annoyances. Today, a network security breach can shut down a company's most important operations, thus decreasing productivity, jeopardizing data integrity, disturbing customer confidence, affecting revenues, and bringing work communications to a standstill.

In past years, business networks were more self-contained, and it was relatively straightforward to secure them. There were fewer online interactions with partners and customers to deal with and less distributed remote access by employees. As shown in Figure 5-1, the network perimeter was clear, and simpler devices could provide sufficient protection to compensate for any possible security holes.

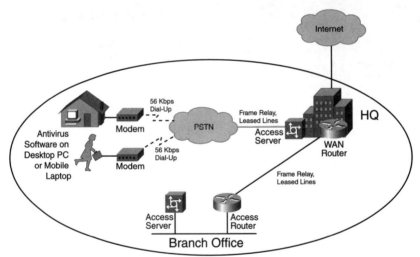

Figure 5-1 *Networks of the 1990s*

The New Environment

As the Internet has matured and wireless and integrated Internet Protocol (IP) networking communications have become more commonplace, business networks have evolved to present significant new security challenges. When businesses open their infrastructures to support collaborative Internet connectivity, teleworking, wireless mobility, and business-to-business application sharing, traditional network boundaries all but disappear. Companies have outgrown security devices designed for legacy networks and at the same time have become more vulnerable to attacks by hackers and other agents. A standalone security product or software package is no longer enough to protect open, distributed, and virtual networks, as shown in Figure 5-2. Instead, an in-depth security solution is needed.

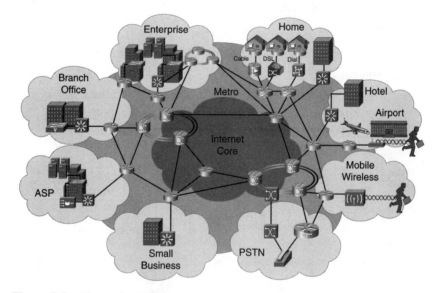

Figure 5-2 *Networks of Today*

Adding to the complexity, many security systems in place today are not network-aware or designed to work with business-class (versus consumer) network services. This situation leaves small-medium businesses especially vulnerable to an increasingly sophisticated array of network attacks.

Growing Network Attacks

The number of security incidents is growing exponentially. Attacks are getting more sophisticated and, at the same time, much easier to deploy, as shown in Figure 5-3. The reasons for this trend include the following:

- Increasing complexity of networks

- The acceleration of public Internet access

- The adoption of always-on broadband

- Wireless LANs (WLANs)

- IP telephony

- Advanced technologies that enable teleworking and a more mobile workforce

- The continuing implementation of e-business applications such as e-commerce, customer relationship management, supply chain management, and web marketing

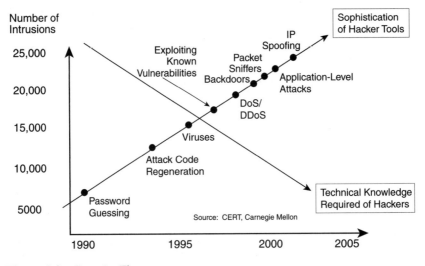

Figure 5-3 *Security Threats*

What this dynamic environment means is that security solutions cannot be static, and they should be re-addressed regularly, because new threats to security are constantly appearing. As new threats arise and business models and supporting networks change, organizations must dynamically evolve their security solutions as well.

Sources of Security Attacks

An often-overlooked yet potentially devastating form of network threat comes from inside a business's local network. There is so much focus on outside attacks that many people forget about those that come from inside the network—from the local area network (LAN). Internal attacks often can be the toughest to combat. How do you prevent high-level employees from selling trade secrets over the Internet? Do you restrict their access to only those secrets, or do you restrict their ability to access the marketplace while at work? Educating the company's network users can be one of the greatest tools for strengthening and enforcing network security.

Small-medium businesses might think they are less vulnerable than larger companies, but research shows that most are extending the reach of their networks (and therefore their security exposure) just as larger organizations are doing. For example:

- Most small-medium businesses have between six and ten remote locations.

- 10 to 15 percent of their workforces telework several times a month.

- About 85 percent of small-medium business workers telework extended hours after a full day at the office.

- Only between 10 and 20 percent of small businesses and a third of medium businesses have already deployed remote-access virtual private networks (VPNs). Yet these numbers are expected to more than triple in the next few years.

The Impact of Network Attacks

Security breaches can compromise application availability, data confidentiality, and data integrity as well as present legal complications. The consequences can be severe, directly affecting a company's bottom line by destroying critical data and resulting in significant repair and recovery costs. Perhaps most importantly, they disturb the conduct of business, which can be tremendously costly. Even the hint of possible security vulnerabilities can be damaging to a company's reputation. Customers, business partners, and employees must have confidence that their information and transactions are private and secure.

One of the biggest challenges for any organization is determining how to cover its bases for all the potential assaults that can occur. A network's security is only as good as its individual elements. It requires that diverse technologies be tightly integrated throughout the whole company network infrastructure. This implies that business decision-makers (and their technology advisors) understand the organization's unique points of vulnerability and risk areas and how to mitigate them. Only then is the organization in a position to protect its network.

Network Attackers Hold the Advantage

A fundamental tenet of computer security is that information defenders (that is, small-medium business management) must always succeed in protecting their systems. If attackers fail to cause disruption on a first attempt, they can try again later, or move on to another target, which might be easier to steal information from, damage, or disable. Businesses must continually block these attackers' attempts to keep their systems up and running and to protect critical information. In that regard, attackers have the easy side of cyber warfare.

A factor that favors the attacker is the proliferation of computer networks and the growing use of Internet connectivity. There are immeasurable upsides to having created a worldwide network of networks such as the Internet, but in doing so, it has become almost impossible to track the number of systems that are interconnected. This can be a serious problem, because many of these networks lack adequate network security and can unknowingly contribute to the distribution of attacks.

Another factor that favors attackers is that they have access to the same technology and/or technical systems information the defender has, such as weaknesses in hardware and software. Although companies that produce IT products try to downplay the weaknesses of their systems and software, it is practically impossible to hide this information from people who are intent on getting it. Websites, user manuals, bug reports, and books provide information about how IT products work and what kinds of weaknesses exist in them.

Attackers are also at an advantage in that they can use the Internet to become members of the same clubs, chat rooms, bulletin boards, and e-mail lists as the defenders. Individuals planning security attacks can easily assume alter-identities and remain anonymous as they enter these websites to seek information that will help them develop information warfare tactics. The openness of the Internet and the freedom to publish almost any type of information in numerous countries has caused the web to become an incredibly rich library for everyone. Unfortunately, this includes those who want to find vulnerability information for their own purposes.

Costs of Network Security Breaches

The security threats that most often and most seriously contribute to small-medium business days lost include virus incidents and website intrusion (by hacking). According to KPMG information security surveys, companies lose an average of 77 days per year as a result of these types of incidents. The revenue impact of company downtime because of security breaches can be significant. More than 70 percent of respondents to a Meta Group survey on qualifying performance loss cited losses of up to $250,000 per hour as a result of downtime. The worldwide impact (that is, the repair cost and revenue loss) of selected high-profile security incidents that ranked high on the international cyber attack index were Nimda worm $635 million, Code Red worm $2.6 billion, and Love Bug worm $8.8 billion. Here are some additional details about these incidents:

- Nimda was spread from client to client via e-mail, from web servers to clients' user devices via browsing of compromised websites, from clients to web servers via various Microsoft directory vulnerabilities, and from clients to web servers via back doors left behind by Code Red worms.

- Code Red was self-replicating code that exploited a known vulnerability in Microsoft servers.

- Love Bug affected systems running Microsoft Windows. It was a program that spread through various means, including e-mail, Windows file sharing, USENET news, and possibly web pages. The people who received copies of the worm via e-mail most likely would have recognized the sender, and the subject line read, ILOVEYOU.

Network security breaches can devastate a small-medium business, particularly in terms of the cost of lost business and worker productivity. The immediate economic impacts are the cost of repairing or replacing damaged systems, disruption of business operations, and delays in transactions and/or cash flow. Short-term economic impacts include the loss of contractual relationships or existing customers because of a company's inability to deliver products or services and a negative impact on the organization's reputation. Long-term there could be a decline in a business's market valuation and stock prices, erosion of investor confidence, and even reduced goodwill standing.

Security intrusions can also lead to bad publicity and legal liabilities, which can negatively affect business continuity. Smaller organizations can be especially hard hit by a compromise in security because of the lack of necessary staff and budget to quickly address a network security problem.

Sources of Security Risks and Vulnerabilities

Worm and virus incidents such as Code Red, Nimda, and the Slammer worm have heightened everyone's awareness of security. Beyond the headlines, however, numerous specific threats have emerged that are particularly troubling for those who are responsible for their organization's network security and privacy. The following seven attack trends are driving the need for defense-in-depth network security systems for small-medium businesses today:

- **Increasing sophistication of attack tools**—Attack tool signatures are getting harder to differentiate from legitimate network traffic.

- **Speed and automation of attack tool regeneration**—Tools now can self-initiate new attacks without human intervention.

- **Faster rate of vulnerability**—Network and computer system security vulnerabilities are doubling each year. Typically, companies cannot install patches fast enough, and hackers discover weaknesses before software and security vendors can fix them.

- **Penetrability of firewalls**—Today, many technologies get past typical firewalls. These include the Internet Printing Protocol (IPP), Web-based Distributed Authoring and Versioning (WebDAV), and certain code, including ActiveX, Java, and JavaScript.

- **Growth of asymmetric threats**—Attacks in which multiple hackers attack one business target are mounting.

- **Increasing infrastructure attack threats**—Distributed denial of service (DDoS), self-propagating worms, and Domain Name Server (DNS) attacks can lead to caching of bogus information.

- **Attacks on routers**—Traffic is directed to routers rather than through them, which can lead to DoS (denial of service) events or unauthorized redirection of traffic.

There are many sources of threats to computer security, including criminals, cyber terrorists, industrial spies, foreign countries in conflict with targeted nations, disgruntled employees, and amateur hackers. Each of these groups has different motivations and poses a different type of problem. The reasons that hacking and intrusions occur vary just as much as the type of intruder:

- Organized criminals are economically motivated. They seek information that can be sold or used to extort money from victims.

- Terrorists are politically or religiously motivated.

- Industrial spies seek competitive information.

- Disgruntled employees often want to damage systems or obtain information to embarrass their employer or former employer.

- Amateur hackers attempt to prove their prowess and earn esteem from their peers.

As networks have become more inviting targets to these intruders, the number of potential internal and external threats has grown. The number and variety of viruses are also spreading faster than ever as e-mail usage grows. Newer, more powerful viruses can distribute themselves throughout an entire network infrastructure, attaching themselves to applications and data files and even moving between the two. A sophisticated virus can spread to millions of computers via the Internet in just hours. It can cost billions of dollars to eradicate.

E-business environments are particularly challenging to protect because of their large number of sites. More companies extend their networked applications to remote offices and to teleworking employees or partners. They need to provide the same level of service to these individuals that is available to their colleagues at the corporate office. And that means IT administrators are faced with the challenge of protecting diverse environments and multiple locations.

Potential assaults can be divided into two categories—internal and external. Employees, consultants, and visitors make up the former category, and hackers and their unwitting accomplices (whose e-mail programs infect PCs with viruses or Trojan horses) are included in the latter category.

Hacker Attacks

To guess passwords, hackers use sophisticated random-number generators. Port scanners gain unauthorized access to systems. For remote access, they rely on keystroke-capture software that's planted on a system, sometimes through a worm or Trojan horse that is disguised as a game or screen saver. Some hackers use IP spoofing, which falsifies a legitimate host IP address and to gain access. And they rely on an array of other techniques that can cripple systems and destroy data.

Hackers are the most widely known external security threat. They exploit security weaknesses to disable a network, steal, or destroy information. The most commonly used hacker attacks include the following:

- **IP spoofing**—A hacker, inside or outside a network, pretends to be a trusted computer. He can do this by using an IP address that is within the range of trusted IP addresses for a network or an authorized external IP address that is trusted and to which access is provided. IP spoofing attacks frequently become the basis for other attacks. A classic example is launching a Denial of Service (DoS) attack using spoofed, forged source addresses to hide the hacker's identity.

- **Denial of Service (DoS) attack**—An intruder overloads an IP network to cause DoS. Flooded with packets, the network cannot handle legitimate traffic and cuts off valid users, such as employees, customers, and business partners. DoS, in which a single machine attacks a single target, and Distributed Denial of Service (DDoS), in which multiple machines attack a single target, are among the most difficult attacks to completely eliminate. Because of their ease of implementation and potentially significant damage, DoS and DDoS attacks deserve special attention from network administrators. They are different from most other attacks because they are generally not targeted at gaining access to a network or the information on it. These attacks focus on making a network unavailable for normal use. This is typically accomplished by exhausting some resource limitation on the network or within an operating system or application.

- **Application-level attack**—These attacks enter a network through a computer program and are targeted toward servers running specific network services such as e-mail or voice mail.

- **Trojan horse attack**—This is a backdoor path into a system that can be created during an intrusion or with specifically designed Trojan horse code. An intruder can repeatedly use the back door to enter a computer or network. Often, after a system has been invaded, the hacker uses the back door, unless the backdoor is detected and patched, to gain access to other systems or to launch DoS attacks.

- **Virus**—Viruses compromise data or applications and are one of the more prevalent forms of attack. They can be divided into four basic types, depending on how they reproduce and transport themselves:
  - Program viruses attach to executable files.
  - Boot viruses infect the system information on a disk.
  - Multipartite viruses infect both the system and files.
  - Macro viruses attach to routines in applications.

- **Man-in-the-middle attack**—This is essentially a form of eavesdropping that occurs when a hacker has access to packets transferred between a small-medium business network and any other network (for example, that of an Internet service provider [ISP]). Such attacks are often implemented using network packet sniffers and routing and transport protocols. The possible uses of such attacks are theft of information, hijacking of an ongoing communication session (to gain access to private network resources), gathering traffic analyses (to derive information about a network and its users), instigating DoS, corrupting transmitted data, and introducing new information into network sessions.

- **Social engineering**—This is obtaining confidential network security information through nontechnical means, such as posing as a technical support person and asking for people's passwords.

External threats like these are not the only challenges to network security. Computer crime surveys by the FBI have determined that up to 60 percent of attacks are initiated from within a company. Some attacks are premeditated and complex, and others are performed unintentionally by a worker.

The original designers of the Internet never anticipated the kind of widespread adoption the Internet has reached today. As a result, in the early days of IP, security was not designed into its specification. For this reason, most IP implementations are inherently insecure. That is why it is important to understand and be able to combat the multitude of security attacks that can occur in a small-medium business network.

The Defense-in-Depth Security Solution Approach

Network security and security policies are absolutely critical to ensure the integrity of company information. Typically, small-medium business decision-makers and IT administrators rate network security as a top concern. Yet they often approach it in a piecemeal fashion. Many companies explore robust security only after a crisis. Relatively few organizations engage in defense-in-depth—a proactive, systemic, integrated approach to network security that is broader in coverage than just a firewall at the company perimeter.

Comprehensive in nature, defense-in-depth aims to achieve the goal of unbreakable network security. This is a vital requirement in a world where security threats are running rampant. There is a need to identify potential exposures and their risks so that security policies and solutions can be developed to minimize the risks.

Because of the complexity of networks and the proliferating points of exposure, small-medium businesses must think in terms of whole security solutions rather than individual security products. For example, most companies deploy firewalls at the network perimeter. But a firewall cannot protect against attacks or accidental damage by employees inside the network, or even against external threats such as the Nimda worm, which bypassed firewalls and caused billions of dollars in damage. This damage would have been preventable with the addition of an intrusion detection system integrated with a firewall.

Adopting a comprehensive security strategy defends against highly sophisticated attacks, which can occur at multiple locations in a business. Business resilience requires the three Cs of conscious, conscientious, comprehensive attention to prevention, detection, and reaction to information security and privacy threats.

Defense-in-depth security solutions are intended to counter the new generation of complex threats. The ultimate goal is to deploy capabilities that create an intelligent, self-defending network that identifies attacks as they occur, generates alerts as appropriate, and then automatically responds without user intervention. This will become increasingly important as data, voice, and video converge onto a single network and as wireless LANs become more common. But the success of all security systems depends on integrated policy, management, and network monitoring.

Where to Apply Network Security

A discussion of defense-in-depth must begin by identifying the three principal parts of the network where integrated, embedded security must be applied:

- **Network edge (or perimeter)**—The periphery of the business network that connects the LAN to the WAN

- **Campus network (or LAN)**—Includes desktops, file servers, file backup or storage systems, and software

- **Remote-access network**—For workers in remote locations and teleworkers who need to communicate securely

Security mechanisms must counter threats in each part of the network. In choosing security products, remember that they should be easily integrated into a total, end-to-end security solution. These complementary products should strike a balance between providing access and providing protection. Five basic functions should be combined to develop a comprehensive network security solution, as shown in Figure 5-4. They are discussed in detail in the following sections.

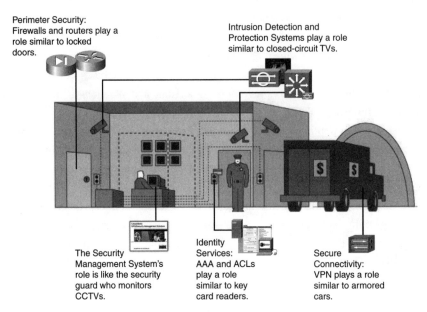

Perimeter Security:
Firewalls and routers play a role similar to locked doors.

Intrusion Detection and Protection Systems play a role similar to closed-circuit TVs.

The Security Management System's role is like the security guard who monitors CCTVs.

Identity Services: AAA and ACLs play a role similar to key card readers.

Secure Connectivity: VPN plays a role similar to armored cars.

Figure 5-4 *Defense-in-Depth Network Security*

Perimeter Security

Extended perimeter security is needed to control access to critical applications, services, and data so that only authorized users and information can pass through the network. Extended perimeter services are delivered via firewalls, purpose-built appliances, and router access control lists (ACLs). Company firewalls are a necessity at the perimeter of the business, where the company LAN and WAN connect. They analyze all incoming and outgoing data traffic on a network and allow only authorized traffic access. Firewall functionality is often integrated into switches, routers, or network appliances to handle packet inspection, internal address blocking, and hazardous-content detection.

Even with company firewalls in place, it is a good idea to install personal firewalls on employees' PCs that are used to access the network remotely. This strategy protects those PCs from being hacked and, in some cases, also monitors outgoing traffic to alert users when an unauthorized program tries to send data across the Internet. ACLs are another extended perimeter security capability. ACLs work with routers, switches, and firewalls. They are used to set up filters that define the permission rights (read, write, or execute) each user has to network resources such as file directories or individual files. This filtering is handled based on criteria such as sender address, destination address, or network protocol.

Identity Services

Identity services are based on the authentication, authorization, and accounting (AAA) of users. AAA services help identify users, ensure that only authorized users gain access to a network, and control their privileges on a network. Access control, including AAA identity services, access control servers, and certificate authorities collectively identify users and control what they are permitted to do on the network. Identity services are made up primarily of authentication systems and can be supplemented with public key infrastructure (PKI) products. PKI systems use digital certificates and smart cards for additional security to ensure that only trusted users are involved in Internet transactions.

Real-Time Intrusion Protection/Detection Systems

Intrusion protection systems/intrusion detection systems (IPS/IDS) systems monitor for and block attacks. These are real-time vulnerability scanning tools that proactively search for security holes before hackers can take advantage of them. They are designed specifically to provide denial of service (DoS) protection, antihacking detection, and defense for e-commerce business applications.

Intrusion detection is the ability to analyze data in real-time to detect, log, and stop network misuse or attacks as they occur. Host-based IDSs are software agents that secure critical network servers and desktops that contain sensitive information. Network-based systems monitor activity on a specific network segment. Unlike host-based agents, network-based systems are usually dedicated platforms.

Secure Connectivity Solutions

These systems protect traffic across a network. Virtual private networks (VPNs) with encryption capabilities are an example of a connectivity solution that allows small-medium businesses to use an insecure Internet for confidential communications. They operate over public networks but use the same security, management, and quality of service (QoS) policies applied to private networks.

Because VPNs use an existing shared WAN infrastructure, costs to operate them are lower and deployment is faster than with traditional private networks. They provide access control and data encryption. VPNs are especially useful for companies with workers who require remote intranet access. Such access might be needed while working at home or on the road; in public access areas such as hotels, airports, and convention centers; and in branch offices. By using VPN functionality, remote workers can connect to their company network without the risk of a hacker or thief intercepting confidential data. VPNs can also be deployed within a LAN, their functionality integrated into switches or routers.

Security Management Systems

These systems monitor and analyze traffic and devices for their adherence to or violation of established security policies. A management infrastructure acts as the glue between the individual elements of a security solution. It gives IT administrators the ability to manage individual devices and entire systems. And for medium and larger businesses, these systems can support more advanced sets of security rules and policies. Security and policy management should be centralized to allow administrators to manage individual devices and total systems, even those that are remote.

Network Security Best-Practice Fundamentals

Security threats attack different parts of the network, so it's essential to deploy and manage network devices on all layers of the network. This strategy of defense-in-depth helps stop a threat in case it bypasses one particular area of a network.

Best-practice case studies and blueprints for end-to-end security strategy development and systems design are available from selected vendors. They spell out fundamental network protection concepts such as the following:

- An effective security solution must continually evolve and change to accommodate new threats or business requirements.

- All points of access on the network are security targets and must be protected accordingly.

- A successful security solution requires comprehensive, integrated safeguards throughout the entire network infrastructure—not just a few specialized security devices.

- Security solutions must be modular to be cost-effective, scalable, and flexible.

- A layered, defense-in-depth strategy ensures more-complete protection to a business to minimize its areas of potential vulnerability.

A comprehensive approach to network security actually delivers new business-enabling advantages and better ways of operating. In the end, defense-in-depth lets organizations minimize their total threat exposure and maximize their business opportunities.

Security Policy Requirements

As part of the security process, organizations must study and understand threats to their networks, design a security policy tailored to meet these threats, and deploy the appropriate solution. A security policy affects all parts of a company. It should be created by a collaborative process that involves participation from IT, human resources (HR), legal, administrative, and executive teams. The elements of a security policy include the following:

- A concise statement describing the purpose of the policy document and how updates will be handled

- A description of the policy's scope of information and covered resources

- Roles and responsibilities for employees

- Security practices regarding network design, third-party connections, remote access, name/password management (including provisions for when an employee leaves the company), and so on

- Acceptable use policy (AUP) for network and Internet access

- Incident response procedures for various threat levels

Basic Considerations for Wireless LAN and IP Telephony Technologies

Wireless LANs (WLANs) and IP telephony (IPT) are becoming increasingly popular network solutions among small-medium businesses. Because of their widespread deployment and their flexibility of use in a variety of applications, these technologies present special security challenges to business leaders. The issues involved are important enough to be addressed in a company's network plans. They also should influence solution investment decisions. The following two sections provide a snapshot of basic technology-specific security factors with which decision-makers should be familiar. More in-depth discussions of security issues and potential solutions relevant to these technologies may be found in Chapter 7, "Wireless LANs (WLANs)," and Chapter 8, "IP Telephony and Multimedia Communications."

Wireless LAN Security Basics

There is no need to forego the use of wireless systems in a business if the proper security precautions are observed. The productivity and flexibility benefits of using wireless systems are too good to pass up.

Using WLANs for connectivity in a room, a building, or even an entire business campus is becoming commonplace among small-medium businesses. Giving workers the freedom of mobility while at the same time denying unauthorized access to corporate information on a wireless network is a vital concern. As is true of wired networks, WLANs also require multilayered, defense-in-depth security. Like wired LANs, WLANS can use techniques such as mutual authentication between clients and Remote Access Dial-in User Service (RADIUS) servers. They also use different techniques, such as dynamic per-user, per-session key generation. See Chapter 7 for more details on WLANs and related wireless security specifics.

Because radio waves travel through ceilings, floors, and walls, the information carried by them can be received by unintended recipients on different floors, or even outside a building. Without rigorous security measures, installing a WLAN can be the equivalent of putting easily accessible Ethernet ports everywhere, including the company parking lot.

Security for wireless LANs can be fairly complex. To achieve maximum security, organizations must do the following:

- Be sure to turn on wireless devices' embedded security features. Most wireless fidelity-certified products ship with these features turned off.

- Implement both authentication, which ensures the identity of users, and encryption, which prevents the reading/understanding of data, thereby ensuring that data remains undecipherable.

- Secure LAN privacy by segregating wireless users onto vitual LANs (VLANs), perhaps with limited access rights.

- Use VPN solutions for remote users.

- Adopt two-way, mutual authentication between clients and servers to ensure that wireless sessions will be almost impossible to hack. One-way authentication is not enough.

IP Telephony Security Basics

IP telephony (IPT) technology—the convergence of voice, data, and video on a single network—offers small-medium businesses the opportunity to reduce communications costs and complexities as well as the ability to enable productivity gains. But the key to adopting such a technology, and realizing its benefits, is having the confidence that comes from knowing that the company network is secure and protected while people use it.

This trend of telephony and computer systems convergence has exposed IP voice systems to the same types of abusers who have traditionally limited their efforts to attempted breaches of data networks and systems. It is critical that business and technical decision-makers ensure that their company adopt proper safeguards to minimize the opportunities for such integrated network system attacks. Chapter 8 provides more details about the specifics of IP voice technologies and how to prepare an IPT network to prevent and deal with security threats.

IPT systems can deliver greatly expanded flexibility, functionality, and usability over traditional voice systems. The benefits they offer have led to increasingly widespread adoption. This, in turn, has increased their vulnerability to unauthorized access by intruders intent on inflicting denial of service (DoS) attacks or causing the total shutdown of business networks. It is important to keep in mind that the telephony servers used for IP voice systems are just as vulnerable to attacks as data servers. An attacker penetrating a call server can do any of the following:

- Change call-forwarding information
- Interfere with the operation of the telephony network
- Plant viruses and worms that can cause disruption of service and business operations

Comprehensive, Business-Class Network Security

An integrated, comprehensive security solution eliminates the interoperability and management issues, functionality gaps, and scalability constraints associated with bringing together individual security devices from multiple vendors.

Organizations that adopt business-class security solutions and back them up with appropriate policies and physical security greatly reduce their risk of theft, vandalism, or business interruptions. Although there's no way to avoid all risk, companies can make it more difficult for hackers and thieves to damage or compromise a network. In the end, it's all about playing the odds.

Implementing a network security solution can prevent costly security intrusions, reduce overall infrastructure costs, and enhance productivity. The paybacks include the following:

- **Reduced costs**—A study conducted jointly by Griggs Anderson and the Gartner Group market analysis firms found that small-medium business security investments resulted in an average annual savings of $426,000. Total costs of connectivity, telecommunications infrastructure, and maintenance were reduced in nearly 90 percent of companies.

- **Enhanced productivity**—The same study found an average employee productivity improvement of more than 3 hours per week, which was reflected in the bottom line.

- **Reduced security intrusions**—Damages caused by a security breach are lowered. Less data is lost, fewer IT hours are devoted to correcting problems, and fewer bouts of negative publicity occur (avoiding damage to the company image).

A well-planned, well-executed, comprehensive security plan helps mitigate the following:

- System penetration by outsiders
- Theft of proprietary information
- Financial fraud
- Virus and worm attacks
- Denial of service (DoS) incidents
- Insider network abuse
- Legal liabilities resulting from a breach

In addition, robust network security can be a business enabler that allows companies to deploy functionality for significantly boosted productivity, efficiency, and information reach. For instance, a secure network ensures that remote users can access the corporate network and conduct business confidently and cost-effectively no matter where they are. Moreover, secure networks let companies work more fully with customers, suppliers, and other business partners. This enables real-time, collaborative applications and open processes such as e-commerce, e-procurement, and supply-chain management.

The most significant benefits of an effective network security solution come from the absence of intrusions and attacks. These benefits can be difficult to measure, because it might not be possible to know what attacks would have taken place without an effective, secure network in place. An in-depth network security solution has other, less-tangible but equally important benefits, including customer and partner confidence in the business and management's confidence in its capacity for business continuance in the event of a disaster.

Network Security Decision Criteria

Secure network connectivity offers protection for growing companies that depend on the Internet to conduct their business. A company is considered a leading e-business (and therefore web-strategic) if the majority of its revenues are generated through web-based applications. If that is not currently the case, it is critical to consider where the business is going and how it will grow. Even if it is only minimally web-based or using e-business applications such as salesforce automation, Internet marketing, or supply-chain management, it might be moving in that direction. If so, management needs to think about how to achieve improved network security as the company expands and becomes more Web-strategic.

Here are some factors to consider when assessing an organization's e-business or web-strategist ranking:

- **E-commerce system in place**—Organizations that have a web storefront and that use web-based permission marketing to customers rank higher. Those with none rank lower.

- **Plans to install an e-commerce system**—Organizations that have plans to install an e-commerce system rank higher. Those with none rank lower.

- **Website**—Organizations with a robust website that profiles a company and its products and that provides other detailed information content, online tools, and resources rank higher. Those with none rank lower.

- **Internet connectivity**—Organizations with Internet connectivity accessible to the majority of employees rank higher. Those with none rank lower.

- **Teleworking and remote access**—Organizations that support employee teleworking and remote access from public venues and while traveling on business rank higher. Those that don't rank lower.

- **Web-based business-to-business transactions**—Organizations that support online transactions and real-time collaboration with partners, suppliers, and other businesses rank higher. Those that don't rank lower.

Defense-in-Depth Security: Candidate Criteria

A small-medium business with any of the following requirements is a prime candidate for an integrated, defense-in-depth network security solution:

- Ranks high on the e-business/web-strategist assessment scale

- Needs to offer partners, customers, and employees different levels of access to company resources via dedicated or dial-up connections

- Runs broadband, wireless, and/or IPT Internet connections

- Operates an internally hosted website or any website that handles sensitive e-business transactions

- Has employees who telework or connect to the network while traveling

- Operates a firewall at the company periphery as the company's only network safeguard

- Employs security products from a variety of vendors

Building Blocks to New Network Security Solutions

There are four areas to consider when planning a new or upgraded network security solution:

- **Strategy**—Identify the company's most critical applications, most likely network threats, and an acceptable level of risk to define the company's security needs and objectives. Articulate clear business value benefits of a comprehensive security solution. Prepare a rough return on investment (ROI) calculation. To calculate the basic annual break-even point, the potential economic impact from a substantiated threat should be divided by the total number of users. Many organizations will find that they need to spend beyond a break-even point to meet legal, regulatory, or contractual compliance obligations.

- **Process**—Clearly define the methods and practice for implementing a network security solution. What security solutions are currently in place? What are the company's security policies or concerns? Will policy changes or greater formalization be required?

- **People**—Training, organizational culture, and organizational structure must support the company's security strategies and goals. Do in-house staff have the skills, resources, and equipment to implement an effective security solution? Is it necessary to hire consulting expertise or to outsource systems design, development, service, and ongoing support?

- **Metrics**—Consider reductions in lost revenues from security breaches, improved customer satisfaction, and increased employee productivity resulting from the uptime and use of secure systems.

Summary

Over the past several years, Internet-enabled business (or e-business) has improved small-medium businesses' efficiency and, in many cases, stimulated growth. E-business applications such as e-commerce, customer relationship management, remote access, and supply-chain management let these companies streamline processes, lower their operating costs, and improve customer satisfaction. Such applications require networks that accommodate voice, data, and video traffic and that are available and scalable enough to support increasing numbers of users and information capacity while sustaining acceptable performance. However, as networks enable more applications and are available to more users in more locations, they also become increasingly vulnerable to a wider range of security threats. To combat the threats and ensure that the business is not compromised, defense-in-depth security must play a major role.

Security threats that most often and most seriously contribute to small-medium business days lost include virus incidents and website intrusion by hacking. These incidents are characterized by seven primary attack trends that drive the need for a multitiered defense-in-depth approach to security systems. Some of the attacks originate internally to companies, and others are from external sources. No matter what the source, network security and security policies are critical to ensuring the integrity of company information and the resilience of the business.

Certain advanced technologies, such as WLANs and IP telephony present unique security challenges. Business leaders must understand the issues that such technologies raise and create network plans and investment criteria that address them.

CHAPTER 6

INTRANETS, EXTRANETS, AND VIRTUAL PRIVATE NETWORKS (VPNs)

As businesses grow, they need to connect an increasing number of users across campuses and remote branch offices to share information and resources. The traditional way to handle this was to build a private, intracompany wide area network (WAN). For a small or medium business, that kind of private WAN can be prohibitively expensive to build and manage. Dedicated, leased lines and the equipment that works with them to interconnect offices can be expensive, and each location to be connected must have its own leased line and equipment. Virtual private networks (VPNs) are an affordable alternative to leased-line networks for small-medium businesses. VPNs deliver private network-like connectivity without the high cost of dedicated line systems.

Distributed work environments, increased employee mobility, supply chain complexity, and the growth of virtual organizations are now more commonplace. The decision processes and connectivity methods that worked when employees were together in a few common buildings are no longer practical or effective. Employees now continue to work while on the road or after hours at home. Being able to adapt to this evolving distributed decision-making model is the key to small-medium business agility and, ultimately, to competitive success.

When considering technologies and communications methods for a distributed commercial business environment, it is important to consider four web-based options:

- The Internet
- Intranets
- Extranets
- VPNs

The Internet

Everyone is familiar with the Internet, the global network of networks. The Internet has become an essential tool for small-medium businesses to send and receive e-mail, establish e-commerce storefronts, and access the web to do research and keep in touch with business partners and customers. Nearly all successful businesses will attest to the fact that using the Internet has helped them build and sustain vital relationships. Managers and employees alike are growing comfortable with the idea of functioning in an e-workplace. In fact, it is getting to the point where the "e" almost seems redundant, because so much of business is conducted electronically. Work is increasingly organized around the sharing of knowledge, functional skills, and best-practice processes and not around physical location.

The Internet is the perfect medium for boundary-free business computing. Perhaps less well known than the Internet, but equally important, are two related types of networks—intranets and extranets that are shown in Figure 6-1. They really build on the Internet model, taking it one step further and making it even more valuable to small-medium businesses and members of their supply chains. In coming years, they will likely become increasingly important and widely deployed. There is no doubt that the Internet, intranets, and extranets are remaking the workplace and bringing about new levels of efficiency, productivity, and global reach. They are also likely to become the precursors and drivers to the development of a wider range of web services based on software architectures and of more-intelligent information-retrieval and data-mining tools.

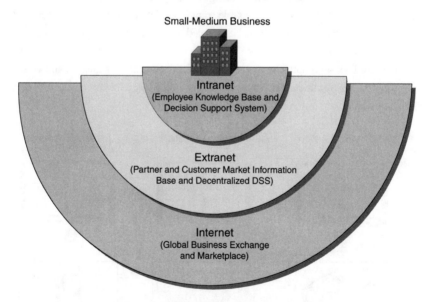

Figure 6-1 *Intranets, Extranets, and the Internet*

Intranets

An intranet is a private network that uses standard Internet protocols and browser-based client/server IP (Internet Protocol) applications. It is open only to the employees of a single organization. *Collaborative workspace* and *company portal* are other terms that sometimes are used to describe an intranet. Intranets are internal communications vehicles and knowledge bases that serve as a company-wide information system that is intended to benefit all departments.

Although they are logically internal networks, intranets are not physically constrained to just one geographic location of a company. In fact, an intranet can be as big as any given community of interest; there are no size limits. Intranets can be used locally or spread across regions and even continents. As such, they support flexible, decentralized decision-making and business communications. Control mechanisms in the form of usage policies can be applied within them to limit certain types of information access to specific groups.

Intranets differ from the groupware of the mid-1990s, which was essentially workgroup software for document sharing, e-mail, and collaborative authoring. A significantly broader and more flexible range of business processes, forms of information, and tracking tools can be enabled with a company intranet than was possible with groupware. Also unlike legacy groupware, intranet technologies can be employed for back-end data storage as well as for front-end user queries and content development. As intranets continue to evolve, they are driving greater process efficiencies, as illustrated in Figure 6-2.

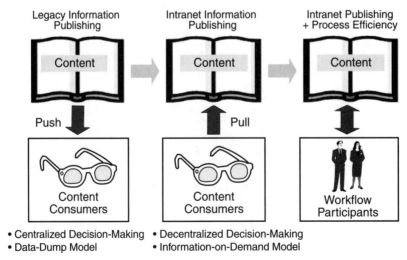

Figure 6-2   *Intranets*

Extranets

Extranets fill the gap between the Internet and intranets. They are most often business-to-business (B2B) intranets that allow controlled, secure access between a company's intranet and authorized, authenticated users from outside the business. An extranet can be viewed as a secure part of a company's intranet that is made accessible to select other companies and customers and allows collaboration with them, as shown in Figure 6-3.

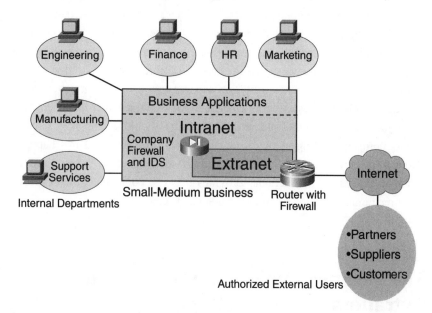

Figure 6-3   *Extranets Enable Collaboration*

Like intranets, extranets are not constrained by geographic locations. During the past several years, the scope of business collaboration has continued to extend from predominantly within companies to outside them, bringing in new participants and processes. Extranets are valuable for supporting all stages of intercompany collaboration, from brainstorming and planning, to data collection, analysis, and consensus building, to project execution. Working together in business is vital to achieving successful results. Working together effectively and efficiently across company lines can affect competitive differentiation and the degree of success. Increasingly, besides B2B interactions, extranets also are being used to simplify and extend customer interactions and provide customers with greater self-sufficiency. Examples of business-to-consumer (B2C) extranet applications include Internet banking, in which customers log on and can conduct secure transactions in their accounts, and retail customers having access to credit card accounts, order shipping status, and so on.

As intranets extend beyond company boundaries into extranets, some of the most critical issues and biggest challenges are those of information security, access control, and ongoing management. These issues can overshadow the benefits of using an extranet if they aren't addressed properly. Most company information is not for external consumption. As sections of the company intranet are partitioned for extranet use, it is important to ensure that there is no seepage of access by outsiders into a company's private and confidential information. VPNs can address some of these security challenges (as discussed later in this chapter). Other methods of defense-in-depth security that should accompany VPNs to protect companies using extranets (and intranets) are discussed in Chapter 5, "Network Security Basics." When designed and used correctly, extranets provide a safe way to allow transactional activities between companies. This can save small-medium businesses significant amounts of money.

The Business Value of Intranets and Extranets

As previously mentioned, intranets and extranets can change the way a small-medium company operates and communicates, both internally and externally, encouraging more collaboration and greater productivity. The result is both strategic and tactical benefits. Both technologies go a long way toward establishing the foundation for networked virtual organizations of individuals who work together toward common goals without the physical constraints of having to work in a single office building.

If the intranet or extranet is applied to improve business processes as well as to publish documents, it can contribute significantly to increasing efficiency (by as much as 40 percent, according to at least one market analyst, The Giga Group [http://www.gigagroup.net]). Indeed, intranets and extranets can benefit virtually every department in a company. They can help in the following ways:

- Encourage better decisions, collaboration, and sense of community, because they link the computers, data, business applications, experience, and knowledge of the people within an organization or across organizations.

- Reduce the costs of producing, accessing, and distributing information by automating processes and providing a central portal for data dissemination.

- Enable just-in-time delivery of information to improve customer responsiveness, resulting in productivity gains and customer loyalty. (A well-designed intranet should include a search engine that lets employees find what's needed quickly.)

- Reduce the cost of deploying client/server solutions. Because intranets and extranets use standard browsers on client devices, they eliminate the need to update client software on every device whenever a new business application is implemented.

- Can be integrated with legacy information systems such as groupware and other databases.

- Reduce travel costs.

Intranets can boast the added upside of being fairly simple to get up and running. The basic technology assets involved in intranets are often already available in small-medium businesses. These assets include PCs, network foundation elements (switches, routers, client adapters, cabling), web servers and server software, business application software and user licenses, broadband WAN access services, and VPN clients and concentrators for secure remote access. Because intranets are based on the Internet, they use the same familiar interfaces and offer similar search, retrieval, and information access features. What is needed in each business depends on the types of applications that are to be run. A qualified consultant or reseller working with in-house IT staff can help assess needs and recommend the appropriate integrated business solutions.

Applications Best Suited for Intranets and Extranets

The types of information exchanged on intranets and extranets can vary, depending on the company operating them. It is a good idea for a company to prepare written policy guidelines for the types of content that are acceptable, particularly because some organizations operate not only companywide intranets but also departmental and personal sites.

Despite their differences, intranets and extranets often are used for fairly similar applications. Intranets enable these applications within a company, and extranets extend them to select third parties. The most common types of applications deployed on intranets and extranets include the following:

- **Collaboration**—Teams of employees, partners, suppliers, and sometimes customers collaborate on business processes such as product development or order fulfillment via real-time document exchange or web conferencing.

- **Publishing**—Companies can make a wide variety of information available, including company news, product catalogs, price lists, product bulletins, HR benefits, cafeteria menus, and so on in varied multimedia formats.

- **Training**—E-Learning is delivered to users at their desktops.

- **Transactions**—Database searches, report generation, and forms completion (insurance, payroll, benefits, 401(k) enrollments, and more) can all be available online at any time.

- **Process tracking**—Workflow procedures, project management schedules, and order status tracking can be easily accessed.

- **Directories**—Users can quickly retrieve company and external phone directories, customer and competitor information, and much more.

- **Online tools**—Internet access, information backups, software tools, and technical support knowledge bases all can be made available through intranets and extranets.

Intranet and Extranet Selection Criteria

It is important to ensure that both intranets and extranets:

- Are easy to set up, configure, and support.

- Deliver the needed functionality. The company must decide whether applications will be mostly dynamic discussion- and collaboration-based or more static and publishing-based.

- Support third-party solutions and tools.

- Provide reliable quality of service.

- Scale as the business and the number of network users grow (or shrink).

It also is critical to allocate adequate staff to maintain and update content, or intranets and extranets will lose their value. Analysts estimate that 18 percent of printed business materials become outdated within 30 days of their release. At that rate, 70 percent of the information would be obsolete within 6 months.

Usually the initial justification for many intranets is the decreased cost of producing, accessing, and distributing information within a small-medium business. The upfront costs of installing an intranet are relatively low. It is the costs of ongoing production and content maintenance that can add up. On the other hand, documents that are printed and mailed not only are costly to produce, but also are often obsolete by the time they are received. Documents published online can, at the least, be updated without printing or distribution costs.

Time-savings are another cost justification factor that businesses must consider. The average knowledge worker spends approximately one quarter of each day looking for information. Assuming that equals 2 hours per day, per knowledge worker, at an average salary of $85,000 per year, Table 6-1 summarizes the value of the time that could be saved with the use of an intranet.

Table 6-1 *Representative Cost-Savings from Intranets and Extranets (by Number of Users)*

Size of Small-Medium Business	Annual Dollar Savings Potential
50 employees	$1.1 million per year
100 employees	$2.1 million per year
500 employees	$10.6 million per year
1000 employees	$21.3 million per year

Another prime factor that can be used to justify the adoption of an intranet or extranet is productivity increases. Business issues are resolved more expeditiously than might be possible otherwise. Actions are taken quickly. More can be accomplished in less time and with higher quality, given the currency and scope of information available for reference. Market analysts have found that many companies adopting an intranet have realized paybacks in as little as 6 to 12 weeks following their deployment.

VPNs

With a virtual private network (VPN), a small-medium business can use the public network for secure connections that support either site-to-site connectivity or remote access. VPNs link members of a community of interest who are in geographically dispersed locations. They have all the characteristics of a private network, but communications are less costly to users because they occur over the public network. By using a VPN, a company achieves levels of privacy, security, quality of service (QoS), and manageability that are similar to networks built entirely on dedicated, privately owned or leased carrier facilities.

A company using a VPN, however, pays only for the bandwidth actually consumed. As such, VPNs provide a simple and cost-effective alternative to leased lines as a means to extend company data networks to remote offices, mobile users, and even teleworkers. If they are implemented correctly, VPNs are transparent to users, and users feel as if they are directly connected to the company LAN, not some remote site.

VPNs are the technology of choice wherever secure data links are required between businesses. Services such as videoconferencing, e-commerce, IP telephony, distance e-learning, and other business-critical applications can be transported easily via VPNs between key business constituents.

The three types of VPNs are as follows:

- **Remote-access VPNs**—These connect teleworkers and mobile users to the company network.

- **Intranet VPNs**—These connect campus-based and branch office employees.

- **Extranet VPNs**—These enable company-to-company collaboration and coordination by giving business partners, suppliers, and sometimes customers secure limited access to the company network.

Benefits of VPNs

VPNs offer distinct advantages over traditional leased-line networks. The following are some of the most compelling advantages of VPNs:

- **They are more affordable than private networks**—They offer lower capital and operating costs. The lower cost of transport bandwidth and backbone equipment, plus a reduced need for in-house equipment, contribute to substantially lower cost of ownership and operation with VPNs. Ubiquitous Internet access through carriers' local points of presence means that business users can connect to the main office from home or while traveling by using local access numbers. This reduces or eliminates long-distance and 800-number charges.

- **They are more agile, flexible, and scalable**—Because VPN links are easy and relatively inexpensive to set up, add, and remove, they can be applied more responsively to changing business demands. Extending the company network to the offices of a new acquisition or branch, or adding new vendors to a supply chain extranet, become simple tasks that are quickly accomplished with a VPN. By using the Internet as the medium for their internal networks, companies make it possible to extend corporate systems to anywhere the Internet is accessible.

- **They are reliable for anywhere, anytime access**—VPN users have the same access and logical view of central services (such as e-mail, directory, internal and external websites, security, and other shared business applications) as those at the main office. Although they might reach these resources over very different paths, the underlying network is invisible to the user.

- **They can leverage public broadband access services for other applications**—Companies subscribe to DSL, cable, Frame Relay, and other broadband services to access the Internet more effectively. By combining encrypted VPN tunnels with these high-speed broadband Internet services, small-medium businesses can allow their remote users to experience LAN-like speeds and always-on access to the company LAN. With broadband VPNs, business applications run in real-time.

- **They are capable of management outsourcing**—Much of the engineering management and administrative workload required to set up and operate a VPN can often be outsourced to a network service provider. Managed VPNs let small-medium businesses concentrate on their core business and reduce the overall resources they must devote to IT and communications infrastructure management.

How VPNs Work

The objective of a VPN is to provide private networking services over a shared communications infrastructure. A public packet network (typically the Internet) or a service provider's telecommunications backbone network is used to establish private, secure connections between remote offices or employees and their main business office. The company's branch office LANs and remote users are connected to the provider network with the same types of access methods used for Internet access (DSL, cable, Frame Relay, T1, and so on).

VPNs usually have several different security and service control features, including tunneling, encryption, and QoS. Each is discussed in detail in the following sections.

Tunneling

Tunneling creates a temporary point-to-point connection between a remote site and a central site, blocking access to that connection by anyone other than the people communicating from both endpoints. It essentially involves repackaging data from one network into the transmission protocol (or native language) of another for data transport. At the sending end of a tunneled transmission, data packets are wrapped (or encapsulated) with new header information. This allows an intermediary network (such as the Internet) to recognize and deliver them to the proper destination. At the receiving end of the transmission, the tunneling protocol envelope is stripped off, and the original packet is transferred to a LAN for delivery. Figure 6-4 shows how VPN tunnels securely interconnect communities of users to enable the use of intranets and/or extranets across the public Internet.

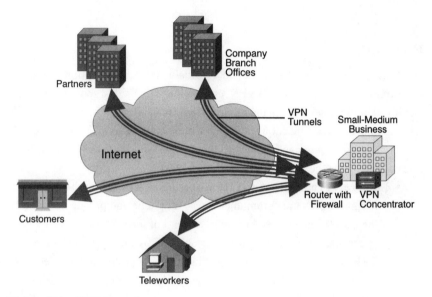

Figure 6-4 *VPN Tunnels*

Several different tunneling protocols have evolved and are in common usage for VPNs. The ones that can arise in discussions with service providers, resellers, or other vendors are

- **L2TP**—Layer 2 Tunneling Protocol
- **PPTP**—Point-to-Point Tunneling Protocol
- **MPLS**—Multiprotocol Label Switching
- **GRE**—Generic Routing Encapsulation

It is not necessary for small-medium business decision-makers to choose among them when evaluating whether to adopt VPNs. However, it is useful to recognize that these protocols support tunneling of data packets between business sites. Some are more complex, yet feature-rich, than others. Service providers mix and match their use of the protocols and often combine them as part of their service delivery, charging customers according to the capabilities they want.

Although tunneling allows the actual transport of data over third-party networks, tunneling alone does not ensure privacy. To secure a tunneled transmission against unwanted interception and tampering, all traffic over a VPN should be encrypted.

Encryption

Encryption is what puts privacy in a virtual network. Encryption is essential for secure communications. In a VPN, encryption is applied to scramble the data, making it undecipherable to unauthorized viewers. Data is scrambled on the sending end of the connection and is unscrambled on the receiving end, so it cannot be read or changed while in transit. Important current standards for encryption include the following:

- **Internet Protocol Security (IPSec)** — IPSec is a framework of standards designed to secure communications over public and private networks at the network layer (also known as Layer 3 of the OSI [Open Systems Interconnection] model). It was established by the Internet Engineering Task Force (IETF) to achieve the dual goals of protecting all selected IP packets from unauthorized viewing and defending networks against attacks. IPSec provides end-to-end security in which only the sending and receiving computer endpoints need to know the IPSec settings to communicate. IPSec requires client application software on remote users' access devices (PCs, laptops, handheld computers, and others) to operate.

- **Secure Sockets Layer (SSL)** — SSL is used to authenticate (verify) and encrypt communications between remote clients and servers. It enables a high degree of information confidentiality. Additionally, with SSL, users can detect whether their data has been tampered with during transmission. Unlike IPSec, SSL relies on a clientless (no end-user device software) method of remote access. With SSL, remote access to intranets, e-mail systems, and other TCP applications are handled through a standard web browser. Internet connectivity is required for SSL to operate.

- **Data Encryption Standard/Triple Data Encryption Standard (DES/3DES)** — DES uses a 56-bit secret key encryption system for security. 3DES (DES applied three times) results in effective 168-bit secret key security.

- **Advanced Encryption Standard (AES)** — AES is available in three secret key sizes (128-bit, 192-bit, and 256-bit). The higher the number of bits in the key, the harder it is for hackers to break the key. AES is designed to replace single DES, but it will coexist with 3DES, which will remain a government-sanctioned encryption algorithm for the foreseeable future.

QoS

Quality of Service (QoS) allows a VPN to deliver high transmission quality for time-sensitive applications such as voice and video. QoS cannot be completely controlled independently of the underlying network. This means that potential VPN users must confirm with a service provider that its network can support priority services at desired service levels over a VPN.

VPN Deployment Options

Establishing a VPN requires, at a minimum, access to the Internet or an alternative private IP network. For smaller networks, a value-added reseller (VAR) can be helpful in getting started and sometimes might also provide network access.

In most cases, a managed VPN service is preferable and is less expensive overall for a small-medium business than a company-built and -managed VPN. Managed service providers can offer attractive alternatives. Specific solutions can vary, but in general, VPNs are designed around either customer premises equipment (CPE) or on network-based solutions (sometimes called IP-VPNs). CPE includes VPN access concentrators, routers, firewalls, and other security devices, client hardware devices, and computer software. With IP-VPNs, all the VPN functionality is located in the service provider cloud or central office.

In network-based VPNs, the carrier, on behalf of the small-medium business customer, handles all configurations, changes, and ongoing management. This can be an advantage or disadvantage, depending on how much control over its network a company wants and on how skilled its IT staff is at implementing and managing VPNs. This includes such tasks as establishing any-to-any connectivity between network users; handling network configuration management, security management, and CPE device management; and negotiating and ensuring the performance of service level agreements (SLAs).

In the network-based option, which is the most logical for a service provider, all user authentication is handled by Remote Access Dial-in User Service (RADIUS) servers in the carrier's network. All the encryption and tunneling are activated as soon as the user's IP traffic gets to the carrier network. The advantage of this to a small-medium business is that no new equipment is needed, no capital expenses are incurred, and there is no equipment to become obsolete. It is relatively easy for a business to establish a network-based VPN. It can also be a cost-effective solution to consider, relative to managing CPE internally, in a resource-constrained IT staff environment. The biggest disadvantage of managed-service network VPNs is that encryption and decryption are handled, in most cases, when the traffic gets to the carrier network. Thus, traffic in the last mile between the business user and the service provider point of presence is not encrypted or secured. Because service providers cannot completely secure this local access loop for their customers, this might not be an adequate option for some small-medium companies.

When considering network-based VPN services, small-medium businesses should make sure their carrier:

- Is financially stable, because the critical requirement of running collaborative and mission-critical company communications will be in the carrier's hands.

- Offers sufficient geographic coverage to remote locations where communications might be needed, or has put in place reciprocal arrangements with other carriers to ensure ubiquitous coverage for customers at a cost comparable to that of the business's local service provider.

- Supports site-to-site extranet communications with partners, suppliers, and customers.

- Offers service level agreements (SLAs) that are a guarantee to ensure network performance at agreed-upon levels, tiered by subscription price. Key factors to be included in an SLA are network uptime, free/busy time ratios, minimum connect speeds, and network latency. It is also important to read the fine print about how the service provider monitors performance levels and how it issues credits if service falls below contracted levels.

- Delivers QoS capabilities for running real-time, delay-sensitive applications such as voice and video over VPNs.

Summary

Small-medium businesses must be able to support a distributed workforce's ability to gather and/or share information and to make timely decisions. The flexibility to do so affects company revenue gains, productivity improvements, and cost-savings. The value of the Internet for achieving such business goals can be extended to remote workers, partners, and customers with the use of intranets, extranets, and VPNs.

Intranets are essentially private networks that use standard Internet protocols and browser-based client/server IP networking. Although they are internal company networks, they are not limited to a single geographic site. They can extend across regions and continents. Extranets are most often business-to-business networks that enable collaboration and secure access between a business's intranet users and authorized users from outside the company, including partners and customers. Intranets and extranets are well-suited for business applications, including transactions, collaboration, process tracking, online training, and so on.

VPNs have all the characteristics of a private network, even though communications with them are less costly to users because they occur over the public network. Generally, VPNs also are more agile, flexible, and scalable for their price than dedicated, leased lines. With VPN, businesses gain a variety of security and service control features, such as tunneling, quality of service (QoS), and encryption to protect the confidentiality of the data they transmit.

CHAPTER 7

WIRELESS
LANs
(WLANs)

Small-medium business leaders must grapple with a productivity paradox that can affect company growth. Employees often spend less than 30 percent of their time each day at their desks, yet this is the one place where they have the easiest access to company information, business applications, and the Internet. For the other 70 percent of their workday, business professionals are at meetings in conference rooms or colleagues' offices, visiting customers, on the road for business travel, and even teleworking from home (full-time, part-time, or extended hours). This disconnect between places of work and ready information availability can impede rapid, well-informed decision-making and, by extension, business development.

The old paradigm of workers being tied to their desks from 9 to 5 has been replaced by one in which they are untethered. Workers are moving around to collaborate with others throughout the day and are working at home evenings and weekends after spending some time with the family. An adjunct to this newfound mobility is the fact that employees increasingly rely on a variety of devices to do their work. Analysts estimate that, on average, knowledge workers carry two or three devices, including laptops, handheld computers, cell phones, pagers, and so on. The business requirement that characterizes this environment and that should be addressed is that of network flexibility to enable information access under varied conditions.

The bottom line is that now it is essential to extend the employee productivity zone beyond the traditional desktop. Wireless technologies offer a solution for bringing the functionality of the desktop to wherever employees need to conduct work, thereby providing the flexibility necessary for worker mobility. With wireless LANs (WLANs), employees can access the online tools that help them be productive anytime and anywhere. But it is important to remember that not all wireless solutions are created equal. Consumer-class wireless systems might not hold up to a small-medium company's critical applications and security requirements.

When considering the adoption of wireless technologies, business decision-makers should ensure that their users are provided secure, easy-to-use, high-speed access with personalized, location-specific services. IT staff must deliver such solutions affordably, rapidly, and scalably, for use by a variety of devices, in multiple locales. A network is useful only if it is convenient and accessible to authorized users, wherever they are working. Wireless technologies offer the untethered mobility and remote-access flexibility required to address and solve the small-medium business productivity paradox.

Wireless networking technologies make particular sense for use in any vertical market that has highly mobile workforces, including healthcare, education, retail and wholesale, public safety, professional services, real-estate and construction, insurance, utilities, and so on. The real power of wireless communications to small-medium businesses (and larger businesses, for that matter) is the ability to optimize communications, improve responsiveness to customers, increase revenues, and accelerate process efficiencies and decision-making within organizations and with external partners and suppliers. Wireless delivers the power to get things done faster and with greater potential payback.

Wireless Networks and Their Components

Networks based on wireless technologies are not new. They have been available for decades. In wireless networks, communications take place through the air using radios and antennas rather than via physical, wired cable connections, as is the case with Ethernet LANs. In fact, wireless systems can be thought of as the truly literal ether networks.

Various types of wireless networks are in use today. WLANs for high-speed data and voice communications are part of a broader landscape of wide area and personal area wireless technologies (including infrared, microwave, satellite, cellular telephony, cordless phones, and paging systems). Some of these technologies may be combined with WLANs in a complementary way to conduct business communications. As shown in Figure 7-1, these technologies range from very low speeds to very high speeds and to those that operate across tens of feet to thousands of miles. This chapter focuses on WLANs because of their ability to integrate data and voice, deliver business-class high-performance connectivity, and interoperate with other intelligent networking technologies and software applications.

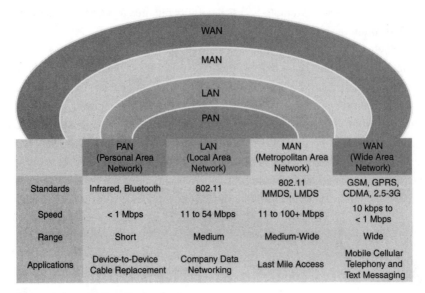

	PAN (Personal Area Network)	LAN (Local Area Network)	MAN (Metropolitan Area Network)	WAN (Wide Area Network)
Standards	Infrared, Bluetooth	802.11	802.11 MMDS, LMDS	GSM, GPRS, CDMA, 2.5-3G
Speed	< 1 Mbps	11 to 54 Mbps	11 to 100+ Mbps	10 kbps to < 1 Mbps
Range	Short	Medium	Medium-Wide	Wide
Applications	Device-to-Device Cable Replacement	Company Data Networking	Last Mile Access	Mobile Cellular Telephony and Text Messaging

Figure 7-1   *Wireless Technologies*

In general, WLANS perform functions similar to their wired equivalent, Ethernet. Because of their similarities to Ethernet, WLANs have sometimes been called wireless Ethernet. The main difference is that WLANs operate using radio frequency (RF) signals. These radio signals communicate within cells called basic service sets (BSSs), which cover roughly circular areas. A small business might need only a single cell, whereas a medium business is likely to need multiple cells if the intent is to extend coverage to most or all employees in the company.

WLANs can be used either to extend the reach of a wired LAN or in place of one, as shown in Figure 7-2. It is important to remember that, even in a predominantly wireless environment, some wires are still needed to handle certain connections. The most popular WLAN technologies in use today are 802.11b and 802.11a. A newer technology that is likely to find great value in small-medium business networks is 802.11g. The features, advantages, and disadvantages of each of these technologies are discussed later in this chapter.

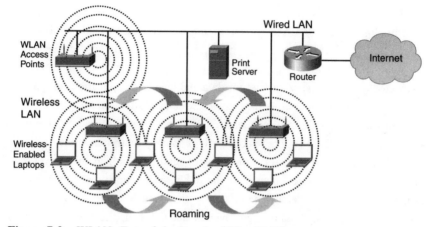

Figure 7-2 *WLANs Extend the Reach of Wired LANs*

WLANs are composed of two basic components: access points (APs) and client adapters. Available in a variety of form factors, APs act as the infrastructure in a wireless network and as a connection point between a wired and wireless network. APs can be thought of as wireless hubs in each wireless cell. In a multicell network, APs are placed throughout a building or in a networking *hotspot* such as a hotel or airport. This lets users equipped with WLAN adapters move throughout an area while remaining connected to the wireless network. WLAN client adapters are network interface cards (NICs) that let users transmit and receive information between a computer (laptop or desktop) or handheld device and an access point. They employ low-power radio transmitters and antennae and function similarly to traditional wired NICs.

Because of the rapid adoption of WLAN technologies by businesses, most computer manufacturers are now building computers, especially laptops, with integrated wireless functionality. Ultimately, this could eliminate the need to insert external wireless NICs for WLAN access.

In addition to wireless hardware components, authentication and encryption are required to secure WLAN communications. These capabilities are embedded in the adapter, access point, and back-end wireless authentication servers. A wireless server can be a Remote Authentication Dial-In User Service (RADIUS), Lightweight Directory Access Protocol (LDAP), or other server already in place to enforce user access rights. A scalable network management system also might be required as WLANs expand. See the later sections "WLAN Security" and "Adoption Considerations," which appear later in this chapter.

One benefit of using radio waves (versus infrared, which sends bursts of invisible light) is that WLANs do not require line of sight to send data from one user to another. Data can travel through walls, windows, and floors, depending on the materials used in construction. The benefit of this is that users can stay connected to the company intranet for data and business applications usage or to share access to the Internet as they move around an office building or campus. With proper WLAN design, seamless roaming can be provided, in which users stay connected without having to constantly reconnect their computers.

WLANs can affordably serve the needs of small-medium businesses yet scale to meet the needs of larger enterprises and public-access hotspots with thousands of users. The key is to deploy the system so that their roaming features provide users with ubiquitous, uninterrupted coverage and secure application connectivity.

WLAN Applications

The killer app for WLANs is mobility. The goal is to provide users with access to the same types of online productivity tools and applications they normally have at their desktops, whether they are at work, at home, or on the road. These include customer relationship management (CRM), salesforce automation (SFA), e-learning, and supply-chain management tools and applications. As shown in Figure 7-3, WLANs can effectively serve users within buildings, between buildings, in public hotspots, and in their homes. They also can be used for networks in motion.

Building-to-Building WLANs

Public-Access Hotspot WLAN

In-Building WLANs

WLANs in Motion

WLANs at Home

Figure 7-3   *WLAN Application Venues*

WLAN applications can be classified into four basic categories:

- **Campus mobility**—Workers maintain wireless connectivity while moving within a building, between campus buildings, and even while in courtyards or plazas outside.

Using wireless virtual LANs (W-VLANs), portions of a single wireless network can be segregated and secured for separate use by internal users and external users (such as company visitors, travelers in airports, hotel guests, and airplane passengers). Functionally, it is as though the users of each W-VLAN are on completely different networks (intranet, extranet, or guest network). With the use of a W-VLAN, any small-medium organization can set up a wireless network to handle the information exchange necessary for internal staff operations and to provide controlled, open portions of the network for the use of outsiders. The communications that occur on these various networks do not intermingle. As shown in Figure 7-4, WLANs allow network partitioning for user access control. A single wireless network can be made to appear as though separate, private networks (called virtual local area networks [VLANs]) exist for different user groups that are internal and external to the company. For more information on VLANs, see Chapter 4, "Network Foundation Technologies—Switching and Routing."

- **Teleworker mobility**—Full-time, part-time, or extended-hours teleworkers can install wireless in their homes for remote access to the company intranet or the Internet. A WLAN would be used in the home, combined with a high-speed broadband access service such as DSL (digital subscriber line) or cable modem for wide area connectivity.

Home-based WLANs enhance a worker's productivity much as they do at the company office. They provide the flexibility to work where the employee feels comfortable, not by tethering him or her to the one room or space that has all the requisite telecommunications, electrical, and network hookups. According to industry studies, employees who work at home generally invest 2 hours more per day than those who don't. These studies also found that teleworkers tend to feel more satisfaction in their jobs as a result of achieving a better work/life balance. Furthermore, employees who are set up with WLAN facilities to work at home provide business continuity insurance for a company in the event of a disaster, outage, or weather condition that prevents productive work from being accomplished at the office. If that is not stimulus enough, many state and local governments are mandating the implementation of telework programs as a means to improve air quality and the environment in their region.

- **Public-access hotspot mobility**—Ethernet-speed high-performance wired and wireless connections to the Internet and the corporate intranet are available in public-access hotspots, allowing employees to stay responsive and productive while on the road. Hotspots are typically placed in locations frequented by business travelers, such as airports, hotels, coffee shops, convention centers, and train stations.

- **Networks in motion**—Mobile vehicles such as planes, trains, trucks, and public safety vehicles (police cars, ambulances, and fire trucks) can be outfitted with WLANs that work in conjunction with computers, routers, switches, and wide area wireless technologies (such as cellular) to enable real-time information access and continuous network connectivity.

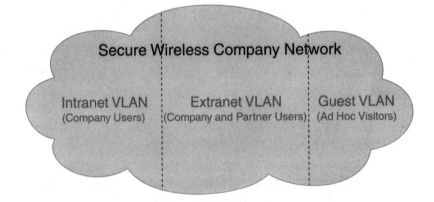

Figure 7-4 *Wireless Virtual LANs*

WLANs can play a vital role in achieving competitive advantage for small-medium businesses and their mobile professionals, such as salespeople, as this representative day-in-the-life business scenario illustrates:

Marie logs on to the web using her home-based WLAN and confirms the airline reservations for her business trip later that day. She then accesses the company intranet using virtual private network (VPN) software, sends some e-mail to colleagues and customers she will be meeting with during her trip, and checks the weather at her destination to know what to pack.

At the airport, while waiting for her flight, Marie logs on to the airline lounge's hotspot WLAN and uses her handheld computer (also equipped with VPN software) to download driving directions from the destination airport to her hotel. She then checks for responses to her e-mails. That evening, having arrived at the hotel, she again goes online, this time using the hotel's high-speed in-room connection, and downloads some additional slides for her presentation from the company intranet. She also checks the latest price list and discount schedule for the products she will be discussing with her customer.

At the customer's office the next day, a question arises about one of the products. Because this office has a WLAN in place with partitioned open access (a W-VLAN) for visitors, Marie can access her company's intranet and retrieve the technical documentation that answers the customer's questions—on the spot. The customer agrees to purchase the products if they can be delivered within 3 weeks. If not, the customer will go to a competing vendor. Marie checks the intranet again, this time for inventory and production lead times. Seeing that she can make the requested deadline, she and the customer close the deal. Marie immediately places the order and requests expedited delivery.

Back at the airport, while waiting to return home, she sends an e-mail to her manager, the regional sales vice president, letting him know that the deal closed and they have just exceeded quota. Marie then logs into the company e-sales portal to register her sale and ensure that her commission is accounted for. Finally, she enters her trip expenses and sales report into the system and logs off. She is left with just enough time for a dash to the gift shop to get those all-important trip souvenirs for her two young children.

Marie's applications of WLANs and VPNs, coupled with broadband access technologies, are ones that make sense for any small-medium business with field personnel who want to access sensitive company data.

Other examples of more niche vertical market applications in which WLANs can be employed by small-medium businesses include but are not limited to the following:

- **Public safety agencies**—WLAN and computer technologies, when combined in police and other emergency vehicles, provide more robust, on-demand information than is possible with standard two-way radios. Using WLAN-based networks in motion, information such as real-time video surveillance, mug shots or structural diagram transmissions, and law enforcement database queries on suspects are all possible. This enables faster decision-making and better preparedness. Handoffs of vital information relating to an ongoing emergency can also be conveyed between agencies as needed for faster problem resolution (whether burglary, fire, or medical crisis). These wireless public safety systems also allow emergency personnel to generate incident reports quickly and remotely—perhaps from their favorite coffee or donut shop hotspot. This saves them the time of continually returning to the office to access or submit information.

- **Hospitality businesses**—Small-medium hotel owners can provide business travelers with fast, convenient wireless check-in and high-speed secure Internet or intranet access from their hotel rooms, meeting rooms, and other public spaces. Such services represent customer-valued, revenue-generating amenities that differentiate the hotels that offer them and provide a competitive advantage by attracting more guests. The network infrastructures that are established to benefit guests can also be leveraged to improve operational efficiencies within the hotels and resorts that offer them.

- **Educational facilities**—Preschools, kindergarten-to-secondary schools, colleges, and universities can all benefit from full WLAN connectivity in classrooms, libraries, offices, cafeterias, and dormitories. Ready access to the Internet, shared multimedia applications, and software downloads by students, teachers, and administrators can enhance learning as well as improve administrative processes. A wireless network-enabled educational facility also allows security personnel and parents to monitor classrooms, playgrounds, or campuses for safety. It permits teachers to stay in touch with the administrative and custodial offices no matter where they are.

- **Health care providers**—WLANs in healthcare practitioner offices, hospitals, and clinics let doctors improve the speed and quality of diagnostics with faster access to test results, electronic images, or online patient databases. WLANs also help doctors stay current on the latest advances from medical journals or pharmaceutical companies. Nurses and pharmacists can use WLANs to confirm medications and treatments before administering them to patients. This is an effective means to improve accuracy and reduce errors and potential liabilities. WLANs also reduce dependency on limited-functionality, one-way pagers in patient care by allowing for voice over wireless LAN (VoWLAN) phones for two-way conversations.

- **Retailers and wholesalers**—WLAN-enabled computers can be used to scan bar codes on receiving docks and at store shelves or cash registers for inventory tracking purposes. Clerks can use WLAN phones to call their colleagues and ask for price checks or to locate products on shelves or in back-room inventory. Applications such as these enable just-in-time inventory management, reduced inventory costs, and improved customer responsiveness and service. Secure WLANs also can be used at the point of sale for high-speed credit card verification and purchase authorization.

These are just a few examples of the many small-medium vertical-market uses of WLANs. What typically occurs is that after a wireless network has been installed, the company that deploys it finds unique and innovative ways to apply the WLAN to grow the business.

WLAN Business Value and IT Benefits

WLANs are cost-effective and relatively fast to implement for extending the reach of company networks to a distributed and mobile workforce. They are compatible and interoperable with existing wired networks and are comparable to them in function. Industry studies have found that in companies with wireless networks, workers connect to the company intranet almost 2 hours more per day and achieve roughly 70 minutes per day in time-savings. This is an average productivity increase of more than 22 percent. When this increase is multiplied by the number of employees in a company, it is clear that a small-medium business can realize substantial productivity gains with WLANs in place.

Other market studies have found that the average business professional spends up to 48.8 hours a month in meetings, and as much as 50 percent of that time is wasted because information necessary for making group decisions is not readily available during the meeting. In contrast, when users and meeting rooms are equipped with WLANs for connectivity to the company intranet and the Internet, productive work can be accomplished.

Extending wireless network access to employees who are mobile and often dispersed around the workplace affords business advantages such as the following:

- Convenient access to information allows for more informed real-time decision-making.

- Improved responsiveness to colleagues and customers leads to greater customer loyalty, increased word-of-mouth business, and revenue growth.

- Just-in-time order processing and inventory management are possible.

- Access to the company intranet and the Internet is available in worldwide public, wireless hotspots.

- Wireless allows the delivery of information to places where cables cannot reach.

- More efficient use is made of office space, because users working effectively offsite frequently need less dedicated space at the office. At the office, shared user spaces (a concept called *hoteling*) can be created to replace individual offices or cubicles. This reduces the company's real-estate footprint and associated operations expenses.

- The company can continue to operate after normal business hours and across multiple time zones, resulting in less business downtime.

It should be evident that the business value of wireless mobility is about more than just the convenience it offers workers. Small-medium companies can realize significant profit gains as a result of the increased productivity, competitive advantages, and business efficiencies that are enabled—for a small, per-user daily IT investment. Wireless mobility also is about more than the gee-whiz factor of a no-wires approach to handling the same old functional processes. Wireless actually has the potential to transform and improve business models.

Beyond the business benefits, IT staff also can realize technical benefits with WLANs, including the following:

- Affordable, high-speed network service delivery

- Support for converged data and voice applications

- Rapid network deployment at the office and at teleworkers' homes

- Compatibility with existing networks (including wired Ethernet LANs and cellular mobile voice services)

- Support for virtual LANs (VLANs), virtual private networks (VPNs), and Internet Protocol Security (IPSec), as well as wireless-specific security technologies

- Network scalability and flexibility, including the modularity to put in place an infrastructure gradually, as needed, without having to overbuild

- Always-on access wherever the WLAN is deployed

- Business resilience as a result of alternative connections to wired networks for access to corporate resources

- Better utilization and leveraging of existing technology investments, including laptops, printers, servers, data and voice networks, and software applications

- Lower total cost of ownership (TCO) than for wired technologies, including capital expenses, ongoing management, and technical support

WLAN Technology Basics and Issues

WLANs are based on IEEE (Institute of Electrical and Electronics Engineers) 802.11 standards. The most widely implemented WLAN standards-based solutions are 802.11b and 802.11a. Another newer standard, 802.11g, is likely to join them as a popularly adopted wireless option, suitable for small-medium businesses, as shown in Table 7-1. These technologies are being adopted for use either singly or in combination technology (dual-mode and tri-mode) products.

Table 7-1 *Comparison of IEEE WLAN Standards*

Features	802.11b	802.11g	802.11a
Spectrum band	2.4 GHz	2.4 GHz	5 GHz
Speed	11 Mbps	54 Mbps trending toward 128 Mbps over time	54 Mbps
Nonoverlapping channels	3	3	8
Coverage	Up to 150 feet indoors and 700 feet outdoors	Up to 150 feet indoors and 700 feet outdoors	Up to 50 feet indoors
Availability	Widely adopted worldwide.	Widespread adoption is expected based on prestandard product sales. The IEEE standard was ratified in the second half of 2003. Interoperates with 802.11b.	Standardized for use in the U.S. Early adopters are enterprises and medium-sized companies seeking high performance.

802.11b

802.11b (pronounced "eight-oh-two-dot-eleven-b") WLANs have been around the longest. The first products were introduced in 1999. They also have the most extensive installed base of users in businesses and public-access hotspots around the globe. These networks offer performance comparable to that of wired Ethernet LANs—that is, 11 Mbps data rates. They have the added benefit of being able to support three channels of user traffic at average distances of up to 150 feet with a single access point (AP). Outdoors, 802.11b APs can reach about 700 feet when coupled with directional antennas. If bridges are used for building-to-building communications, signals can travel for up to 1 mile. With proprietary manufacturer enhancements, bridging can be extended to as much as 25 miles.

A single 802.11b access point can theoretically support up to 255 simultaneous users. But given the 11 Mbps bandwidth ceiling, 20 to 25 users would be a more realistic number for which to plan. To cover more distance and handle a greater number of concurrent users, more APs would have to be installed to form a network infrastructure of slightly overlapping WLAN cells. This multicell wireless network is called an *Extended Service Set* (ESS). It is important to remember that the actual distances across which wireless signals travel might be less than their theoretical limits. Like other high-speed communications technologies, WLANs have distance and performance trade-offs to consider. Wireless, with its over-the-air transmission method, has the added consideration of being affected by factors such as construction materials used in the building, the building's shape, the density of people occupying the space, and placement of access points.

802.11b WLANs operate in the 2.4 GHz radio frequency band. That is the band reserved for industrial, scientific, and medical (ISM) usage and is the same band used by microwave ovens and some cordless phones. The 2.4-GHz band is an unlicensed frequency, which means that networks using it can be operated without a license from the Federal Communications Commission (FCC). A couple of spectrum-management techniques are used with 802.11b WLANs. In small-medium business environments, the one that is most widely deployed is called *Direct Sequence Spread Spectrum* (DSSS). DSSS is used by 802.11b. An earlier alternative is *Frequency Hopping Spread Spectrum* (FHSS). FHSS also was supported in the earlier version of 802.11 at speeds of 1 and 2 Mbps.

DSSS is a technology that helps alleviate various forms of interference and signal jamming. It also supports communications by multiple concurrent users. With DSSS, signals are spread out, which helps make company information transmissions harder to intercept and, therefore, more private. As a further protection, encryption is used. Only people with the proper spreading code can decode the signals.

The advantages of 802.11b WLANs include the following:

- The technology is mature and reliable.

- Products are readily available and affordable.

- They integrate easily with wired Ethernet LANs or they can stand alone.

- Products are certified for mixed-vendor device interoperability by the Wi-Fi Alliance. The term *Wi-Fi* (short for *wireless fidelity*) is sometimes used interchangeably with 802.11b WLANs. The Wi-Fi Alliance (formerly known as the Wireless Ethernet Compatibility Alliance

[WECA]) is an industry body that tests WLAN products for their performance levels relative to the IEEE 802.11b standard specifications and for their ability to work as they should across different vendors' product lines.

Products that pass the Alliance's testing criteria get the Wi-Fi seal of approval. When employees of a small-medium business are mobile and want to use their company WLAN devices beyond the boundaries of the office, such as in a hotspot, it is important to know that their WLAN devices will interoperate with whatever WLAN products are deployed in the public space. On the road, worker productivity benefits are contingent on businesses and service providers deploying Wi-Fi–certified products to help ensure this communications flexibility.

- Fewer access points are needed for more coverage area as compared to 802.11a. This means that less capital investment is required.
- 802.11b WLANs are deployed worldwide and can be used by business travelers in public-access hotspots.

Here are some disadvantages of 802.11b WLANs:

- They support only three nonoverlapping channels, which limits the number of simultaneous users who can be supported.
- They operate at 2.4 GHz, which is susceptible to interference from microwave ovens, cordless phones, and other devices that use that radio frequency band.

802.11b WLANs can be right for small-medium businesses if the following are true:

- They operate in a transaction-intensive environment.
- The employees travel a lot and need remote access to the company intranet or information systems while in other locations.
- Keeping costs low is a key adoption criterion.
- Some network users already are using 802.11b LANs.

802.11a

802.11a WLANs were standardized by IEEE at about the same time as 802.11b, but the first products were not introduced into the market until early 2002. With 802.11a networks, users get roughly five times the performance of an 802.11b network (54 Mbps is the theoretical transmission rate, but the actual throughput is about half that) and five more nonoverlapping channels, for a total of eight simultaneously usable channels. The trade-offs are that 802.11a WLANs consume more power, and their cell coverage is only up to 50 feet from the access point. To avoid the frequency interference issues of 2.4 GHz WLANs, 802.11a networks operate in the higher 5 GHz spectrum band, which is also unlicensed.

802.11a uses a different spectrum-management technique called *Orthogonal Frequency Division Multiplexing (OFDM)* for greater channel availability, user support, and data rates than are possible with DSSS, used with 802.11b. Organizations that want maximum performance and usability from their WLANs choose 802.11a. However, it is important to keep in mind that 802.11a is not backward-compatible or interoperable with 802.11b WLANs and is not available or standardized worldwide. The lack of worldwide compatibility is related to spectrum conflict issues in regions outside the U.S. An FCC proposal currently under consideration will add more frequencies to those allowed for 802.11 LANs. If it passes, worldwide interoperability becomes a possibility.

The advantages of 802.11a include the following:

- At 54 Mbps, its data speed exceeds that of 802.11b (11 Mbps), but not 802.11g, which also supports up to 54 Mbps.

- 802.11a operates in a different frequency band than 802.11b and does not interfere with it. In fact, some dual-mode 802.11b/a combination products have been released so that businesses can capitalize on the best features of both technologies.

- The larger number of channels and higher bandwidth it provides let more concurrent users (up to 255) share the network without interference from neighboring access points.

802.11a also has disadvantages:

- 802.11a is not backward-compatible with 802.11b technology, so the two wireless systems cannot interoperate. Moreover, 802.11a client devices cannot work with 802.11b access points widely installed in public-space hotspots.

- 802.11a requires more access points to cover a given area because the distances over which each operates are shorter than for 802.11b. This is a cost as well as a design factor.

- 802.11a consumes more power than 802.11b, which could drain users' laptop computer batteries.

- 802.11a is not as mature an installed technology as 802.11b.

- 802.11a is still undergoing Wi-Fi Alliance interoperability testing.

- 802.11a is costlier than 802.11b systems.

802.11a WLANs can be right for small-medium businesses if the following are true:

- High bandwidth is needed for streaming video or other dynamic multimedia content.

- The business is growing quickly, and there is a need for the greater capacity of more channels.

- The office building contains many 2.4 GHz wireless technology interferers, such as microwave ovens, cordless phones, Bluetooth wireless devices, and so on.

- There is currently no WLAN in place in the business.

- Cost is less of an issue than performance.

802.11g

802.11g is the latest addition to the alphabet soup of WLAN options. Like 802.11a, it offers high-performance data rates of up to 54 Mbps with development trends moving toward 128 Mbps. Unlike 802.11a, it operates in the 2.4 GHz spectrum band and therefore supports only three nonoverlapping transmission channels. It is backward-compatible and interoperable with the large installed base of 802.11b WLANs. 802.11g also operates over longer distances than

802.11a and typically sustains higher performance. It is similar to 802.11b, but with higher data rates. With the exception of speed, its advantages and disadvantages are comparable to those of 802.11b WLANs. For users with 802.11b WLANs already installed, the compatibility of the two technologies provides for an easy and gradual migration path from 802.11b to 802.11g.

An important factor to keep in mind is that if 802.11g and 802.11b WLAN equipment is installed together in a mixed-mode wireless network, the two systems work together compatibly, but the data rates of the 802.11g systems fall back to the performance level of 802.11b. Specifically, if an employee has an 802.11g wireless NIC in his laptop and it associates for wireless connectivity with an 802.11b access point, that user will not achieve speeds greater than 11 Mbps. However, if the access point is 802.11g (or a dual-mode 802.11g/a), the user will get the full throughput possible if no 802.11b clients are on the WLAN.

Another important factor to keep in mind is that the IEEE 802.11g technology standard was ratified in the latter half of 2003. This means that standards-based products became available toward the end of 2003 and the early part of 2004. Wi-Fi Alliance interoperability testing will have to be conducted as well. Prestandard 802.11g products have been on the market since early 2003. Their manufacturers vow to make them IEEE standard-compliant with simple firmware upgrades rather than requiring customers to make additional investments in completely new products.

Voice over Wireless LAN (VoWLAN)

Packetized IP voice also can run over 802.11 WLANs for use by employees moving around within an office, retail associates working in a warehouse or on a sales floor, and people in call centers. It can be used by nurses, doctors, educators, and IT staff, among others. Voice over Wireless LAN (VoWLAN) also can increase staff reachability and improve their productivity by adding voice telephony to other WLAN applications. The initial adopters are likely to be small-medium businesses with specific vertical market applications, such as those just mentioned.

The first generation of products uses 802.11b. They are available in different form factors, such as telephone handsets or handheld computers with softphone applications software and wireless NICs installed. These WLAN phones deliver many of the voice and messaging features business users have come to expect in legacy PBX-connected phones and wired IP telephones. Examples of such features include multiline appearances and extensions, calling name and number display, call waiting, call forwarding, call transfer, redial, call mute, "you have voice mail" displays, and so on.

The most notable benefits of combining telephone and data traffic on a WLAN are that can achieve not only greater mobility for users but also more robust use of the network infrastructure to lower total cost of ownership (TCO). Using WLAN phones eliminates the need for cabling and recabling portions of a business as users change where they are working.

More widespread adoption of VoWLAN products and technology is likely to follow the completion of the IEEE 802.11e Task Group's standards for wireless quality of service. The IEEE 802.11e Task Group is defining the network traffic prioritization capabilities that are needed to support real-time, multimedia, delay-sensitive voice traffic over WLANs.

The other key factor in wireless voice transmission is security. Current security methods used for wireless data transport are applicable to VoWLANs as well. As new WLAN security enhancements for WLANs are introduced (such as those being investigated in the IEEE 802.11i Task Group and the Wi-Fi Alliance), they will continue to be added to VoWLAN systems as well. In the meantime, if VoWLAN is a desired capability, it is important that the underlying WLAN have the coverage, performance capacity, and security not only to support the small-medium business's data traffic, but also its voice traffic (or a portion of it).

WLAN Security

It is ironic that two of the biggest advantages of WLANs—the ability to provide network access to mobile workers anytime, anywhere and the ease of rapid deployment—are also the factors that often lead to potential adopters' greatest concern—security risks. It's a fact that over-the-air data transmissions are easier to intercept than wired communications. For that reason, some small-medium businesses dismiss WLANs out of hand and decide not to deploy them. They wrongly assume that wireless networks cannot be made secure. Sometimes, that assumption is based on several-years-old press headlines about the weaknesses of static wired equivalent privacy (WEP), the earliest and most primitive form of WLAN security. Significant wireless security developments have occurred since that time, partly spurred by the headlines, resulting in what are now effective and proven business-class wireless security techniques.

Like any information security system, though, even the newer, more rigorous security methods will continue to evolve and improve. Security developers cannot rest on their laurels, or clever hackers will find ways to breach even the strongest protection systems. It is critical for IT staff to stay current with the latest security advances for both wireless and wired networks.

The only alternative to adopting the best available security methods is not to use wireless networks at all. But the company that takes that approach loses access to the valuable business productivity benefits and process efficiencies that WLANs offer. Besides, if a company does not install a business-sanctioned WLAN, it is likely that some employees will plug their own access points into the company network for mobile convenience. Analysts estimate that 30 percent or more of APs in businesses are unauthorized access points. These rogue APs represent a significant security risk to companies for several reasons:

- All Wi-Fi–certified products ship with their security features turned off. IT staff turns these features on before deployment. Employee-installed APs might not have the security features activated.

- APs installed by workers are probably not known to IT and therefore are not monitored by them. Anyone with an 802.11 client device (employee or not, authorized or not) could access the company network via these rogue APs, even from the street outside the building.

It does not matter if an employee's intentions are innocent when an unauthorized wireless system is installed. Outsiders can take advantage of the unguarded pathway into the company network it offers. Rogue WLAN APs are roughly comparable to leaving the office doors unlocked at night. Anyone who wants to enter and rifle through files and confidential data can do so. The best way to anticipate and avoid rogue WLANs is to deploy a company system with the appropriate safeguards, including employee usage policies.

Network security is not just a techie issue. The company's intellectual property assets (and often those of customers, partners, and suppliers) are potentially at risk. Business and technical leaders together need to be informed of the best alternatives for securing the confidentiality and privacy of their company information. They should also ensure that whoever is installing their WLAN system has taken the appropriate factors into account.

Organizations have basically four different WLAN security deployment blueprints from which to choose, as shown in Figure 7-5. They range from completely open access to limited security to multilayered enhanced security to virtually impenetrable approaches for those away from the office.

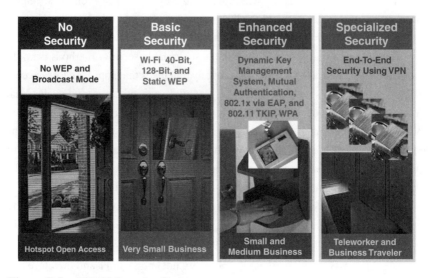

Figure 7-5   *WLAN Security Options*

It is possible to combine more than one of these (such as enhanced plus specialized) in a single network implementation. The options are described in the following list. The technical terms within each description are addressed in the following pages:

- **No security**—Open access WLANs, although acceptable for public wireless hotspots, are unsuitable for business environments.

- **Basic security**— Security that relies only on static wired equivalent privacy (WEP) keys might be all right for very small home-based businesses with just a few employees and no proprietary information. But it is a risk, even for them, to rely on minimal information security for business operations.

- **Enhanced security**—Small-medium businesses (of 20 or more employees) need multilayered wireless security methods that include IEEE 802.1*x* with Extensible Authentication Protocol (EAP) for strong, mutual authentication and key management, plus WEP with Temporal Key Integrity Protocol (TKIP) enhancements for encryption. The new Wi-Fi Protected Access (WPA) standard is one option for enhanced security.

- **Specialized security**—For small-medium business teleworkers and professionals who are on the road and using public WLANs, the most secure type of remote access, virtual provate networks (VPNs), should be adopted.

No one approach is right for all environments. A fair amount of art and science come into play in selecting and deploying WLAN systems and their associated security. It is best to enlist a knowledgeable consultant or other trusted advisor to assess what is appropriate for a particular company's network. The type of security adopted depends on such factors as size and dispersion of the network, amount of remote-access traffic, level of security required, budget, and so on.

As a general rule, four types of enhanced features should be considered for adoption as part of a robust WLAN security implementation for small-medium businesses:

- **User-based authentication**—Device-based authentication means that a wireless adapter contains authentication information. With device authentication, an intruder can gain network access by stealing or simulating an employee's wireless device (PC, handheld computer, WLAN phone, and so on). With a user-based approach to identity verification, personal passwords and logins must be supplied. The assumption is that only an authorized company user should know this information. That makes the user-based authentication approach preferable.

- **Dynamic, session-based encryption keys**—By default, 802.11 uses static WEP keys that must be changed manually. The same key is used often enough for a hacker to capture packets and determine the encryption key. Dynamic session keys are changed every time a user tries to authenticate to gain network access and automatically, at fixed intervals, throughout the time a user is online (called a *session*). Per-session, per-user keys are more difficult for intruders to crack than static WEP keys, which remain unchanged.

- **Mutual, two-way authentication**—Mutual authentication, in addition to validating the credentials of users attempting to log on to the network, also verifies that the access point through which they plan to connect is valid and authorized to provide such access. Mutual authentication ensures that a user does not inadvertently associate with a rogue AP. This mitigates *man-in-the-middle* attacks, in which a third party can intercept and tamper with a user's data.

- **Centralized management**—Authorization credentials are stored in a central database. This eliminates the need for such information to be distributed to every access point (AP), thereby reducing the vulnerability of authorization and usage policy systems.

Some of the key technologies involved in WLAN security systems are discussed in the following sections.

SSID

A *service set identifier* (SSID) is a unique label that distinguishes one WLAN from another. Wireless client devices such as laptops use SSIDs to establish and maintain network connectivity. A wireless NIC in a user's device must have the same SSID as the access point (AP) with which it wants to associate. Because wireless devices must present the correct SSID to access the AP, the SSID could be viewed as providing very simple password protection. But because users typically configure their own systems with SSIDs, they are widely known, easily shared, and not exactly a secret. This minimal level of security is compromised even further if an AP is configured to broadcast its SSID, which is the default. When this broadcast feature is enabled, any user's computer, even if it is not configured with a specific SSID, can receive the SSID and access the broadcasting AP. This is useful in public-access hotspots, but it isn't good at the office. SSIDs, therefore, should not be considered a viable security approach for small-medium business WLANs.

Even though SSIDs should not be used alone for robust security, they do offer some viable security-related functionality. Business-class wireless access points are generally designed to support multiple separate SSIDs. Consumer devices usually support only a single SSID. The availability of multiple SSIDs in an access point translates to more flexibility for IT staff when they are deploying a shared WLAN infrastructure. The various SSIDs can be used to logically divide an access point so that it appears as though several APs (virtual APs) are functioning on a single hardware platform. If a network uses VLANs (see Figure 7-4), individual SSIDs could be assigned to each VLAN to securely separate different user groups and their wireless-enabled business applications.

Static WEP

Wired equivalent privacy (WEP) is intended to protect the privacy of data being transmitted between a user's WLAN device and an access point by encrypting it. WEP uses a symmetric key encryption algorithm called RC4 (Rivest Cipher 4, also known as Ron's Code 4). When WEP is used, data is encrypted before being sent and is decrypted upon arrival at its destination. If an access point uses WEP and a client device lacks the correct WEP key for the access point, the client cannot communicate with the AP or gain access to the company network behind it.

WEP is used with 40-bit and 104-bit shared-secret keys. An additional 24 bits, called the *initialization vector* (IV), is appended, resulting in 64-bit and 128-bit encryption keys. Because of this, 802.11 WEP is alternately shown as using 40-, 64-, 104-, or 128-bit keys. Unfortunately, some of these keys are relatively easy to crack. A competent hacker can retrieve a 40-bit key in a few minutes and gain access to a company's network. 128-bit keys are harder to crack. Static WEP encryption should be considered particularly vulnerable to attack. It is applicable only for use on the very smallest (fewer than ten users), tightly managed networks with low security requirements. For most small-medium business networks, including those with fewer than ten employees, the use of static WEP keys is insufficient for WLAN security.

Ideally, employers should change their employees' WEP keys regularly to minimize the risk of WLAN attacks. If someone leaves the company, all static WEP keys must again be changed. The challenge is that there is no easy way to handle this reset process, because keys must be entered manually on all employee wireless devices and access points. No mechanism exists to centrally manage static WEP keys and control user access into the WLAN. When all these factors are added together, the bottom line is that static WEP, as a security mechanism, does not scale and is insufficient to protect a small-medium business's WLAN.

Securing a small-medium business WLAN takes more than SSIDs or static WEP keys. It should include at least the following three critical security components:

- **Authentication management for intrusion protection and access control**—This is provided by 802.1x coupled with a RADIUS (Remote Authentication Dial-in User Service) server, wireless client devices, and access points. Small businesses without a RADIUS server should have an alternative method of user authentication.

- **An authentication algorithm to prevent access fraud and verify user credentials**—This is usually Extensible Authentication Protocol (EAP) or some vendor-proprietary derivative.

- **A data privacy algorithm for sending authenticated transmissions confidentially**—This can be provided by TKIP with message integrity checks (MICs).

IEEE 802.1x with EAP

802.1x provides WLANs with strong, mutual authentication between a wireless client device and an authentication server. It also provides dynamic per-user, per-session encryption keys, removing the administrative burdens of deriving and manually distributing keys with static WEP encryption. 802.1x's dynamic keys help prevent network eavesdropping. Its mutual authentication capability ensures that sensitive information is sent only by legitimate users over legitimate networks, not to rogue APs that could lead to the interception of users' identity credentials and company data.

The IEEE 802.1x standard is for port-based network access control. It was originally designed to support authenticated access for wired Ethernet networks. It is now used extensively on WLANs as well. Under the standard, when a user connects, the port is blocked until after authentication. Networks can then authenticate devices attached to a specific LAN port or deny access if authentication fails. After the user supplies a username and password, his wireless client device interacts with the RADIUS server through an access point. If the RADIUS server authenticates the client, the server and client set up a single-session, single-user encryption key. The RADIUS server transmits that key to the access point and assigns it to the client. The five consecutive steps involved in this process are shown in Figure 7-6 and are described in the following list:

Step 1 A user requests network access. The access point (AP) prevents network access.

Step 2 Encrypted user credentials are sent to an authentication server.

Step 3 The authentication server validates the user and grants the authorized user access rights.

Step 4 An AP port is enabled. Encrypted and dynamic WEP keys are assigned to the client.

Step 5 The wireless user can now access network services and applications securely.

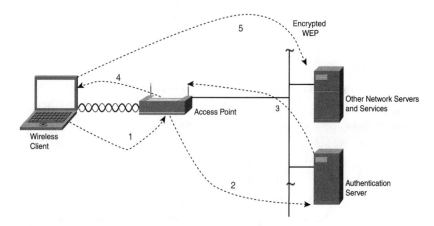

Figure 7-6   *802.1x WLAN Security*

802.1*x* does not require a specific protocol for authentication. Instead, it specifies that EAP be used. EAP is an encapsulation protocol that allows the use of different authentication protocols. This means that EAP serves as a conduit for other authentication protocols. For 802.1*x* with EAP to operate, the proper software must be installed on wireless NICs, APs, and the RADIUS server.

802.1*x* has the following advantages:

- It is standards based.

- It offers flexible authentication to IT administrators, who can choose the type of authentication method they want.

- It is scalable.

- It can be centrally managed.

- It delivers client keys that are dynamic and therefore harder to break than those of static WEP.

- It supports more transparent roaming because authentication of users is centralized.

TKIP with Message Integrity Checks

Temporal Key Integrity Protocol (TKIP) provides enhancements to 128-bit encryption. One such enhancement (called *per-packet, per-session key hashing*) changes the encryption key with each packet. This helps combat common WLAN hacking tools that take advantage of the weakness in WEP encryption when keys are not changed in each session. For now, TKIP uses the same RC4 encryption engine used by WEP, but the weaknesses of WEP are all addressed. An encryption method based on the Advanced Encryption Standard (AES) is being considered to replace RC4.

An additional feature of TKIP is message integrity checks (MICs, also sometimes called Michael). With this enhancement, a digital signature is included with every packet to mitigate man-in-the-middle attacks. The intent of TKIP with MIC is to assure businesses that their wireless communications have not been tampered with during transmissions.

VPN

End users require secure, easy-to-use, high-speed access wherever they go—especially from hotel rooms, airports, and other public-access spaces, but also from their homes while teleworking. Virtual private networks (VPNs) are widely deployed to provide remote workers with secure access to company intranets via a dedicated path over open, untrusted networks, such as the Internet. The same VPN technology used for wired remote access networks (see Chapter 6, "Intranets, Extranets, and Virtual Private Networks [VPNs]") also can be used to secure wireless communications.

VPNs can be considered a complement to 802.1x with TKIP. They ensure confidentiality, integrity, and authenticity of data communications across public networks. A VPN secures WLANs by overlaying IPSec on top of 802.11 WLAN traffic. Confidentiality is achieved through the use of an encryption standard such as 3DES (pronounced "triple dez") or AES.

The VPN approach for secure remote wireless communications offers advantages such as these:

- Existing VPN deployments in many business networks can be leveraged for wireless remote access. This brings the added benefit that IT staff are already familiar with them.

- Consistent network access interfaces are provided to users in different locations, whether at work, at home, or on the road.

- VPNs are scalable from small to large numbers of 802.11 WLAN users.

- VPNs provide isolation of traffic destined for the company intranet until VPN authentication is performed.

- There is no need for WEP keys because security measures are created by the VPN channel itself.

- There is lower IT administration for 802.11 APs and client devices because VPN concentrators can be centrally administered. This means lower staffing resource costs.

IEEE 802.11i and the Wi-Fi Alliance's WPA

A new security standard for wireless is being developed by the IEEE 802.11i Task Group (TGi) to address the user authentication and encryption weaknesses of WEP-based wireless security. As an interim measure before the acceptance and ratification of the full IEEE 802.11i standard (expected sometime in 2004), the Wi-Fi Alliance released Wi-Fi Protocol Access (WPA) in mid-2003. WPA is composed of those elements of 802.11i that are stable and ready to be deployed on companies' existing 802.11 equipment with a software upgrade. Cryptographers have examined WPA to ensure that it passes key integrity tests and have given it their approval. When the IEEE 802.11i standard is released, it will be backward-compatible with WPA while also adding new functionality such as AES.

WPA's key components include the following:

- IEEE 802.1*x* server-based authentication framework with EAP.

- TKIP with MIC.

- Key hierarchy and management features.

- Cipher and authentication negotiation, which reduces the transfer time between access points. This is important to users of Voice over WLANs (VoWLANs) to keep voice calls from being dropped.

With WPA in place, VPNs are most highly recommended for WLAN users for public access and home connections back to their company. WPA should offer sufficient security for most small-medium business main office and branch office WLAN communications.

Smaller companies that don't have a RADIUS server can instead use WPA's Pre-Shared Key (PSK), a shared-password–based authentication method that relies on AP-based distributed security policies. No authentication server is involved with PSK. If there is a match in keys between the user's WLAN device and the AP, a four-way handshake generates a session key. Although PSK does not offer the advanced features found in RADIUS-based authentication methods, it should be adequate for most smaller WLANs.

WLAN Adoption Considerations

This section offers a sampling of business and technical factors to consider when evaluating the adoption and deployment of WLANs:

- Business issues:
  - **Productivity gains**—How many meetings per month can be eliminated? How much time will be saved at meetings by having ready access to needed information? How many employees does that affect? How much time can be gained, per day, either in time-savings or longer work hours, on a per-employee basis? How much do productivity benefits increase if wireless is available to workers while they're teleworking at home or while on the road in addition to when they're at the office?

  - **Flexibility**—What is the value of business continuity, resilience, and 24/7 operations uptime, which can be improved as a result of employees being able to conduct productive work in places other than at their desks? Is the hoteling office model being employed or desired? Are WLAN systems needed to communicate and work more effectively with partners who have their own WLAN systems in place? How long would it take the local telephone company or other communications service provider to install a phone or other telecommunications system? What are agility tradeoffs?

  - **Competitive advantage**—Will ready access to information provide more responsive customer service? Will it help capture market share from competitors, resolve business issues faster, improve partner/ supplier interactions, speed time to market, and create new revenue opportunities? For each consideration, the question is "By how much?" for it to be meaningful.

  - **Efficiency improvements**—Which business applications must be supported? Will wireless network-based applications and location-sensitive tools lead to streamlined processes (for instance, between back office and front office workers, or between main office and branch office workers)? Will it stimulate the growth of the business?

- Technical issues:

  - **Security**—How many users will have access to the network? At how many locations will the network be deployed? What volume of remote access is anticipated, and at what times of the day? Which applications and what types of information will be accessed? Will outsiders (such as partners and suppliers) be granted any access rights? Will the WLAN have to interwork with a wired Ethernet network? Must the network be segregated for separate use by different functional departments and/or outside guests?

  - **Performance**—How many network users will access the network concurrently? Will they access the network from remote locations that might require interworking with mixed-vendor WLAN equipment? What types of applications will they operate? Will multimedia support be needed (integrated data, voice, and video)? How much bandwidth is needed to ensure acceptable response times? Over what distances must WLAN communications be transferred? How many hours of network availability are expected per day? Are there any radio spectrum interferers (microwave ovens, cordless phones, Bluetooth wireless products) in the vicinity of where the network is to be installed? What level of extra investment in battery power for end-user devices is acceptable to get greater WLAN performance? Are there areas or rooms where employees regularly gather for meetings or other group work? Will the company's last mile WAN access service become a bottleneck to WLAN usage?

  - **Scalability**—Is the number of network users (internal or external) expected to stay static or grow? Will the number of locations to be networked increase? Does the company require the flexibility to grow the network modularly?

  - **Deployment**—How quickly does the network have to be installed? Are indoor and outdoor connectivity desirable? Is a wired network already in place? Are individuals in-house qualified to conduct a site survey for access point deployment? Is delivering power over the LAN infrastructure desired to save significant costs by eliminating electrical cable, electrical outlet, and uninterruptible power supply installations?

If so, an intelligent switch with inline power capabilities should be purchased along with the WLAN system, or an existing network switch should be upgraded to handle this.

– **Network management**—How many staff are available to conduct ongoing network maintenance and end-user technical support? How important is it to be able to detect rogue access points? Is centralized support needed for configuration, monitoring, troubleshooting, and performing network upgrades? How automated should upgrades be? Is a self-healing network important to ensure uptime? Is there a willingness to outsource management of the wireless network or portions of it to an outside service provider?

WLANs do not necessarily have to be deployed company-wide to be useful. They are modular and can evolve as needed. For organizations trying to assess payback, it might be wise to equip a highly mobile workgroup with wireless access in their laptops and deploy a few access points in key meeting rooms and common areas of the company as a pilot. That way, the capital investment will be small, and the company can start to determine whether the enhanced collaboration, communications, and productivity gains are such that they justify a wider-scale deployment.

Another option to consider, for companies that are interested in the potential benefits of WLANs but that might not have the resources to deal with them in-house, is managed WLAN services. Managed WLAN services are provided by selected value-added resellers, interexchange carriers, local exchange carriers, and Internet service providers (ISPs). Certain small-medium businesses might find these managed offerings the most cost-effective way to achieve the benefits of WLANs. The following are some service capabilities to ask providers about when considering a managed WLAN as an option:

- Bundling of broadband access services (DSL, ISDN, PRI, Frame Relay, and so on) with the managed WLAN service

- Type of WLAN security and managed VPN capabilities offered

- Ability to integrate the WLAN into an existing wired Ethernet LAN

- Availability of 24/7 technical support

Summary

Small-medium business leaders often face a productivity paradox that can affect company growth. The one place where employees have the easiest access to company information, business applications, and the Internet is the one place where they spend the least amount of work time—at their desks. Wireless technologies offer the kind of untethered mobility and remote-access flexibility that is needed to address and solve this small-medium business productivity paradox.

WLANs are cost-effective and relatively fast to implement. They extend the reach of wired LANs or can be used alone. They also operate across various distances of up to a mile (just over a kilometer) without special connections such as bridging.

The killer app for wireless is mobility. Applications for WLANs can be classified into four primary categories: campus mobility, teleworker mobility, public-access hotspot mobility, and networks in motion. WLANs make sense for use in any vertical market sector in which employees are mobile—at work, at home, or on the road. Companies that already employ WLANs find that they improve workgroup collaboration, increase customer responsiveness, enable just-in-time order processing and inventory management, make more efficient use of office space, reduce business downtime, and so on. Users praise the flexibility that WLANs deliver to enable voice and data communications applications.

For all its benefits, the one concern that many small-medium businesses express about WLANs is security. Potential adopters need not let such concerns become an impediment to implementation. Effective WLAN security solutions exist, are proven, and are commercially available. With proper planning, business-class wireless solutions, and conscientious usage, companies should feel confident that information transmitted over the air will be secure and private.

CHAPTER 8

IP TELEPHONY AND MULTIMEDIA COMMUNICATIONS

When it comes to voice systems, small-medium business decision-makers might well ask, "If it ain't broke, why fix it?" After all, telephones have been used commercially practically since the day Alexander Graham Bell first introduced his harmonic telegraph and asked his partner, Mr. Watson, to "Come here" from another room. It is reasonable that today's business leaders would question why they should adopt voice systems based on Internet protocols and move away from a long-established telephone system. The answer is simple. Bell's invention was indeed radical back in 1877 for enabling mass communications. But in the intervening years, times have changed, and business models have changed with them. What was technologically innovative in the late nineteenth century to support and develop an industrial economy can now be limiting and inflexible to growing organizations with distributed workforces, mobile employees, real-time collaboration requirements, e-commerce sales methods, and a high dependence on rapid, personalized customer care. Internet protocol telephony (IPT), the next phase in the evolution of voice systems, will support such practices and propel businesses to deliver more competitive services and products.

Change is an expected occurrence in company telecommunications. Business voice systems are not static. Market analysts report that each year 10 to 14 percent of small-medium organizations replace or upgrade their telephony systems. Key business drivers that move these companies to integrate IP voice and video systems with data networks as part of the upgrade process typically include the following:

- Desire to move away from a 7-to-10-year proprietary system lock-in when a private branch exchange (PBX) lease or key system contract expires (or the system hits its user expansion ceiling)

- Intent to add productivity-enhancing, revenue-generating software applications

- Need to achieve greater process efficiencies and cost-savings

- Desire to increase flexibility to support the addition of new offices, moves to a new building, and hiring or reallocation of more employees

Add to these drivers the business priorities of customer care, employee mobility, and collaboration, as previously indicated.

The integration of voice, data, and video onto a single network, versus separate networks for each technology type, is called *convergence*. Convergence can play a critical role in helping a company identify new ways to generate revenues, reduce operational costs, increase organizational flexibility, and generate a sustainable competitive advantage. Whether for customer relationship management (CRM), e-commerce, workforce optimization, or other business initiatives, a converged network provides the necessary foundation to decrease implementation times, support robust applications within and outside the company, and maximize an organization's combined IT and telecommunications investments.

Converged networks also can reduce a company's total cost of ownership (TCO), not only for establishing a network infrastructure, but also for ongoing maintenance and upgrade costs as shown in Figure 8-1.

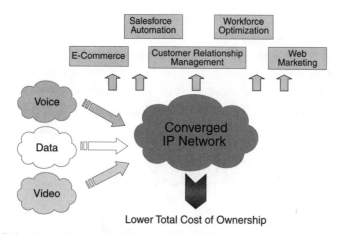

Figure 8-1   *Voice, Data, and Video Networks Converge with IP*

Although IP telephony (IPT) and converged multimedia networks can deliver significant benefits to their users, they might not be for everyone. If all a small business needs to do is place and receive phone calls, such a system would be overkill and not worth the investment to implement it. But companies that face the same challenges and priorities as those highlighted previously should explore IPT and weigh it relative to other alternatives. IP data communications is already the global standard. IP voice and multimedia communications have been slower to develop but are now proven, reliable, and high quality and are rapidly gaining market acceptance. They are being deployed across companies of all sizes and are likely to displace traditional circuit-based systems over time.

What Is IP Telephony?

IP telephony (IPT) allows the combining of separate voice and data infrastructures onto a single, converged network. The resulting network can support phone communications with the same quality and reliability as traditional telephone company-provided circuit-switched voice networks. The biggest bonus is that IPT also adds support for applications that deliver a richer, sometimes more streamlined, communications experience to its users.

IPT runs over a local area network (LAN). Therefore, it is well-suited for communications within a building or between buildings scattered across a campus. A complementary technology, voice over IP (VoIP), runs over wide area networks (WANs). VoIP can transmit voice over a public WAN (such as the Internet) or a private, company-owned WAN. As is the case with data networks, a complete IP-based voice system should combine both LAN (IP telephony) and WAN (VoIP) capabilities. Sometimes these terms are used interchangeably. In this book, the umbrella term IP telephony is used for simplicity's sake to represent IP voice systems for LANs and WANs, as shown in Figure 8-2.

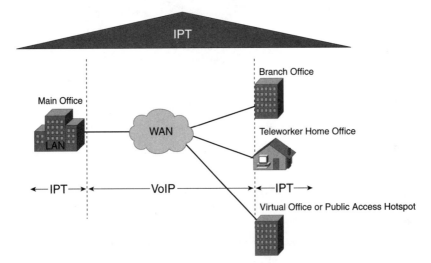

Figure 8-2 *IPT—An Umbrella Term for LAN IPT and WAN VoIP*

IPT systems are designed to interoperate with legacy private branch exchange (PBX) and wide area public switched telephone network (PSTN) systems. They provide comparable features to these legacy offerings but also include web-based individual and workgroup productivity and call-management applications. The result is that Internet business solutions such as customer care, sales force automation,
e-commerce, and others can be deployed more effectively. One way to look at IPT is that with it in place, a company's phone system is raised to be on par with its computer system in the areas of features, usability, and business productivity.

An IPT system has five major components, as shown in Figure 8-3 and as described in the following list.

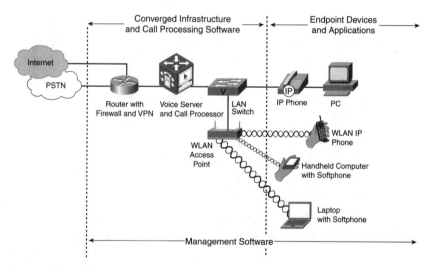

Figure 8-3   *IPT Components*

- **Converged IP network infrastructure**—This is the underlying foundation that supports voice and video on an existing data network or that is integrated as part of a new network installation. Infrastructure elements include switches with inline power, routers, *gateways* (the translating devices between traditional telephones and the Internet), *gatekeepers* (which provide centralized call management functions such as network address translation, bandwidth management, authentication, and so on), conference units (to manage multiparty conferences), security appliances, and intelligent services software.

- **Endpoint devices**—Endpoint devices are designed specifically for voice and mixed-media communications over an IP network. They enable mobility and the ability for employees to make and receive calls from anywhere on the network where work is being conducted. IP telephones, handheld computers equipped with softphone software to emulate the functionality of IP phones, and wireless LAN IP phones (discussed in Chapter 7, "Wireless LANs (WLANs)") are included in this category. These endpoint devices have LCDs (liquid crystal displays) that support the display of diverse application content and soft keys that make using the various functions within the applications intuitive. This means that, unlike PBX systems, there is no need to remember arcane random code numbers to perform a specific function. Instead, users simply read what their options are on-screen. If workers are familiar with web logic and uniform resource locator (URL) links, they will find the same types of information lookup logical on business-class IP phones.

- **Application software**—Applications can enhance individual employee and workgroup productivity, support collaboration (even between users in remote locations), improve customer service, and help reduce costs. An in-depth discussion of IPT applications appears later in this chapter.

- **Call-processing software**—This extends telephony functions such as call setup, forwarding, and teardown to the IP network. It also creates new telephony functions that are uniquely delivered in an IP environment and that are not possible with legacy telephone systems.

- **Management software**—Management applications provide graphical user interfaces (GUIs) to simplify systems administration, ensure consistency of user experiences by providing common access methods anywhere on the network, and ensure reliable interworking between all components of the IPT system.

Small-medium business decision-makers may choose from two primary adoption approaches to IPT systems:

- **Pure**—This is a solely IP-based solution including hardware, software, services, and applications. No integration or coordination between premises-based legacy telephone and IPT systems is required with this option.

- **Hybrid**—This approach combines a legacy circuit-switching infrastructure and IP-enabled systems. Typically, in this model, circuit-switched systems are used at the company's main office and IP systems are used at branch offices. Hybrid systems are most often adopted by companies whose PBX systems are not depreciated but who want to start introducing employees to IPT's expanded functionality gradually until older systems can be replaced entirely.

In addition to choosing whether to adopt a full or partial IPT system, small-medium businesses can select from three deployment options: single site, multisite with centralized call processing, and multisite with distributed call processing. The choice of model depends on such factors as the number of system users, the number and types of devices to be connected, geographic distribution of users and devices, features and services desired, ease of administration required, scalability needs, disaster-recovery specifications, and so on. Here are some basic guidelines to consider when deciding between these models:

- **Single site**—This is for organizations that want a communications system that operates within a single building or campus. This is essentially a LAN-only implementation.

- **Multisite with centralized call processing**—This option is for organizations that need to communicate across a LAN at a main site, as well as across the WAN to smaller remote branch offices and/or teleworkers' homes. Also, there is a desire to simplify management of the IPT network by having a single call-processing system at a central site where IT staff are based.

- **Multisite with distributed call processing**—This is a more complex option for businesses usually with more than 500 system users. These businesses typically operate multiple branch offices (of at least 50 users per branch) across geographically large distances. Several, or all, of these branch locations operate their own IPT call-processing system, and IT staff are distributed across sites to manage and administer the various systems.

In many small-medium businesses, voice system implementations are not brand new (sometimes called greenfield). Companies that already have a legacy voice solution employed can replace or complement it with IPT, as shown in Figure 8-4.

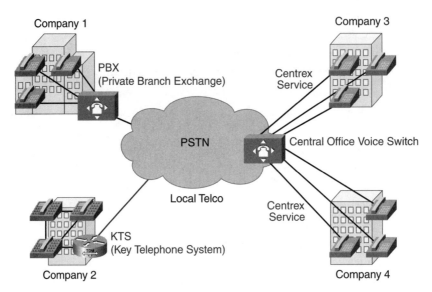

Figure 8-4 *Key System Versus PBX Versus Centrex Implementations*

Legacy systems that might be in place include the following:

- **Centrex (Central Office Exchange Service)**—Centrex is essentially a PBX in which call switching is handled at a local telephone office rather than on a company's premises. Separate phone lines are delivered to each employee by the local telecommunications carrier.

- **Key Telephone Systems (KTSs)**—Key systems are basic-functionality customer-premises phone systems that are designed primarily for use by very small offices of fewer than 25 users.

- **PBXs**—Private Branch Exchanges (PBXs) are private company premises-based digital phone networks, most often used by medium-to-large companies.

Centrex

Centrex is a switching service that provides companies with telephone lines that have capabilities similar to those offered on a PBX or key telephone system. Unlike a PBX or KTS, however, Centrex does not depend on call-processing equipment being located on the premises. Instead, equipment is housed at a service provider's local point of presence, and companies subscribe to a service. Centrex differs from basic business lines in that it typically has an average of 100 built-in features. It can be grouped with other Centrex lines for delivery to a small-medium business site. A basic business line is a standalone service; extra charges are applied whenever extra features are added to it.

Key Telephone Systems (KTSs)

A KTS is a customer premises-based communications system that links every phone in an organization to every other phone using a complex cabling arrangement. These systems perform basic intercom, paging, and call-processing functions (such as answer, dial, hold, forward, and conference). A KTS traditionally has been the first system purchased by small businesses.

Key systems derive their name from the multiline keyset phones that are used with them. These phone handsets have buttons (keys) associated with each phone extension. The keys light up to indicate whether a given phone is active (lit) or inactive (unlit). These visual display systems provide very small businesses with a relatively low-cost, simple-to-use, entry-level telecommunications system. The downside of key systems is that they become obsolete as soon as a business expands beyond 20 to 25 employees. Furthermore, they are extremely limited in flexibility as far as adding applications or managing system changes. They do not provide intelligent routing capabilities or links to other voice systems. For these reasons, a key system is not a good choice to support a company that plans to grow.

Private Branch Exchanges (PBXs)

A PBX is essentially an automated digital switchboard operator that remembers where everyone is and switches telephone calls between the appropriate parties. Legacy PBXs are based on centralized intelligence, so their management and control are handled via a single console. Because this console is often directly connected to the PBX, a network engineer or administrator must be physically present to handle network management.

Specialized personnel are also needed to program employee moves, adds, and changes (M.A.C.s), a function that companies frequently outsource to service organizations. The complexity associated with PBX M.A.C.s can increase operations costs and decrease the flexibility of PBXs for small-medium businesses.

Another flexibility issue to be aware of with PBXs is that they are typically designed for a certain size of business. When a growing company outgrows the capacity of its PBX, there is no scalability headroom. The company has to replace the PBX and upgrade to a higher-end model. Plus, a typical PBX lease locks its customers in for a 7-to-10-year contract period.

On the plus side, PBXs offer more voice features and functionality than KTSs and they are available in models that handle up to several thousand lines. This expanded capacity is significantly more costly than key systems.

Some of the most common PBX basic features are

- Speakerphone
- Mute
- Call forward
- Call transfer
- Call park
- Conference
- Caller information display
- Programmable keys
- Music on hold
- Last number redial
- Shared line ringing

Beyond these basic features, PBX systems also provide advanced functions:

- **Voice mail**—Practically ubiquitous, voice mail supports automated answering, message retrieval and forwarding, and customizable outgoing message capabilities.

- **Automated attendant**—This feature is sometimes called a *digital receptionist* because it directs calls without the need for a live operator.

- **Conference bridge**—This function allows multiparty voice calls.

When weighing IPT system investments, a significant point to keep in mind is the flexibility that IPT delivers versus older, circuit-switched legacy voice systems. IPT can be location- and service provider-independent, spanning local area networks (LANs), MANs (metropolitan area networks), and wide area networks (WANs). Devices can simply be plugged into an IP network and be visible to the entire enterprise. No provisioning services are required at a telephone company's local switching office, which greatly speeds installation time. Management can be handled via the web from any point on the organization's IP network. Additionally, businesses can benefit from the inherent scalability and reach that the IP infrastructure provides, as well as the value gained from interoperability between voice and computer systems.

The variety of choices involved in selecting an appropriate IPT voice system, and the importance of integrating it properly with data and/or legacy voice networks, makes it vital that a qualified (ideally, vendor-certified) consultant, systems integrator, value-added reseller, IPT vendor, or other trusted advisor be enlisted. Ideally, this advisor should be tapped to assist small-medium business staff with the planning, design, and installation of either a pure or a hybrid IPT system. The advisor should also suggest how best to optimize ongoing operation of the system after it is installed.

IPT Applications

A key driver motivating most organizations to migrate their voice traffic to run over an IP network is the ability to gain access to innovative horizontal and vertical industry-specific applications. IP-based applications go beyond the basic (dial, forward, mute, and others) and advanced (voice mail, automatic call distributor, three-way calling, and so on) voice services found in legacy telephone systems. IPT systems deliver those capabilities and more.

As a rule, IPT applications are designed to extend beyond the fundamentals to improve organizational productivity and competitiveness while reducing operations costs and increasing efficiency. Because of this, IPT networks are being adopted by increasing numbers of small-medium business users in a variety of vertical industries. As they integrate IP voice systems into their daily business and network operations, innovative new services and applications continue to emerge.

For now, IPT applications generally fall into four business value categories: productivity improvement, customer care, cost-savings, and safety and security. The following list highlights examples of popular killer apps that map to each of these categories and that are already in use among small-medium businesses:

- Productivity improvement:
    - Unified messaging
    - Presence-based services
    - Instant messaging
    - Remote/mobile access
    - Directories
    - Self-service
    - Scheduling
    - Multimedia conferencing
    - Videoconferencing
- Customer care:
    - Call center/Help desk
    - Click-to-talk
    - Bulletins and broadcasts
    - Self-service
    - Directories
    - Customizable services
    - Database access
    - Videoconferencing
- Cost-savings:
    - Toll bypass
    - Time card tracking

- Purchase tracking
- Event reporting and tracking
- Electronic transactions
- Call recording
- Safety and security
  - Identity verification services
  - Alerts/emergency messages
  - Silent alarms
  - E911
  - Call recording
  - Attendance tracking
  - Zoned paging

These leading IPT business applications operate on IP phones alone or in combination with a PC. They deliver functionality that can be tailored to suit the needs and business practices of different vertical industry sectors and organizations. Each one is described briefly in the following sections.

Productivity Improvement

The following applications can be used to improve productivity:

- **Unified messaging**—This supports a universal inbox that links e-mail, voice mail, and fax so that messages in each medium can be provided to workers in the other formats. For example, e-mail or fax messages can be forwarded to a voice mail box for employees to retrieve and listen to while on the road. Voice mails can be directed to e-mail systems for listening to when it is more convenient, and so on. The key to successful unified messaging is to create a tight linkage between PCs and voice systems.

- **Presence-based services**—These services let users specify where they want to receive information while at home, on the road, and so on. This service can be integrated with a unified messaging application for even greater application customization.

- **Instant messaging**—This enables real-time short messaging services between a sender and receiver of information across an IPT system. Messages appear on the IP phone display.

- **Remote/mobile access**—A single network connection provides workers with access to either voice services, data services, or both from home, on the road, or at remote branch, customer, or partner locations.

- **Directories**—Directories provide lists and guides to virtually any topic of interest to the organization, such as employee names, company locations, locations with product in stock, calls received, calls placed, and so on.

- **Self-service**—These applications let IPT system users handle transactions on their own to expedite needed responses or information gathering, such as registering for courses, checking account balances, and more.

- **Scheduling**—Such applications let users view schedules of events and activities, milestones, and so on. Users also can create calendars or project road maps for others to view.

- **Multimedia conferencing**—By combining voice, video, and data systems, users can collaborate using online, real-time shared whiteboards. All users can see what is written or drawn on a computer screen as it is entered. Users can conduct simultaneous IPT-based discussions.

- **Videoconferencing**—This is another multimedia application that mitigates the need for conference bridges. It enables shared, real-time network meetings, including audio, video, and graphics among groups of workers, partners, or customers. With IPT, desktop videoconferencing has evolved from being an informal tool for connecting two parties online to a geographically independent meeting tool.

Customer Care

When it comes to the crucial category of customer care, a number of useful functions exist:

- **Call center-Help desk**—IP call center or help desk applications offer the flexibility to distribute calls anywhere on the IP network. As a result, it is easy to move call center staffers from one location to another or even allow them to work from home.

- **Click-to-talk**—Web-based call centers let users talk with a call center agent without disconnecting from the Internet. The agent can track a caller's actions online and eliminate the delay between making contact with a caller and providing him with a reply to his questions. This boosts responsiveness and can lead to a competitive advantage in help desk and e-commerce offerings.

- **Bulletins and broadcasts**—News alerts can be broadcast across the display screen of IP phones, sometimes in lieu of paging services, depending on the user's application.

- **Self-Customizable services**—Users can program features into an IP phone to suit their personal preferences. Examples include wake-up calls in hotels, special ring tones, audio or text alerts when product orders are ready to ship, and so on.

- **Database access**—IP phones (or softphone-enabled handheld computers) can be used as database access appliances in lieu of PCs. This is useful for gathering information on topics of timely interest, such as traffic conditions, weather forecasts, stock prices, flight or public transport schedules and status, location of automated teller machines (ATMs), dates and locations of events and activities, and so on.

Cost-Savings

A number of IPT applications help out with cost-savings as well:

- **Toll bypass**—IPT across wide area networks eliminates the need to incur expensive long-distance toll charges for calls placed to branch offices or other remote locations. Voice and fax calls are carried across the company IP network as part of a stream of data traffic, so they bypass telecommunication carriers' voice billing systems.

- **Time card tracking**—Users "punch in" and "punch out" at work by entering their employee or visitor identification code into the IP phone system. This provides accurate, real-time record-keeping and tracking.

- **Purchase tracking**—Lists of goods such as office supplies, retail stock, and so on are made available on an IP phone application that can be used not only to place orders but to track purchases as well. By integrating this application with data networks, such lists can be filtered to display only those items the individual viewing the list is authorized to order.

- **Event reporting and tracking**—Tasks that require check-in can be set up to notify potential handlers of specific tasks they need to address and their priority order. After completing the required task, the handler can register the activity, or trouble ticket, as closed. This application is useful for security staff, engineering or housekeeping workers in hotels, those who replenish or locate stock in retail/wholesale/manufacturing businesses, realtors who must attend property inspections or tours, and so on.

- **Electronic transactions**—IPT applications can be used for credit card verifications at a point of sale, electronic funds transfers, online approvals, and so on.

Safety and Security

The all-important concerns of safety and security have a variety of possible applications:

- **Identity verification services**—Photos and personal information shown on an IP phone display let staff or security personnel ensure that someone is who they claim to be.

- **Alerts/emergency messages**—Messages can be flashed across an IP phone display screen, much like the alerts that appear at the bottom of TV screens during other programming. This function can be used to draw attention to urgent news, to specify an action that should be taken, or to provide warnings about imminent or ongoing incidents.

- **Silent alarms**—With the push of a single IP phone button, an outgoing call for help can be sent in the event of danger.

- **E911**—Alerts go directly to police, fire, and ambulance. They use the standard emergency 911 dial code that also identifies the calling party's phone number and location.

- **Call recording**—Portions of IPT calls can be recorded at the push of a button to document and verify verbal agreements made during the course of a call or to identify harassing phone callers.

- **Zoned paging**—This sends a selective broadcast alert to a subset of users on an IP phone system.

The use of IPT is not limited to or biased toward any one particular vertical market. Deployment is spreading across all verticals. Industries that are realizing business value by adopting IPT systems and applications include but are not limited to the following:

- **Real-estate**—IPT-enabled unified messaging applications are adopted to help make constantly on-the-move agents more accessible and productive. IPT lets them work effectively untethered from their desktops in favorite spots such as coffee shops (where they can combine IPT and wireless Internet access) or at home. By using IP-unified communications, agents can save an average of 20 to 25 minutes per day by handling their messages more efficiently.

- **Legal**—Law firms earn revenue based on billable time with clients. And lawyers spend a lot of time on the phone. Therefore, it is inefficient for them to maintain separate phone and accounting systems. Traditionally, lawyers have kept manual, running diaries of call records and then entered those records into the firm's billing system at month's end. This procedure can send IT systems' utilization skyrocketing. Using IPT as an alternative approach, call usage can be tracked daily and combined with an automated back-end application that imports call data into a billing system. This method streamlines operations, frees lawyers to spend more time on billable hours, and provides faster cost recovery to law firms. Additionally, the IPT system can support critical tools such as a company directory with one-touch dialing, an on-screen litigation resource directory, an expert witness directory, on-screen expense account balance reports, and breaking news or other firm alerts. An emerging application, handled via IPT and computer systems combined, is that of videoconferencing for predeposition planning, deposition taking, and even remote trials.

- **Education (K-12 and university)**—IPT supports schools, libraries, and affiliated local government agency offices. In K-12 (a U.S. designation for kindergarten through twelfth grade) environments, schools are paid a per diem fee for each student in attendance. Truancy can have a monetary impact on schools as well as cause teachers, administrators, and parents to fear for the safety of students who are unaccounted for. As a result, IPT student attendance management is a valued application that allows teachers to take attendance in the classroom and that informs them of preapproved absences. Photos of students can be included so that new or substitute teachers can verify students' identities. Integrated e-mail systems can be used with an attendance application to alert parents that their children are not in school. Other IPT educational applications include the following:

  – Electronic hall passes issued via the IP phone

  – Online faculty phone directory

  – Student management functions, such as early dismissal approvals, enrollment in daily activities, and so on

  – Faculty bulletins

  – Visitor/intern control, a security measure that supplies digital pictures of visitors, contractors, and interns

  – Timekeeping (for temporary and hourly personnel)

  – Teachers can use IP videoconferencing to allow their classes to interact and communicate with students in other districts and even around the world. This broadens students' learning horizons by offering them global "field trips."

- **Hospitality**—IP screen phones in hotels' guest rooms can serve as an information portal for any of the following:

  – Ordering hotel room service or food delivery from affiliated outside restaurants

  – Renting DVD movies or audio CDs from nearby video stores

- Selecting hotel or spa services such as wake-up calls, housekeeping or engineering support, massages or facials, and so on

- Accessing weather reports, flight information, and more

- Obtaining electronic concierge assistance with local entertainment, dining, transportation, golf, and so on

Access to information and services in this way is less invasive and more efficient than having to tune the TV to a constant and linear hotel services broadcast channel. For frequent or long-term guests, an IPT system can remember and save individual phone numbers or preferred speed dials. Numbers can be retained even if guests move from room to room. For internal operations management, IPT phones can be tied into the property management system (PMS) for automated operations such as check-in/ check-out, housekeeping room readiness status updates, wake-up calls set by staff, and so on.

- **Finance and banking**—High-quality service can be a key differentiator in a customer's choice of financial service providers. Sales of existing products and services can be stimulated through the use of multimedia IPT systems combined with automated teller machines (ATMs) and kiosks to market and advertise products and promotions and to build awareness of financial services. Branch employees can be provided with a complete view of every customer's accounts to ensure that the most appropriate sales or service employee answers a call from a customer. IPT systems also can be used to distribute training content to all branches as part of a desktop videoconferencing system. Loan or interest rate information can be pushed to loan officers, and accompanying automatic callback services can be set up to ensure that customers are satisfied with loan application procedures and results.

Business Benefits of IPT Systems

Most small-medium business leaders report that they start realizing benefits from their IPT systems either upon initial installation or within 6 months of deployment. They are usually surprised by this, having expected that it would take considerably longer to derive measurable value from their investment. When decision-makers discuss the benefits of IPT to their organizations, the four value categories they most often cite are the following:

- **Individual employee productivity gains** — The business case for IPT is usually based first and foremost on measurable gains in employee productivity. Solutions that increase an individual user's work output are rated most important because of the constant value they deliver throughout market downturns, hiring freezes, and even business upturns.

  IPT is put to use reducing the time employees spend retrieving and responding to e-mail, voice mail, and faxes. This time averages 2.5 hours per employee per day. Analysts report that unified messaging applications (those that let workers access and immediately respond to voice, fax, and e-mail messages from any IP phone or PC anywhere) can help companies gain at least 30 to 40 minutes per day of effective work time per employee.

  Other IPT applications, such as personal communications assistants, online directories, remote/mobile access, and videoconferencing, let users achieve even more results faster.

  Converged IP applications also help businesses reduce downtime, because employees can work equally well in virtual offices anywhere on the network as they would in their primary workplace. The additional work time gained from remote staff can add up to more than 4 hours per branch office employee per week and 5 hours per teleworker per week. This totals 28 or 33 days per year, respectively. When those numbers are multiplied by the total number of relevant employees (and their loaded salary costs), the productivity gains to an organization are significant.

  Although all employees become more productive as a result of IPT systems usage, those who tend to experience the greatest personal productivity benefits are customer service agents, IT staff, and the sales force.

- **Workgroup productivity gains**—Small-medium business decision-makers also turn to IPT to realize benefits that result from knowledge sharing and collaboration between cross-functional teams across the entire company and with key partners and suppliers. The applications most commonly mentioned by business adopters as helping to achieve workgroup productivity benefits are two-way videoconferencing and multimedia conferencing (including shared whiteboard applications) and one-way broadcasts and instant messaging.

- **Customer care and responsiveness improvements**—A frequently quoted business statistic claims that it costs five to ten times more to acquire a new customer than it does to retain an existing one. Assuming that this is true, the ability to deliver outstanding customer care is a critical driver of competitive advantage for businesses of any size. It also can help control marketing expenses. IPT systems often are mentioned anecdotally as being successful in helping organizations increase customer satisfaction. Empirical research bears this out. Studies have found that 60 percent of users with IPT systems running multimedia contact centers, online showrooms, and self-service web applications reported that their deployments provided them with differentiated service capabilities and customer retention advantages versus competitors.

In call center environments, IP-unified communications support small-medium businesses by helping them respond more quickly to customer inquiries. Integrated click-to-talk capabilities let customers talk live with customer service agents when online self-service is insufficient. And intelligent automated e-mail responses provide a quick way to reply to customer requests with an anticipated callback time. The callback time can be based on the call center's workload to ensure that customers know that they are not being ignored. This helps set realistic expectations as to when they will be served.

Companies that run business-critical e-commerce systems with integrated IPT capabilities say the key benefit of these systems is that they provide a rich, online customer experience with service levels comparable to those of bricks-and-mortar stores. In some cases, business owners combine online and physical storefronts to achieve the best possible blend of local and remote customer interactions.

- **Cost-savings and operational efficiency improvements**—Last but not least in benefit priority, small-medium business leaders find that IPT systems reduce infrastructure equipment costs (CAPEX), minimize staffing and facilities costs (OPEX), and increase workflow efficiency and company flexibility. Specific benefits include the following:

  - **New office openings can be completed more quickly** —IPT systems can be provisioned in just under 4 weeks on average.

  - **Less capital investment is required**—IPT equipment is not as costly as PBX systems for the scalability it offers.

  - **Less cabling is needed than with traditional voice systems**—Less cabling reduces design and installation charges.

  - **System flexibility and ease of use are improved**—Workers can use an IP phone handset that resembles a regular desk phone but that has a larger screen display and soft key functionality. They can use a software-based softphone that loads onto desktops, laptops, and handheld computers. Softphones are especially useful for mobile workers who want to continue using IPT while passing through travel hotspots, at home, at branch offices, or at other nonstandard work locations. Moreover, users can use the same phone number in any of these locations.

  - **Ease of scalability**—An IPT system can grow quickly, simply, modularly, and cost-effectively as a small-medium business grows.

  - **Faster moves, adds, and changes (M.A.C.s)**—This is the most common benefit cited by technical decision-makers, because it can reduce IT support and administration costs by as much as 70 percent. Small-medium businesses whose staffs are highly mobile or that undergo rapid employee turnover and frequent restructuring can save significantly on each M.A.C. A move averages 1.5 hours. As companies increasingly focus on teaming and collaboration, employees also might move more frequently to be closer to other team members for project work.

    With IPT systems, all a user has to do is unplug the IP phone from the network outlet in her office and plug it in at a new (or temporary) location. This is the equivalent of carrying a laptop computer to another place in the office to do work. The network recognizes the device and allows it to access authorized services from wherever it is attached. Because of the ease with which moves can be made, savings are accrued by eliminating the need to pull new cabling, to reconfigure existing cabling, or to pay experts to handle the move. Junior-level staff can handle M.A.C.s, or they can be carried out via employee self-service.

– **Reduced IT staffing and administration costs**—IPT call processing can be centrally managed to reduce the need for onsite IT staff at all company locations. Centralized management also makes it easier and less costly to integrate new IPT applications. And it reduces the need for IT staff to travel as frequently to remote offices, which can save a company the equivalent of roughly 19 workdays per year.

Because IPT features are easier to use than those of legacy PBXs, IT employees also spend close to 6 hours less per week providing phone support to workers.

– **Reduced PSTN bills via toll bypass**—IPT reduces PSTN voice charges by using the company data network to transport voice traffic. IP-based voice technology can virtually eliminate toll calls regionally, nationally, and internationally.

– **Decreased office space rental expenses**—More employees can work productively from home or another remote location and appear to others as if they are at the office.

The bottom line is that with the right IPT system in place, companies heighten their ability to respond quickly to changes in the market and realize a wealth of business and technical benefits. Benefits include productivity gains, increased customer satisfaction, cost-savings, and improved safety and security.

IPT Technology Overview

Traditional voice communications are provided over circuit-switched networks using the public switched telephone network (PSTN). With legacy circuit switching, a 64 Kbps link is dedicated to connecting directly between two endpoints for the duration of a call. It doesn't matter if the sites are separated by wide areas or are local and connected by a PBX—the principle is the same.

As soon as this short-duration dedicated link is established, it cannot be used for any other communications. Because voice conversations are more sensitive to delay variations than data transmissions, to be understood they must be sent without any interruptions or delays. The circuit-switched PSTN has traditionally provided high-quality, high-reliability (referred to as *five nines*,—99.999 percent availability), low, fixed-latency (minimum delay), bidirectional (full-duplex) service that is needed to enable two-way conversations. The main shortcomings of circuit switching are its inherent lack of network flexibility, limited productivity and vertical market applications support, and the inefficiency it creates by relying on dedicated connections. In spite of these shortcomings, most business voice traffic is still circuit-switched. But that is changing as IPT makes its way into small-medium businesses, as illustrated in Figure 8-5.

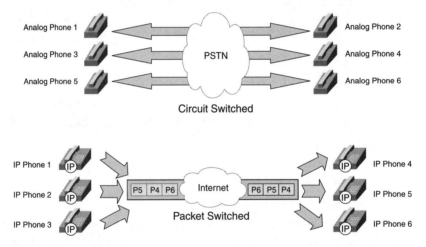

Figure 8-5 *Circuit-Switched Versus Packet-Switched Voice*

IPT does not use circuit switching. IPT is based on packet switching. In packet switching, links are not reserved for specific users' voice conversations. In fact, quite the opposite is true. Voice traffic is broken into chunks called *packets*. Each voice packet contains its own destination address and is routed across a network. The packets that comprise a single voice conversation may take different network paths and can even be interwoven with other types of packet traffic (such as data and video traffic) before reaching their intended destination. At that endpoint, the packets are reordered in their proper sequence for delivery as a recognizable voice stream. Although this process might seem as though speech could end up garbled, packet-switching systems handle such transfers almost instantaneously. IPT technology has matured to the point where there is no noticeable delay as parties converse.

IPT Protocols and Standards

Depending on the telephony or multimedia services and business applications a company wants to employ, different IPT standards and protocols can be adopted. These signaling standards ensure that the information needed to establish, terminate, and otherwise control call processes in an IP environment are provided when and where needed. They also help avoid degradation of voice services operating between IP networks and the PSTN. A variety of signaling standards are available. Two of them are most suitable to support the scale and needs of small-medium business IPT systems: H.323 and Session Initiation Protocol (SIP). They are compared in Table 8-1 and are briefly described in the following sections.

Table 8-1   *H.323 and SIP Signaling Standards Compared*

H.323	SIP
ITU standard	IETF standard
Designed on legacy circuit-switched signaling models	Designed for use on IP networks and the Internet
Supports multimedia	Supports multimedia
Older, most prevalent standard (especially on LANs)	Newer standard
Complex protocol	Relatively simple protocol
Difficult to customize	Easy to customize

H.323

H.323 is the most prevalent wide area IPT standard. Developed by the International Telecommunication Union (ITU) standards organization, it is a multimedia (audio, video, and data) conferencing protocol that defines standards for communicating over packet-switched networks. In addition to call control (setup and teardown), H.323 includes algorithms for converting call streams to communicate between packet networks and circuit-switched networks and voice compression processes to keep network bandwidth requirements in check. Furthermore, it includes capabilities to ensure multimedia communications' quality of service (QoS) by defining how voice should receive priority over other IP traffic on a LAN or WAN. In doing this, H.323 supports the reliable delivery of delay-sensitive, real-time voice (a capability that is not naturally inherent in IP).

H.323's operational richness comes at a price. Although it has been useful to kick-start the transition from legacy circuit switching to IPT, its circuit-switched heritage makes it complex to implement, resource-intensive to operate, and difficult to scale. It is often called a *heavy* protocol because of that complexity.

Another drawback of the standard is that four versions are available, and the ITU continues to enhance H.323 to improve its performance. Technical decision-makers evaluating H.323-based IPT systems should keep this standards fluidity in mind. Even if products are designated H.323-compliant, they will not necessarily interoperate with each other in an end-to-end system unless all products involved use the same version of the standard. If some products use a vendor-proprietary implementation and others do not, or if different versions of H.323 are running throughout the network (for instance, one product is version 2 and one is version 4), they likely will not interoperate easily, if at all. That could result in the small-medium business having to dedicate costly IT resources and/or hire outside experts to resolve the incompatibilities. Even with these quirks, H.323 is well-established and will be around for the foreseeable future. Because of its complexity, however, those in the industry ultimately expect it to be replaced by SIP.

SIP

SIP was developed as an alternative to H.323 by a different standards group, the Internet Engineering Task Force (IETF). It was developed specifically for use in an IP environment. It is a control protocol for creating, modifying, and terminating point-to-point and multiparty IPT or IP videoconferencing sessions.

SIP can be used to support end-to-end mobility, presence-based, and instant messaging services. It integrates equally well with legacy circuit-switched telephony networks, WWW, and e-mail systems. It also is more scalable than

H.323. The upshot of all this is that SIP is becoming the IPT protocol most preferred by users. Many of its supporters have been known to proclaim, "SIP happens."

SIP offers benefits such as the following:

- It is extremely efficient, offering faster call setup with fewer steps than H.323.

- It is less complex, which gained it the moniker of lightweight standard. It requires less memory and processing power than H.323.

- It is more intuitive in addressing procedures. The scheme it uses is the same as IP addresses, which consist of a user (or host) name and a domain name. Specifying addresses is similar to the Hypertext Transfer Protocol (HTTP) syntax of web browsers. The advantages of this are that SIP addresses can be processed easily by existing IP servers. Users who are familiar with e-mail or Uniform Resource Locators (URLs) can use them for SIP dialing rather than having to remember a separate system of phone numbers.

- Because SIP is less complex and generates less overhead than H.323, it is also better-suited for use in small, mobile devices such as handheld computers and laptops.

IPT Voice Quality

One of the most critical technical dimensions to evaluate and handle without compromise in an IPT system is voice quality. Workers and business executives have every expectation that their office-based voice system will be on par with legacy, circuit-switched telephone systems. Most small-medium business users tend to be more forgiving of systems used while mobile or on business travel. This is a result of the voice quality they are used to with their cellular phones. To achieve the desired quality level for all relevant work locations, it is important to ensure that quality of service (QoS) specifications are addressed as part of an IPT system. QoS factors include the following:

- **Latency (or delay)**—This is the time it takes from when one person begins to speak until another person hears what the first one said. Real-time, two-way voice conversations are intolerant of too much delay. So

IPT systems must be able to guarantee low latency. This delay is usually measured in milliseconds. Latency of less than 150 milliseconds (for one-way traffic) and less than 250 milliseconds (for round-trip or two-way traffic) is generally considered the absolute ceiling for high-quality IP voice services. It is the same level of delay that users get with circuit-switched voice services delivered via satellite.

- **Jitter (or delay variation)**—This occurs when voice packet arrival times fluctuate. Jitter requires buffering voice traffic. Packets are held for a period of time before they are forwarded to control the rate of flow. The unfortunate side effect of buffering, however, is increased latency.

- **Packet loss**—Packet loss is a normal occurrence on packet networks. It can be caused by links overloaded with traffic, too many packet collisions on a LAN, and other reasons. In voice transmissions, if packets are dropped or other data errors occur at a volume greater than roughly 5 percent of the total number of packets, an audible pop is heard. Packet loss, therefore, has a significantly higher impact on voice traffic than it does on data traffic, such as e-mail. Data traffic is more forgiving in this respect.

Business-class IPT QoS should include provisions for managing delay, jitter, packet loss, and bandwidth efficiency for voice calls. To ensure traffic integrity across all these dimensions, QoS does the following:

- It prioritizes one type of traffic over another. Traffic prioritization becomes even more important when traffic flow is heavy—an increasingly common situation for most networks.

- It prevents or delays the transmission of low-priority traffic, when needed, to avoid network congestion.

- It controls the rate at which individual applications transmit their packets.

Networks rely on a variety of QoS mechanisms, in the LAN and the WAN, to achieve peak performance with converged traffic. QoS mechanisms include the following:

- **Packet classification**—This is a way to recognize application packets moving across a network.

- **Marking**—This uses classification information to tell network equipment how to handle packets.

- **Enforcement**—Policing schemes establish and ensure different classes of service (CoS).

QoS comes in three basic flavors. When deciding on QoS for a converged IPT network, companies should consider which of the following types of service levels, or classes, they prefer:

- **Best effort**—This class has no QoS at all. Traffic simply moves across the network with no guarantees.

- **Differentiated service (DiffServ)**—This is sometimes called *soft QoS*. DiffServ treats specially marked packets better than others. However, there are no hard-and-fast guarantees.

- **Reserved service**—As its name implies, reserved service reserves network resources for specific traffic. Called *hard QoS,* reserved service ensures that the most sensitive traffic gets priority access to network resources over all other traffic.

The type of QoS selected for a small-medium business depends on the applications to be run, what the network infrastructure can support, and the company's cost sensitivity. QoS technology can help ensure optimal network performance in IP converged networks that support business-critical applications and communications among supply chain partners, customers, and remote workers.

IPT Security

As small-medium business executives evaluate the adoption of LAN and WAN IPT systems, it is critical that they ensure security as an integral element. Voice systems running over IP networks are just as vulnerable to attack as the rest of the company data network, and they must be protected accordingly and in depth. Chapter 5, "Network Security Basics," provides an overview of network security considerations and technology basics. There is no need to rule out the use of IPT systems for fear of security breaches. Proven solutions exist to ensure adequate security. The first step in addressing potential breaches is anticipating what the possible assaults might be.

Here are the most common attacks to which IPT systems can be subjected:

- **Denial of service (DoS)**—DoS attacks can overload IPT server or client devices and shut down the network's availability.

- **Viruses, worms, and Trojan horses**—These can be time-triggered to execute attacks on servers and client devices and to damage their performance levels.

- **Packet sniffing**—Sniffing taps or intercepts conversations by capturing transmitted packets. It compromises company information privacy.

- **IP spoofing**—Unauthorized users impersonate trusted parties to commit toll fraud (theft of long-distance service) or to hijack others' transmissions.

- **Voice over Misconfigured Internet Telephones (VOMIT)**—Misconfiguration enables eavesdropping on others' conversations.

In these attacks, several things are at risk technically:

- The reliability and functionality of the entire IPT system

- The infrastructure network on which the IPT network is built

- The information that is exchanged

- Possibly even identity information belonging to the parties engaged in communications

It is for these reasons that security must be an integral part of an IPT system and not an afterthought or acquisition planned for some future date.

Security capabilities that should be part of the checklist for an IPT system include the following:

- **Identity authentication**—Authorized user and device authentication is needed to prevent rogue devices or unauthorized users from gaining access to the company IPT network.

- **Voice encryption**—This is required for communications over the Internet or other insecure media.

- **Data and voice network segmentation**—An IP voice network should be logically segmented (or segregated) from the IP data network to increase attack protection. This does not mean that two IP network infrastructures are needed. Rather, technologies such as stateful firewalls, access control policies, and virtual LANs (VLANs) can be used to keep the segments separate. Segmentation coupled with a switched (rather than a shared) infrastructure reduces eavesdropping, guards against denial of service attacks, and protects against spoofing voice segments of the network. *Stateful inspection firewalls* should be used to filter traffic. Stateful inspection firewalls are those that check not just packet header source and destination information but also packet contents up through the application layer. Firewalls must be intelligent enough to open only properly negotiated and authenticated connections and to close the connections when an IPT session is over.

- **Secure IPT servers**—A call server is one of the basic differences between an IPT system and a traditional PBX. IPT call servers are often based on a vulnerable operating system (OS) such as Windows or UNIX and are connected to the data network. As such, they must be secured and protected from internal and external attack.

- **Secure remote access**—IP phones, IP wireless LAN (WLAN) phones (discussed in Chapter 7), and softphones (on laptops, handheld computers, or other portable devices) that employees use to connect to the company network via the Internet should be able to use the same remote-access virtual private network (IPSec VPN) client that is used for data. Anti-virus software and personal firewalls on portable devices also should be used for added protection.

IPT systems can be made as secure as legacy voice systems, but the proper elements must be acquired and implemented from day one. Security must be part of a holistic approach to end-to-end converged (voice, data, and video) networking systems. A company's security policy should cover workers' client devices, voice servers, application servers, legacy PBXs, and other key network infrastructure elements (such as routers, switches, gateways, and firewalls).

Reliability/Availability

Most users' experience with legacy telephone systems is that when they pick up a handset they hear a dial tone 99.999 percent of the time. It is sometimes assumed that when voice is merged onto a data network, the combination will become unstable and unreliable. Frankly, a PBX is inherently no more reliable than a data network. Part of what makes a legacy voice system such as a PBX reliable is the company's commitment to invest in the necessary redundancy and power backup systems to guarantee its uptime.

The best way to ensure comparable reliability in IP voice communications is to take the same approach: Use redundancy. First and foremost, it is important to plan an IP network infrastructure for resiliency, because it will serve as the foundation on which an IP voice or multimedia network (and other advanced technologies) is built. Second, redundancy should be integral to the IPT system's call-processing servers, routers, and switches, as well as uninterruptible power supply (UPS) systems. Adopting systems with inline power also helps ensure IPT phone service continuity. Ethernet switches with inline power provide low-voltage power over standard unshielded twisted-pair (UTP) cables instead of using wall power. The voltage that is delivered can power an IP telephone or a WLAN access point (AP). Therefore, it is sufficient to run Ethernet switches on a UPS to maintain IPT service in the event of a building power loss. Inline power also offers another noteworthy benefit: It significantly lowers power provisioning and administration costs.

IPT Adoption Considerations

As mentioned previously in this chapter, if all a company requires is the ability to receive and place calls, an IPT system is not needed. Here are some factors to consider when determining whether IPT technology is right for a small-medium business:

- **Company size and growth plans**—Does headcount fluctuate regularly? Are new offices being opened or consolidated? Do more partners or suppliers need to communicate with staff? Businesses that experience regular change should consider IPT for the scalability; geographic reach; ease of moves, adds and changes; and flexibility to deal with changing business conditions it supports.

- **Technology adoption culture**—Is the company conservative, leading-edge, or somewhere in between? No matter where a company falls within this continuum, there's an IPT deployment model to consider. The solution might be pure IPT or a combination of legacy telephony and IPT.

- **Operational and workplace characteristics**—What are the company's current efficiency or inefficiency levels? What is the effectiveness of workflows and customer service ratings? What is the pervasiveness of employee mobility? IPT systems and applications can improve employee and workgroup productivity, increase customer satisfaction and competitiveness, streamline business processes for greater efficiency and cost-savings, and enable transparent communications among mobile employees in a networked virtual organization.

- **Communication application needs**—Must the system operate locally, remotely (including teleworkers' homes), or a combination? Will a current PBX remain in use until its lease expires? IPT systems operate equally well across LANs, MANs, WANs, and employee homes equipped with broadband access. IPT also integrates with existing phone systems and applications and extends the breadth of functionality they are capable of delivering.

- **Resources**—What is the IT budget? How large is the IT staff? IPT systems can be sized and delivered to fit the resources of small-medium businesses using a variety of platform approaches and deployment methods. Solutions can be self-managed or service provider-managed.

Small-medium business decision-makers should assess other factors. These are things they might be asked by consultants, integrators, value-added resellers, or other advisors. When evaluating the adoption of an IPT solution, consider the following:

- Expenses:
  - What is the current telephony system TCO? Include equipment costs, recurring service charges, administration and management fees, equipment leasing, and other financing costs.
  - How much might these costs increase in the future?
  - Will a PBX (or other proprietary voice system) lease expire soon?
  - How often are outside experts required to make service calls for routine management tasks?
  - How important is a future-proofed platform to investment justification?

- Phone usage:
  - What role do voice communications play in the business?
  - How are calls transferred to users throughout the company today?
  - Can employees perform tasks such as forwarding voice mail between remote offices?
  - Do employees in remote offices have the same access to telephony applications as someone at the main office?
  - How many locations, employees, and partners (and possibly customers) must retrieve voice mail, e-mail, and fax messages?
  - How do customers and partners currently communicate with company employees?
  - Do customers have adequate access to mobile employees?
  - Does the company operate call and contact centers?
- Legacy existing equipment:
  - Are separate voice and data infrastructures being supported?
  - What does it cost to make them compatible with each other?
  - Is it easy to upgrade or scale existing telephony equipment?
  - Does existing voice and data networking equipment meet company needs?
  - Are equipment upgrades or new purchases planned?
  - Is a phased or flash-cut transition needed?
- Customer service:
  - Are employees equipped to best serve customers with current communications tools?
  - Do customers require more personalized phone services?

Business leaders who are considering adopting a new IPT system should keep in mind that it will require the merging of separate voice and data networks into a single, converged network. Convergence subsequently might drive the need for changes to existing IT operations. It also might dictate that IT staff with data-only or voice-only expertise (which is the norm) receive additional training to ensure they have the skills required to operate and manage both technologies.

As soon as the decision has been made to move forward with an IPT system, a PDIO (planning, design, implementation, operations, and optimization) methodology is recommended to facilitate deployment. This commonly used procedure generally ensures the smoothest, most efficient path to integrate IPT into a small-medium business.

Some companies might realize short-term benefits, such as reduced capital expenditures on IPT equipment and the ability to incorporate systems without adding network administration staff, by outsourcing IPT to a managed service provider (MSP). An MSP is most often a specialized systems integrator or a value-added reseller, long-distance telecommunications carrier, or local exchange carrier.

In addition to IP voice services, these providers can often deliver additional bundled capabilities, such as managed security and VPN services. As decision-makers evaluate business case data and weigh IPT investment options, the managed services approach might be one they want to include in the price/performance, functionality, company control, and payback analysis mix. They should be careful, however, to gauge whether the MSP can support the key IPT applications (noted earlier in this chapter) the company wants to operate to achieve its business objectives.

In a managed IPT service, customer premises equipment (CPE) is leased from the service provider as part of a services package. Network infrastructure equipment is hosted at the service provider's site. This could be an ideal option for small-medium companies that do not want to manage their own network equipment or those that are concerned about the technology obsolescence of IT investments. Some service providers also might offer LAN equipment for lease (such as switches and routers). This gear is not specifically IPT-dedicated. Instead, it serves as the network foundation on which IPT and other advanced communications technologies run.

Summary

Small-medium businesses are evolving their voice systems from circuit-switched to IP telephony packet-switched alternatives that better support company mobility, workgroup collaboration, e-commerce, and personalized customer service. Decision-makers are finding that IPT systems have matured to the point that they are reliable and flexible, offer high-quality and rich application options, and can be made as secure as traditional voice systems. And they do so with a lower total cost of ownership than legacy alternatives.

These IPT systems span LANs, MANs, and WANs and can be used for voice and multimedia communications regionally, nationally, and even internationally. They also are adaptable enough to be used on their own or in conjunction with existing legacy telephone systems such as PBXs and the public switched telephone network (PSTN).

A major draw of IPT for most small-medium businesses is the wealth of productivity, customer care, safety and security, and cost-saving applications they support. There are applications for both horizontal and vertical market uses.

IPT technologies are available for purchase or lease in a variety of configurations and options to suit the business practices, scale, application needs, and budget of any small-medium company. Given the breadth of options that are available, decision-makers have a lot of latitude to shape a system that is just right for their organization. The key is to fit the technology to the business's needs, not vice versa. When evaluating IPT alternatives, buyers should not compromise or scrimp on three essential IPT technology components: quality of service, security, and network reliability and availability. These elements are vital, because business continuity and the assurance of resilient and confidential operations depend on them.

CHAPTER 9

EMERGING TECHNOLOGIES

A handful of exciting newer network technologies are expected to become increasingly viable and valuable to medium and smaller businesses during the next few years. Collectively, they can be referred to as *emerging* technologies.

Not all of these technologies are newly emerging, though. In fact, some (such as the various storage networking alternatives and content-delivery networks) have been around for years. They have already proven their value to large enterprises as enablers of more effective, efficient, and innovative business practices, with measurable productivity, business continuity, and revenue impacts. But for many small-medium businesses, they are still considered emerging. This is because, for the most part, they are not appropriately sized, featured, priced, simplified for installation and management, or standardized for the small-medium business.

Early technology adopters might want to jump in feet-first to pilot, deploy, and modify available emerging technologies to suit their needs. But even business leaders who prefer to take a more conservative wait-and-see IT investment approach should monitor the technologies profiled in this chapter for their availability and adoption trajectory among medium and smaller companies because of the business and competitive value they bring.

Other technologies in this chapter (such as Metro Ethernet, IPv6, and Mobile IP) are genuinely emerging and are not yet mainstream, even among larger enterprises. They are still undergoing design and testing in vendors' and service providers' research and development laboratories and in the field. They also are weathering the politics of being defined in standards and industry organizations. Their rollout will be slower and will occur over a period of several years.

Why care about emerging technologies if they cannot be adopted and installed within the next 6 to 12 months? Being aware of them and what they are intended to do can help a company accomplish the following:

- Manage the level of company investment in products or technologies that could be made obsolete by newer offerings.

- Influence the content of the company's network plans (and network infrastructure foundation designs) to ensure that they are flexible enough to accommodate anticipated technology evolution road maps and to allow cost-effective upgrades in the future.

- Stimulate ideas for achieving at least part of their intent in the near term.

The emerging technologies highlighted in this chapter include a mix of local area network (LAN), metropolitan area network (MAN), and wide area network (WAN) technologies—storage networking, Metro Ethernet, content delivery networks (CDNs), Mobile IP, and IPv6. These technologies support increasingly distributed and networked virtual organization structures. They also work together with and extend the capabilities of the advanced and foundation network technologies highlighted in the previous chapters. In fact, together they can be thought of as a set of building blocks to be arranged and rearranged to suit the business needs, priorities, and wallets of small-medium organizations.

Storage Networking

Storage systems are designed to make the right information available to the right people when and where needed. They also are intended to protect organizations from data loss, even in the event of security incidents, computer failures, or other disasters. As such, they must enable 24/7/365 access to company information by employees and, sometimes, partners and customers. The three primary functions of IT storage systems are to ensure the following:

- Ease of data accessibility and availability

- Protection and retention of archival information

- Data recovery for business continuity and resilience

As a business technology category, storage area networks (SANs) are not new. Sophisticated systems are already installed and operating in large enterprises. What is new is that they are increasingly at or near the top of the short list of near-term IT investment priorities for medium businesses.

Business and Technology Drivers

Five business and technology drivers provide the stimulus for medium (and some smaller) companies to adopt storage networking systems: the need to improve productivity and revenues, ensure business continuity, adhere to government regulations, make the best use of installed network infrastructures, and curb IT spending.

Here are some key underlying issues that relate to each driver:

- Improve productivity and revenues:

  - **E-mail aids productivity**—Workers are getting more and more e-mail messages and deleting fewer of them (either through personal choice or government regulation). In fact, analysts expect the volume of business e-mail to balloon into tens of billions of messages before 2007. As such, it is one of the primary users of storage capacity. E-mail is also, coincidentally, one of the first business applications that small-medium business leaders mention when asked which applications contribute to employee productivity. This means that high-capacity storage for and easy access to e-mail is critical.

  - **Multimedia data enables collaboration**—Increasingly, collaborative computing, digital messages, and files are composed of integrated data, voice, and video information. This multimedia data consumes millions of bytes and cannot tolerate network lags during use. This is especially true for interactive customer-facing, training, and business process applications.

  - **E-commerce and call centers personalize service**—Fast, reliable, secure information access is essential to workers interacting with customers online. They need to understand customer transaction histories, buying preferences, and concerns in real-time to deliver personalized service that stimulates loyalty and increases revenues.

  - **Front-office (customer-facing) and back-office (business process) information integration**—This is driving demand for consolidated storage systems to improve organizational process efficiencies and spur creative new ways to generate revenues.

- Ensure business continuity and resilience:

  - **Nominal productivity disruption**—The goal of a business is to avoid any downtime. But if it happens, companies want to be assured that the downtime will be nominal and that no data will be lost in the process.

Most businesses cannot tolerate the loss of productivity or the negative impacts on customer responsiveness that accompany network downtime.

- **Separate storage from servers**—Because more than 60 percent of server failures and 30 percent of business application downtime are caused by legacy storage-related problems, taking a storage networking approach should substantially improve uptime. This approach separates storage from servers and places them on different networks.

- **Improve network management**—Separate storage networks also reduce the logistics nightmare of scheduling data backups. It helps IT better control the volume of network traffic generated by backups or data recovery. Degraded network performance and/or crashes can result when these processes run across a company network.

- **High availability**—Depending on the storage area network that is installed, data can be made available for use 99.99 to 99.999 percent of the time. That translates to an annual IT system downtime (planned or unplanned) of 53 minutes to 5 minutes.

- **Offsite storage**—Offsite storage capabilities that complement onsite networked storage are critical to any business. They should be of particular concern to those whose storage requirements extend into the billions and trillions of terabytes of data.

- **Computer backups**—Disturbingly, it has been found that more than 50 percent of medium companies do not back up their employees' PCs. And almost 60 percent of those that do back up data to a local device. If a catastrophic event occurs that destroys the business's primary server, it is likely that its backup devices and media will also be destroyed. This means that company information and intellectual property assets could be lost along with the backups. This does not have to be the case, because storage networks can mirror data for secure replication at distances of just over 6 miles (up to 10 kilometers) away.

- Adhere to government regulations:

    All companies, but especially financial and health care institutions, are obligated to upgrade their data storage capabilities to comply with a variety of regulations, including the following:

    - **HIPAA**—The Health Insurance Portability and Accountability Act

    - **Sarbanes-Oxley**—The public company accounting reform, financial reporting, and investor protection act

    - **USA PATRIOT**—The United and Strengthening America by Providing Appropriate Tools Required to Intercept and Obstruct Terrorism act

- Make the best use of installed infrastructures:

    - **Leverage Gigabit Ethernet LANs**—Installed Gigabit Ethernet (GigE) LANs and IP infrastructures can be used as an alternative to Fibre Channel to create storage area networks. In many cases this helps more fully use the intelligence and installed capacity of a company LAN while sustaining its high performance. For companies deciding whether to invest in GigE for their infrastructure, its ability to support storage networks should be added to business case justifications and return on investment (ROI) analyses to help prove it in. Information on GigE can be found in Chapter 3, "Local Area, Metropolitan Area, and Wide Area Networks."

- Curb IT spending:

    - **High-capacity storage required**—Market analysts have found that roughly 50 percent of medium businesses consume 200 to 999 gigabits of data storage at their sites. The other 50 percent use anywhere from 1 to more than 2 TB (terabytes or trillions of bytes) of storage. These numbers are significant and continue to almost double each year. Traditional file servers will not scale to handle these capacities.

    - **Disk storage lacks scalability**—When disk storage on servers reaches capacity, new servers must be purchased to handle additional data. Adding more servers not only incurs equipment costs but also requires hiring more administrators dedicated to managing them.

- **SAN management costs less than DAS**—In a storage area network model, costs for IT staff can be reduced significantly. Administrators can support more than 40 percent more storage than in direct attached storage (DAS) environments, and they can do so from a single location.

- **Network storage offers lower total cost of ownership (TCO)**—Because storage networks are separate networks, the initial purchase price might be on the high side relative to direct attached storage. What is important to keep in mind is that the TCO will be lower over time as the number of storage system users and data volumes increases. TCO should take into account hardware (disk drives, tape drives, servers), software, support services (power, cooling, floor space), and staffing expenses.

Advantages of networked storage systems include the fact that they are:

- **Efficient**—Storage is allocated dynamically to ensure the best use of resources.

- **Fast**—Information is delivered to more users, more quickly, than with non-networked alternatives.

- **Reliable and flexible**—Networked storage systems can route around problems and therefore can improve system uptime.

- **Scalable**—New resources can be added quickly to networked storage systems to support distributed and virtual organization information-sharing in growing companies. Even remote workers can get easy access to information.

The near-midterm storage technology trend is toward shared or consolidated storage, in which pooled storage resources are allocated on an as-needed basis. The intent is that servers share fewer higher-capacity disk arrays and tape systems to provide the following:

- High-availability data access

- Reduction in the number of servers required

- Lower network management (overhead) costs

- More fully used storage and network assets

- Improved disaster recovery and business continuity capabilities

The bottom line is that consolidated network storage aims to help IT provide more storage systems value for less cost to the business.

Longer-term, the trend is for the data center and IT to become an information utility, providing centralized information services, of which the storage utility is one. Figure 9-1 shows where storage systems reside in the utility model. As IT evolves toward this pay-as-you-go utility business model, small-medium business executives should watch for additional developments in IP-based storage networking (such as Internet Small Computer System Interface [iSCSI, pronounced "eye-scuzzy"] and Fibre Channel over IP) and the convergence of network attached storage (NAS) and SANs that will extend storage networking capabilities and lower systems costs.

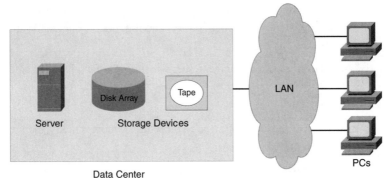

Figure 9-1   *The Future: Storage as an IT Utility*

Storage Technology Overview

Storage systems must balance seemingly conflicting requirements for broad-based, on-demand information access, information asset protection, scalability that supports business growth, and controlled costs of ownership. If those objectives are not challenging enough, serious hurdles to achieving them include the following:

- Lack of scalability of traditional servers
- Unconnected pockets of data that already exist as a result of separate legacy storage systems
- Dynamic and fluid networked virtual organizations and workgroups (company-centric and external, local and remote) that must store and retrieve information.

In trying to achieve these goals, storage systems have evolved through several technology architecture generations, from distributed (DAS) to centralized Network Attached Storage (NAS) to separate storage area networks (SANs). Table 9-1 profiles and compares these storage options.

Table 9-1 *Storage Networking Options Compared*

Features	DAS	NAS	SAN
Number of devices	High. High capital expenditure (CAPEX).	Moderate. Lower CAPEX.	Low. Lower total cost of ownership (TCO).
Performance	Low.	Moderate. Protocol overhead consumes some LAN bandwidth.	High. High-speed data transfers are kept off the company LAN.
Administrative costs/management	High. Requires a large staff.	Moderate. Needs less staff, is easy to install and configure, but lacks high-level software management tools.	High. Fibre Channel configuration is complex. Central software management tools are available.
Security	Poor. Distributed and hard to secure.	Moderate. Fewer locations. Easier to secure.	High if protected with defense-in-depth network security. Fibre Channel provides no inherent security.
Scalability	Easy to add devices.	Moderate. Easy to add devices. Performance can degrade with scale.	High. Can be distributed over local and wide areas. Maintains high performance with scaling.
Storage capacity usage	Poor. 40 to 50 percent of total capacity (inefficient).	Moderate. 75 to 85 percent of total capacity.	High. 85 to 95 percent of total capacity (efficient).
Downtime	High. Down for expansion and reconfiguration.	Low. Storage devices and backups operate independently of servers.	Low. Fault tolerance ensures business continuity.

These three storage technologies are described and compared in the following sections.

DAS with SCSI

In a DAS architecture, storage such as Just a Bunch of Disks (JBOD), disk arrays, and tape backup devices is directly connected via Small Computer System Interface (SCSI). SCSI is a parallel interface for input/output to a server. Direct attached storage is shown in Figure 9-2. This storage is distributed around an organization. Each application's access is limited to its own storage on its own dedicated computing platforms.

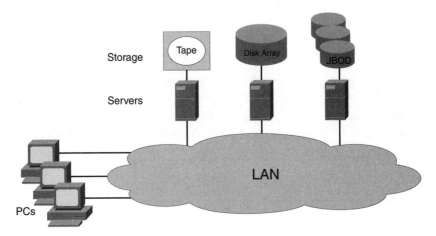

Figure 9-2   *Direct Attached Storage (DAS)*

The DAS approach to storage has a few critical problems:

- Only a few storage devices can be attached to a server, because the number of SCSI interfaces on servers is limited.

- If storage is shared between two or more servers, performance declines significantly.

- Because of DAS's distributed nature, *silos* (isolated pockets) of storage are created. This demands that IT staff manage each storage site individually to monitor storage usage and perform data backups.

- DAS has no storage load-balancing feature, so some servers might have underused storage capacity, and others might exceed capacity. This means that companies might not be getting the full value for their hardware investments.

- A server failure shuts down all data access because the server is the sole owner and route to its storage devices.

- Distributed storage does not give medium and smaller businesses the necessary flexibility, availability, performance, and scalability they need for growth.

NAS

A Network Attached Storage (NAS) device is standalone and self contained, and it connects directly to a LAN rather than to a server. This separation of data from servers is intended to improve network performance as a whole. NASs are devices that contain file systems and that can communicate using network protocols (Fast Ethernet, Gigabit Ethernet, or Fibre Channel). A NAS also can provide file access across a private WAN or the Internet, as shown in Figure 9-3. NAS devices are mostly focused on data and content sharing. They are essentially file servers optimized to deliver documents and files to servers or employees' workstations.

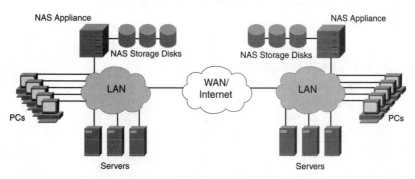

Figure 9-3   *Network Attached Storage (NAS)*

Advantages of NAS systems include the following:
- They can be set up and operated out of the box without complex configuration. As a result, NAS is referred to as *plug and play,* which means it reduces administrative overhead. More NAS devices can be added easily without disrupting the network.

- NAS can be managed remotely through a web browser. This eliminates the need for dedicated staff at branch locations to handle management oversight.

- They scale from multi-gigabytes to multi-terabytes of storage capacity.

- They are attractive for centralizing and sharing storage in mixed operating system (heterogeneous operating system platform) environments.

- NAS can be used to consolidate file servers or DAS storage.

- They provide mirroring to another NAS device or to remote storage devices for backup. *Mirroring* makes a point-in-time copy of data.

- NAS works together with and complements storage area networks.

Disadvantages of NAS systems include the following:

- NAS is not high performance as a result of the protocol overhead it carries. Therefore, it is not very useful for database and video application storage.

- NAS devices have limited flexibility because they are designed as fixed-functionality appliances for file serving or file sharing.

- Most NAS products do not support software that allows separate NAS devices to be managed as an integrated storage system.

- NAS's ability to support multiple operating systems (OSs) will have very little value in a single operating system (homogeneous platform) IT environment.

SANs

Storage area networks (SANs) create a separate and dedicated high-performance storage network that supports any-to-any (or peer-to-peer) connectivity. They offer high-availability data access between storage devices and servers, as shown in Figure 9-4. SANs are network architectures rather than devices. They are typically dedicated to high-volume traffic, such as that for business applications like enterprise resource planning (ERP), customer relationship management (CRM), salesforce automation (SFA), and so on. One of the fundamental principles of SANs is that they offload storage data transfers from the company LAN and WAN to ensure consistently high performance on both networks.

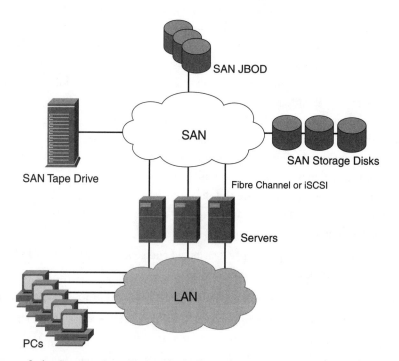

Figure 9-4 *Storage Area Network (SAN)*

The technology that provides connectivity between servers and storage devices attached to a SAN is currently based on Fibre Channel switches and storage protocols. Fibre Channel was developed by the American National Standards Institute (ANSI) to support high-speed data transfer rates (currently up to 2 gigabits per second [Gbps]).

Although Fibre Channel is high-performance, it also is high-cost. It might be affordable to large enterprises, but it can strain the IT budgets of most small businesses and even many medium businesses. iSCSI, approved by the Internet Engineering Task Force (IETF) in February 2003, is intended to reduce the cost of midrange SANs by using Internet Protocol (IP). It also leverages companies' existing Gigabit or Fast Ethernet networks.

iSCSI makes sense for entry-level and midsized SANs. With it, standard Ethernet switching technology is used in the SAN core rather than the more expensive Fibre Channel switches. IP WAN access routers are used to extend the storage network to the wide area for applications such as remote data backup and restore. iSCSI is an attractive option for small-medium businesses because it is easier to install, offers lower-cost connections into SANs, integrates with existing IP infrastructures, and simplifies network management (because Ethernet and IP components are already familiar to IT administrators).

Fibre Channel over IP (FCIP) is an alternative emerging technology to iSCSI for use in midrange SANs. FCIP is well-suited for companies that already have Fibre Channel installed and that want to extend their reach cost-effectively, over longer distances, for remote data backup and restoration.

The advantages of SANs are as follows:

- Data transfers are offloaded from the primary company network to sustain its high performance.

- Servers can be physically distributed and separate from centralized and centrally managed storage devices.

- Each server can assume the job of others that fail or for load balancing.

- Data backups and restorations are transparent to network users. There is no downtime during these processes.

- Multiple servers can access one or more storage resources and still deliver high performance.

- Fewer, but larger, shared storage devices enable streamlined management by IT.

- They can be dedicated strictly as storage networks or, in the case of IP-based SANs, as part of the larger company network.

- SANs scale from departmental and small-office environments to large data center deployments with hundreds of ports.

    – For smaller implementations, a SAN can be built with economical storage devices, such as JBOD.

The advantages of iSCSI or IP-based SANs are as follows:

- They are more affordable to small-medium businesses than Fibre Channel SAN solutions.

- They lower the total cost of ownership Transmission Control Protocol/ Internet Protocol (TCP/IP) to businesses by using existing TCP/IP and switched Ethernet infrastructures.

- There is no need to retrain IT staff or hire outside experts to operate them, because the technologies underlying these SANs are familiar, and IT staff already should be expert in them.

- Their ease of implementation reduces staff overhead costs.

- They extend connectivity so that companies can store and protect data locally (on the LAN), as well as across wider areas up to thousands of miles.

The disadvantages of Fibre Channel SANs include the following:

- They can be costly and complex for many small-medium businesses.

- Technical staff with the expertise to manage them are needed, which contributes to administrative overhead.

- Not all storage applications benefit from SANs' multigigabit bandwidth. In some cases, it might be overkill.

Storage Network Adoption Considerations

Consolidating storage resources through storage networking is about making the small-medium company's business processes (and supporting IT environment) more effective, efficient, and responsive. Consolidation can affect costs, service levels, and business flexibility in the following ways:

- Cost savings can be achieved as follows:

  - Increasing disk usage to 80 percent or more

  - Reducing the number of storage devices (tape, optical, and so on) needed by 50 to 75 percent

  - Reducing staffing costs by up to 80 percent (according to market analysts)

  - Reducing the number of servers required

- Leveraging existing network infrastructure investments for another business-critical application—storage

- Service delivery levels can be improved through the following:
  - Centrally monitoring and proactively managing storage to ensure business continuity and resilience
  - Increasing storage systems performance and information availability to keep pace with real-time business processes and applications
  - Adding new disaster-recovery capabilities (onsite and offsite)

- Business flexibility comes in the following ways:
  - Faster time to deploy applications without downtime
  - Scalability that supports growth and backup without affecting 24/7 applications
  - Providing a reliable network foundation that lets workers (and partners) react quickly to business demands

Business and technical decision-makers should keep the following considerations in mind when planning and evaluating how to invest in storage networking:

- What would happen to the company if its data and intellectual property were lost? From a business standpoint? From a regulatory standpoint?

- What applications will the company run? Will they operate best with NAS, a Fibre Channel SAN, an IP SAN, or a combination? What amount of IT administration will the combined applications and storage systems require?

- How important is high availability of data and information resources for decision-making and/or customer care?

- What are the costs related to scaling an existing storage system?

- What are the risks of continuing to use an existing storage system?

- Will current storage technologies be compatible with emerging storage technologies and interoperate to curb IT administration overhead?

- Which devices will be attached to the storage network now (for instance, servers, blade servers, JBOD storage)? In the next 3 years?

- What are the direct (hardware, software, service contract, and so on) and indirect (testing, training, system transition, and so on) costs for a storage network conversion or first-time installation? How are expenses affected by the use of existing IP and/or Ethernet network equipment?

- What types of network security will be used to protect the storage network?

- Should in-house IT resources be used? Or should a specialized managed storage service provider be contracted to implement and maintain the storage network system? A managed storage service provider can reduce the amount of a company's capital expenditures, help desk calls, IT staff costs, and downtime (assuming that appropriate and enforceable service level agreements (SLAs) are put in place and managed with the service provider). The service provider should also be able to help ensure storage scalability, reliable 24/7/365 storage availability (with 99.99 to 99.999 percent uptime), responsive disaster recovery, local area and wide area company network compatibility and leveragability, offsite storage, and nondisruptive storage installation, backup, and restore operations across the wide area network (WAN).

Metro Ethernet

Metro Ethernet is an emerging high-speed WAN service currently in an early deployment phase by selected incumbent local exchange carriers (ILECs), interexchange carriers (IXCs), competitive local exchange carriers (CLECs), and Internet service providers (ISPs). It delivers Ethernet networking over an optical fiber infrastructure within metropolitan areas (citywide) and beyond. Connection speeds for this service parallel those of local area Ethernet networks: 10 Mbps, 100 Mbps, 1 Gbps, and 10 Gbps. Analysts forecast that this service will begin to take off aggressively toward the end of 2005 and grow rapidly in its adoption from there.

Market Drivers

Business and technology factors that are most likely to drive small-medium business demand for this high-speed service include the following:

- Increasing volume of multimedia content and other business applications that must be shared using high bandwidth

- Growth of high-speed Internet access by higher percentages of workers

- Need to connect remote LANs, branch offices, and data centers that are scattered throughout a metropolitan area with LAN-like performance and response times

- Ability to connect to offsite storage for data backup, information retrieval, and disaster recovery to ensure business continuity

- Need for real-time, collaborative communications with partners and suppliers (and even customers) using a wide-area extranet

- Desire to bridge the bandwidth chasm that exists between LAN and WAN systems' speeds to help reduce communications bottlenecks and possible downtime resulting from congestion at the network edge (where the LAN and WAN connect)

The following are some of the key applications for which Metro Ethernet service is best suited:

- **High-speed Internet access**—Metro Ethernet can be used as a replacement for dedicated private lines, Frame Relay service, and possibly digital subscriber line (DSL), depending on the bandwidth growth requirements the company anticipates.

- **Intersite connectivity**—It can connect remote LANs within the metropolitan area at native Ethernet LAN speeds as if the WAN between them were transparent. This service offering is called Transparent LAN Service (TLS).

- **Server consolidation**—Servers can be centralized at a business's main office for use by branch locations and perform as if they were located at the branch.

- **Hosted service access**—Metro Ethernet can provide access to offsite hosted or managed services.

- **Transport for data storage, backup, and recovery**—Metro Ethernet supports storage systems consolidation.

Here are some advantages that small-medium businesses can gain from Metro Ethernet:

- The price of its customer premises equipment (CPE) is economical compared to the equipment used for other high-speed WAN access technologies, such as T1/E1 and T3/E3 private lines, Frame Relay, asynchronous transfer mode (ATM), and SONET-based optical networking.

- There is less cost per megabit, per second than with private lines.

- Companies can realize cost savings of close to 70 percent over a 3-year period, even with as few as five or six locations online.

- Because Ethernet is a familiar technology to IT staff for the LAN, no special learning curve is required to extend Metro Ethernet to the MAN. Its ubiquity (90 percent of all data traffic terminates on Ethernet ports) coupled with its maturity make it a logical choice for subscribers to achieve comprehensive coverage and adaptability.

- Its performance can scale from data rates of 10 Mbps to 10 gigabits per second (Gbps) in modular 1 Mbps increments.

- Metro Ethernet interworks with and can be combined with existing WAN access service alternatives such as T1/T3 (in Europe, E1/E3), Frame Relay, and ATM. In fact, doing so could be part of a phased migration plan to evolve to Metro Ethernet company-wide (starting with Metro Ethernet to the main office and maintaining existing WAN access services to branch locations).

- It supports service level agreements (SLAs) that ensure that service providers deliver the quality of service they have committed to delivering. The provider must offer subscribing companies credits or other givebacks if it doesn't.

- Metro Ethernet enables rapid service provisioning. Provisioning can usually be accomplished in just over 2 weeks if fiber cabling to the subscriber's building is already in place.

- It provides data transport support to the full range of widely deployed business applications.

Disadvantages of Metro Ethernet for small-medium businesses include the following:

- It requires fiber-optic cabling from the service provider's point of presence to the customer's premises (for the best performance) or to a carrier's termination point, just off the street near the customer's premises. This termination is called fiber-to-the-curb (FTTC). 10 Mbps and higher Ethernet speeds are not yet defined for deployment over copper telephone cables. If this occurs, it would open the market for Metro Ethernet to more businesses.

- Currently, the fiber network infrastructure build-out to small-medium business buildings is limited, and carriers are moving slowly. They complete about a 15 percent infrastructure increase per year because of the high capital costs of deployment, including the complexity of laying fiber. Perhaps most importantly, incumbent providers fear cannibalizing existing services and facilities before they are fully depreciated. The highest likelihood of fiber cable having been run are for companies based in multi-tenant office buildings. In most instances, carriers will have a difficult time justifying the deployment of fiber cable to a standalone, small-medium company.

- Deployments to date have mostly been in Tier 1 and Tier 2 metropolitan areas. Smaller markets are lower on carriers' to-do lists.

- It is difficult for service providers to offer customers end-to-end quality of service (QoS) to ensure data traffic delivery priorities. Best effort (no guarantees) is what customers should expect to receive in the near term. The Metro Ethernet Forum (MEF), an industry and standards organization, is working to address and resolve this issue. Without QoS, real-time multimedia communications are unpredictable, which means they would not be business-class or reliable for business-critical applications.

Technology Overview

Traditionally, Ethernet-based networks have been deployed in enterprise LANs because of their simplicity, low equipment cost, high speed, and multivendor interoperability. Service providers recognize these benefits and have begun to offer Ethernet-based WAN services as alternatives to traditional WAN services such as Frame Relay and dedicated private lines (T1/E1, T3/E3). Figure 9-5 highlights the different technologies used to enable an Ethernet WAN versus a traditional WAN. These traditional services have performance bounds of up to 45 Mbps at the high end. Compared to Ethernet LANs operating at 100 Mbps (Fast Ethernet), 1000 Mbps (Gigabit Ethernet), and 10,000 Mbps (10 Gig), a 45 Mbps data rate seems slow, and it results in some LAN/WAN bandwidth gap.

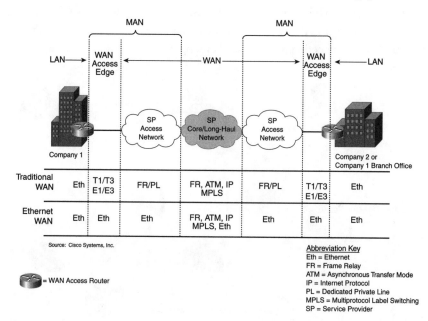

Figure 9-5 *Metro Ethernet Versus a Traditional WAN*

To help close that gap, three basic Metro Ethernet services are currently available from service providers in early deployment (shown in Figure 9-6). These services continue to be refined by the Metro Ethernet Forum (MEF) and its member companies:

- **Ethernet Relay Service (ERS)**—The Ethernet equivalent of Frame Relay and ATM, this is used for point-to-point connections between two sites. Multiple remote sites can be reached using one physical Ethernet connection.

- **Ethernet Wire Service (EWS)**—The Ethernet equivalent of dedicated private lines, this is used for point-to-point connections between two sites. A single remote site can be reached from one physical connection.

- **Ethernet Multipoint Service (EMS)**—The multipoint WAN equivalent of Ethernet LANs, this extends their characteristics across the WAN. A single connection is established among multiple sites.

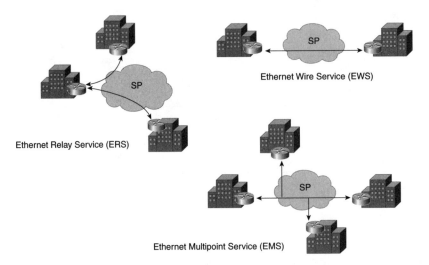

Figure 9-6   *Basic Metro Ethernet Services*

At the customer's premises, a standard Ethernet device interface can connect to the service provider's network and use these services with no additional hardware or software changes.

Metro Ethernet Adoption Considerations

For the more than 65 percent of small-medium businesses that are based in multitenant office buildings, Metro Ethernet is worth investigating if it is available from service providers or is offered by the building's management company as part of a bundle of technology services. However, it is important to keep in mind that this is an emerging and therefore dynamic technology that continues to evolve. Users must be aware of and willing to deal with the kinds of change and service issues that accompany such newness.

Here are some questions a small-medium company should consider when assessing the potential relevance of Metro Ethernet service adoption:

- What applications, business processes, or work-related interactions are driving demand for bandwidth? How will this change over time?

- What are the bandwidth requirements to address those elements?

- Where must service be delivered? How many locations are there? Does fiber infrastructure run to those locations?

- Where is the data center located today? Where will it be in the future?

- What is the current cost of operating the WAN access network? What is the budget that is allocated for WAN access going forward?

- How long has the service provider been offering Ethernet services? Are there satisfied customers who can serve as references for these services?

Mobile IP

A mobile workforce must be able to communicate with customers, partners, and colleagues anywhere, anytime. They also must have easy access to the various business applications, technologies, and digital tools necessary to conduct their work effectively. Mobile Internet Protocol (IP) lets its users stay continually connected to the Internet while appearing as if they are in their primary office, regardless of location. Users do not need to log off, change their IP address, and log on again each time they move about. This is intended to help workers achieve flexibility of workplace and resources accessed whether they are in the office, on the road, at customer sites, or at home by making mobile network operations transparent.

As employees move between different places and networks, connectivity should be automatic. This includes roaming from a wired network to a wireless one or vice versa, and from a LAN to a WAN. All connections should be handled intuitively and with ease for the mobile worker. Mobile IP is making an impact by addressing and delivering on that vision. It is gradually gaining acceptance with selected small-medium business users as a valued emerging technology.

Market Drivers

With the advent of a more mobile workforce, Internet-based business applications, and growth in the adoption of wireless devices, there is a corresponding need for seamless communication between mobile devices and the packet networks to which they attach. Analysts forecast that the number of wireless-enabled mobile devices will surpass the number of wired desktop computing devices within the next few years and that mobile communication will be the predominant form of business communication. These conditions are expected to drive more pervasive adoption of Mobile IP technology by small-medium business executives for use by their employees.

Mobile IP delivers business value by enabling uninterrupted access to such applications as the following:

- Checking and sending e-mail and unified messages while roaming at the office, on the road, or at home

- Accessing remote company intranets via virtual private networks (VPNs), which is important because VPNs are sensitive to IP address changes

- Browsing the Internet to conduct research on customers, competitors, products, and so on

- Downloading or uploading online information files to access information stored in office databases or to transfer files to the office or to partners and customers while at home or traveling on business

- Interactive network meetings for anytime, anywhere computer-based videoconferencing via the Internet

- Internet Protocol telephony (IPT) over wireless LANs for affordable and easily accessible voice communications

- Collaborative computing for sharing information interactively with colleagues and others via PCs as though on a whiteboard

- IP video surveillance for remote, real-time monitoring of office (or other) facilities in lieu of using a closed-circuit TV system

- Mobile health care by physicians, nurses, and so on

Mobile IP has a number of advantages:

- **Boundaryless information flows for mobile workers**—Time and location constraints for information sharing are reduced because workers can conduct business while remote, roaming, and untethered to their desks. Their ability to interact with colleagues, customers, and others to conduct work wherever they are is improved.

- **Improved employee productivity**—The always-on aspect of Mobile IP translates to no work downtime while the user is mobile and roaming.

- **Flexibility**—Workers can connect to information networks and stay connected regardless of the access medium that is available to them (wireless or wired).

- **Greater use (for better ROI) of the company's existing network technologies**—Routers, wireless LANs (WLANs), IPT over WLAN, virtual private networks (VPNs), security services (such as authentication, authorization, and accounting [AAA]), and others are more highly utilized.

Disadvantages of Mobile IP include the following:

- It is still emerging and is not yet widely available among small-medium businesses.

- It will undergo some refinements during the transition from current Internet Protocol Version 4 (IPv4) addressing schemes to Internet Protocol Version 6 (IPv6) addressing.

- Employees' personal downtime can be infringed upon. With Mobile IP, workers can always stay attached to the network. Or, to put it more ruefully, they can run, but they can't hide. No matter where they are, they can receive and reply to e-mails, participate in online collaborative meetings, and respond to customers while appearing as if they are at their primary office.

Technology Overview

Being able to receive data at a mobile device is a difficult networking challenge. The problem is to get data to a device that can be anywhere or nowhere. Nowhere means it could be powered down or out of range of the network system.

With current IP networks, if a worker moves from one network to another without changing his computing device's IP address, he cannot receive data packets on the new network. But if he changes his device IP address when he moves, that device must end its current IP session and completely restart communications. This is true for every time it moves between networks. This process is disruptive, interrupts information flows, and makes it impossible for the worker to conduct real-time communications.

Business mobility requires that employees be able to move between networks with their computers and handheld devices throughout the workday. As they move around, their computing connections and in-progress communications must be kept running. In technical terms, this means that the computer (or other device) cannot change its identity; it must retain its unique IP address.

In conventional IP networks, routing of information is based on fixed IP addresses, very much like how the post office delivers a letter to the address on an envelope. A computing device on a network is reached through the IP address it is assigned on the network. Mobile IP takes this premise and extends it to moving and fixed-location devices. Mobile IP was created by the Internet Engineering Task Force (IETF) as Request for Comment 2002 (RFC 2002). This RFC was ratified in June 1996. With Mobile IP, workers keep the same IP address on their devices while traveling to different networks, even networks using different media or managed by different carriers. This ensures that as business proffesionals roam, they can continue to communicate without Internet sessions or data connections being dropped mid-application.

The IETF solved the mobility problem by allowing each device to have two IP addresses and to create a bond between them. One of the IP addresses remains unchanged as the static home address. It is assigned on the primary workplace or home network. The other is a dynamic care-of address that changes at each new mobile worker location and point of network attachment.

Mobile IP has three major components, as shown in Figure 9-7 and as described in the following list:

- **Mobile node**—Any device (laptop computer, tablet PC, handheld computer, cell phone, and so on) that has Mobile IP software installed. These Mobile IP-enabled devices can change where they attach to networks. A mobile node also can be a router that is responsible for the mobility of one or more entire networks moving together, such as on an airplane, ship, train, or car. A mobile node must be configured with a fixed home IP address and a mobile security identifier that is known to the mobile node's home agent.

- **Home agent**—A router on the home network that serves as the communications base for the mobile node. The home agent establishes a data transfer tunnel to a foreign agent at the mobile node's foreign *(visited)* network through which traffic intended for the mobile node is forwarded.

- **Foreign agent**—This is a router that serves as the attachment point for the mobile node when it roams to a visited network. It also is the tunnel termination point for the mobile node that originates with the home agent. As such, it is the conduit for delivering packets received from the home agent to the mobile node. The foreign agent keeps a constantly changing visitor list that contains information about all the mobile nodes currently visiting its network.

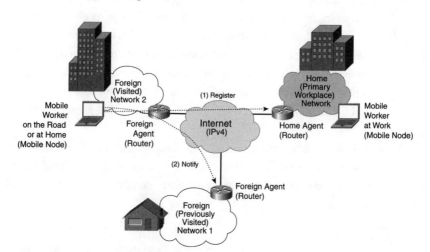

Figure 9-7 *Mobile IP Components*

These three Mobile IP components work together in a three-step operation that entails the following functions:

- **Agent discovery**—A mobile node discovers its foreign agent, home agent, and care-of address (a temporary address to which data packets sent to a mobile node's home address can be forwarded). It does so by listening for advertisements that are sent across the network.

- **Registration**—The mobile node registers its current location with the foreign agent and its home agent. It requests service from a foreign agent on a foreign network. It then informs its home agent of its current care-of address.

- **Tunneling**—A communications tunnel (virtual circuit) is set up between the home agent and the care-of address on the foreign agent. This is so that packets can be routed through it to the mobile node as it roams. When the mobile node wants to send packets, the process is reversed. It uses its home IP address to maintain the appearance that it is always attached to its home network. In that way, even while the mobile node is roaming to foreign networks, its movements are managed automatically and therefore are transparent to users (including company employees and those communicating with them).

Security is important in Mobile IP because mobile nodes move continuously and are often connected to the Internet via wireless links. Security is handled during the registration process. The home agent must be sure it is getting registration requests from authorized mobile nodes and not receiving mobility requests from rogue (illegitimate) nodes. Mobile IP handles this by establishing a security handshake mechanism between the home agent and mobile nodes. For the handshake to work, every registration message from a mobile node must contain its home agent's authentication code, called a Security Parameters Index (SPI), before the mobile node can be issued an authentication key that grants it network access.

Mobile IP is a prime example of IP's evolution from a standard designed strictly for use by immobile computer systems to a technology adapted to the needs of a newly mobile workforce dependent on portable computing and networking devices.

Mobile IP Adoption Considerations

Mobile IP lets network users move from one Internet connection point to another without disrupting application connectivity. Conventional IP, without Mobile IP activated, can only send packets to a fixed IP address in one place. It does not support mobile networking. Although it is not yet widely deployed, Mobile IP has great potential for transparent, uninterrupted business communications for workers who want to move between wireless LANs (WLANs), wireline networks, and even cellular wireless systems.

Here are some of the questions small-medium business leaders should consider when thinking about Mobile IP adoption:

- Is there a plan to deploy workforce mobility services within the organization?

- If so, is there a need for transparent mobility of IP services? At work, at employees' homes, while they are on the road?

- Does the company already use IP-based mobility services/technologies? If so, which ones? How will Mobile IP enhance them? Extend their investment value?

- Which of Mobile IP's features and/or supported applications are most important or desired?

- Is there a need to turn VPN on or off while workers roam? Does the considered Mobile IP technology allow that?

Content Delivery Networks

Content delivery networks (CDNs) and associated caching technologies were introduced during the dot.com Internet boom of the 1990s. They were developed to accelerate web page downloads and make Internet access more responsive for users. Post-crash, this technology is being repurposed to deliver streaming as well as static content for use in such e-business applications as audio- and video-on-demand, e-learning, customer relationship management (CRM), salesforce automation (SFA), and workforce optimization. Large enterprises with many dispersed offices or branches recognize the value of CDNs for internal as well as customer-facing operations. They are gradually beginning to adopt them to more efficiently distribute multimedia data.

Although there is a widely recognized need for speed to enhance business networks, networks need to be smarter too. Another attribute of content networks is that they make networks more intelligent and help create peak IT resource usage by enabling better management of data delivery and access. CDNs do this by identifying and storing the most frequently used information files on caching servers that are located away from the data center and close to the workers who will use them at the edge of the local area network (LAN).

At present, large businesses are the primary users of CDNs. For small-medium businesses, CDNs are still an emerging technology and are likely to remain so for the next few years.

Market Drivers

As the number of users accessing content across intranets and extranets increases, it becomes harder to provide a high level of availability, scalability, and rapid responsiveness from a single data center. CDNs help provide users with the best experience possible by distributing applications and data to servers at different locations throughout a company (as opposed to hosting all files on a single server). CDNs also reduce loads on the company network and IT staff.

Some of the networking applications that are fueling enterprise adoption of content delivery networks include the following:

- The web enablement of enterprise resource management (ERP), CRM, SFA, and supply chain management (SCM)
- Corporate web portals
- Computer-based videoconferencing and IP-televised company meetings
- E-learning and online training
- Mobile applications that require content transformation (format alignment for viewing on different devices' screen size)
- IP telephony application databases
- Multimedia file distribution
- Point-of-sale service kiosks

Here are some benefits that users report after adopting content networking:

- The ability to better build networks that are optimized for e-commerce and web content delivery

- Reductions in employee travel costs to participate in training

- Payback in as few as 6 months

- More data, delivered to more users, at higher quality, for improved business productivity

- Constantly refreshed web and other information content

- Improved network throughput and application updates without having to invest in more bandwidth, servers, or IT staff

- Improved network availability and response times for users

- Consistent overall website performance

- Less network congestion, the ability to handle traffic overflows or surges, and more rapid recovery if servers fail

Technology Overview

The principle behind content networking is to improve web and application content delivery efficiency. To achieve that, content is distributed from centralized origin servers (file servers in which new content is generated or stored) to servers that cache store content at the edge of the network and physically closer to employee workgroups. These caches are designed to speed up data retrieval response rates for workers, put less strain on LAN infrastructures when delivering bit-rich content, and help the using company save money (because caching devices are less-costly networking equipment than servers).

As soon as information is transferred to and stored in a local cache, whenever other workers request the same content, it is delivered to them directly from that local storage device rather than from its origin file server. Workers benefit by getting their requested data more quickly than they would if the request had to be sent to an origin server. A more technical way to describe this is that local caches act as proxies for the file servers that store content in the data center.

There are two basic ways for businesses to acquire content delivery networking capabilities: public content delivery networks and private content delivery networks.

Public CDNs

Public CDNs are managed outsourced services offered by content service providers (CSPs). CSPs host the origin servers that store a subscribing company's original content. They distribute that content to caching servers, which are located in Internet Service Provider (ISP) points of presence (POPs) at the edge of the Internet. A subscriber's employees (and others, such as partners and customers) can be given access to the content. When workers request access, the content is delivered to them from the ISP's cache rather than from the CSP's origin servers.

This approach is all right for distributing content to consumers, but in many instances it is less than effective for growing businesses, especially for use with streaming content such as video-based e-learning or IP television archive access. Random access to rich content such as that can throttle the bandwidth of the public CDN, lower overall network performance, and cause users to experience slow response times.

Private CDNs

Private CDNs, also called *enterprise CDNs*, are owned and operated by enterprises themselves. They are best suited for streaming content applications that are used by a company's workers internally. These systems deliver content to departmental or workgroup caches, which in turn deliver content streams to the appropriate workers via the LAN. They are effective for delivering static content such as large multimedia documents as well as streaming content.

Private CDNs work with and complement company storage networking systems that centrally store and maintain large volumes of company information for access, archiving, and disaster-recovery purposes. Private CDNs also complement content transformation technologies that adapt content designed to be viewed in larger-screen formats (for instance, on desktop PCs and laptops) for readability on smaller displays such as those found on handheld computers, IP phones, cell phones, and other mobile business gadgets.

CDNs generally share three integrated technology components:

- A dedicated server network with some degree of commonly cached content

- A dedicated, intelligent distribution mechanism to streamline data delivery to the edge server network, end-users, or both

- A mechanism to intelligently match requesting users with the most efficient content distribution server

The key equipment used to deliver these capabilities as part of a content networking system is illustrated in Figure 9-8 and is described in the following list:

- **Content routers**—These routers direct workers' requests for content to the best site's content resources using rules for doing so. Rules might include server load limits, acceptable delays, and so on. Content routers can be used at multiple company sites or at managed content service provider points-of-presence to ensure the fastest delivery of content, no matter what its source of origin.

- **Content switches**—These switches address the unique needs of e-commerce and web traffic and are the front-ends to web server farms and groups of caches. They handle data traffic load balancing across web servers and edge devices to ensure content availability, high network performance, reliable security, and network scalability.

- **Content edge delivery engines**—These engines cache information for local delivery to workers. They handle static and streaming media (video and audio).

- **Content distribution and management devices**—These devices contain policies (also known as *rules*) that specify how content transactions should be handled. They also manage bandwidth, measure performance levels, manage synchronization of cached data to ensure that it is current, and log content transactions for billing purposes. Transaction logging is a feature that is immediately useful to content service providers and also eventually to IT staff for internal bill-back purposes, especially as the IT utility model evolves and emerges. In the IT utility model, the IT department functions as an internal data service provider and profit center to the company. Departments subscribe to centralized company data services, and they are charged for their usage on a per-transaction basis—hence the need to track the company's information system transactions with a logging system for billing purposes.

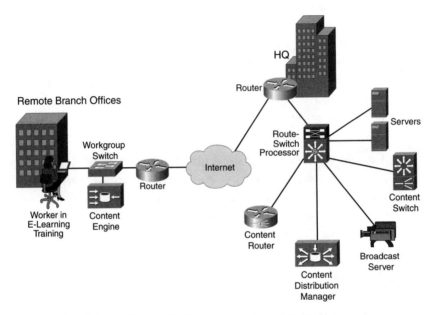

Figure 9-8 *Private Content Delivery Network Architecture*

Content Delivery Network Adoption Considerations

Because of their complexity and the number of components involved, content networking technology currently is primarily targeted at larger enterprises. The options available to potential users are to build and manage their own content networks or to outsource them to service providers.

An important factor to keep in mind when evaluating content networks is that the CDN market has been a volatile one, with players entering, leaving, and consolidating regularly over the years. For the majority of small-medium business executives, it would be preferable for the market to stabilize before they invest in this technology.

Small-medium business leaders who recognize the business and technical value of CDNs and who are willing to adopt a technology that is in its early growth stage should consider the following questions:

- Is there a plan to add streaming video (and/or audio) and other information-rich content to the company website or intranet?

- Can the company network handle the anticipated demand for streaming video without crippling overall site response times?

- For streaming media, will CDN users have to download a specific player to view content? Or can they use HTML, Real Player, Windows Media, or other general-purpose players?

- What is the contingency plan if equipment fails?

- What is the company's bandwidth to and from the Internet?

- What are web application-related bandwidth costs if handled directly by the company or if paid to a third-party host?

- If company servers are colocated at a hosting site, how are they and their content secured?

- What are the logistics of handing over company files to a content service provider for managed service delivery? Is there a tool for converting files to a format the provider can accommodate?

- How financially stable are the businesses of the content networking equipment vendors and/or content service providers that are being considered?

IPv6

Because of the extraordinary growth of the Internet and the proliferation of devices, applications, always-on services, and new populations accessing it, the IP addresses needed to communicate across the Internet are running out. This is similar to growth spurts that necessitate the creation of new telephone area codes. IPv6 and sometimes IPng for IP next generation is intended to remedy the worldwide shortage of Internet addresses. It also will provide other feature enhancements beyond those included in the current scheme, Internet Protocol version four (IPv4).

The Internet Engineering Task Force (IETF) standards organization has been leading the development work on IPv6 since the early 1990s. It was joined in the late 1990s by an industry association called the IPv6 Forum (www.ipv6forum.com/). Work in these groups is ongoing. Their goals are to define feature requirements for IPv6 and how best to create and deploy them. They are also specifying options for managing a smooth migration to IPv6 by users of IPv4.

Market Drivers

The Internet will keep growing as e-businesses and networked virtual organizations expand. That is clear. New markets such as personal mobility, home networking, and office and home control systems are joining existing markets and are taking off too. The devices that operate in these new areas will require their own Internet addresses. Such growth will place even more demands on IPv4 and will increase the already-significant pressure that exists to remedy its address shortage situation.

While companies can use Dynamic Host Configuration Protocol (DHCP) and Network Address Translation (NAT) to assign temporary IP addresses, this should only be viewed as a transitional approach. These solutions do not resolve more serious and fundamental issues. Because Internet control relies on IP addresses to operate properly, the push will be on for a more aggressive transition from IPv4 to IPv6 in the coming years.

Technology Overview

Every computing device on the Internet has a unique numeric IP address. An IP address is typically expressed as four decimal numbers, each between 0 and 255, separated by dots. An IP address looks like this: 145.178.12.3. The IP address represents that device's location on the Internet (much like the role of telephone numbers as locators in legacy telecommunications networks).

The solution to the shortage of Internet addresses is to create a new addressing format. Rather than relying on IPv4's 32-bit address length, IPv6 uses a 128-bit-long address. By accommodating four times as many bits, the Internet address universe will increase from IPv4's 4.3 billion addresses to IPv6's 340 undecillion unique addresses. It is written as 340,282,366,920,938,463,463,374, 607,431,768,211,456, which the website mathworld describes as a "large number." IPv6 developers claim that this address pool works out to a unique IP address for every square inch of the Earth's surface. A fair number of the addresses are reserved for systems operations and will not be available for use by individual devices.

Within the increased address space of IPv6, three types of addresses have been defined:

- **Unicast**—This is used for one-to-one communications. A single device, or interface, is at either end of a connection.

- **Anycast**—This is used for one–to–one-of-many communications. A packet from one device is routed to the nearest device that is listening in an anycast group.

- **Multicast**—This is used for one-to-many communications. A single device sends broadcast messages to many devices.

Besides increasing the IP address space, IPv6 also is intended to incorporate functions that currently are handled as add-ons to the IPv4 system. Those functions include the following:

- **Auto-readdressing**—This allows data packets intended for mobile users to be routed to a new address automatically rather than using Mobile IP's home agent approach. The "Mobile IP" section of this chapter contains more details on home agents.

- **Autoconfiguration of network addresses**—This makes devices more Internet-ready out of the box. Devices are more plug-and-play without needing a lot of manual address configuration.

- **Support for IP Security (IPSec)**—This authenticates senders of information and encrypts the data packets they plan to send to ensure privacy and confidentiality.

- **Priority routing**—This lets users assign delivery priorities to outgoing data packets and therefore manage the quality of service (QoS) level they are afforded.

It will take tremendous effort and many years to complete a full transition of the Internet and its users from IPv4 to IPv6. The IETF has defined three techniques to help with the transition process and to ensure that users' network communications are not affected in the process:

- **Dual stack**—This approach allows both protocols to coexist throughout all, or parts, of a network. This option is likely to be used most often.

- **Tunneling**—IPv6 packets are tunneled through an IPv4 network. That is, IPv6 packets are encapsulated wrapped inside IPv4 packets to mask their differences for easy transmission across a network.

- **Translation**—This uses a gateway to allow IPv6-only devices to communicate with IPv4-only devices or vice versa. This is accomplished by translating packet formats from one scheme to the other.

IPv6 Adoption Considerations

IPv6 is still an emerging technology that is not yet deployed on a broad scale. It has been one of those almost-there technologies for about a decade. Even with transition plans defined for it, IPv6 will still not be a painless move to make. Therefore, its migration roadmap likely will extend over the next 10 to 15 years. It is not expected to be a public capability anytime soon.

Early adopters of IPv6 include software developers, the military, government agencies, academia, and selected research organizations. High-end, medium-sized businesses with global operations might consider migrating to IPv6. This is particularly true for those conducting business in Asia, where IPv6 is mandated for deployment. Businesses must determine if they have the IT resources and if they are willing to work with a technology that is so early in its adoption curve. For most small-medium businesses, it is too early to adopt IPv6.

Summary

A number of emerging network technologies are being readied for adoption by small-medium businesses. Some of these technologies are further along the development and maturity bell curve than others. The options that are included in this survey of what's to come include LANs, MANs, and WANs.

Storage networking makes the right information available to the right people when and where needed. It promotes business continuity and protects companies from possible data loss. Already widely used in large enterprises, storage networks are now increasingly at the top of many medium business' IT investment priority lists.

Metro Ethernet is a high-speed access service that delivers Ethernet networking over optical-fiber infrastructures within metropolitan (citywide) and wider areas. It extends the reach of Ethernet for use in Internet access, intersite connectivity, access to managed services, and storage networking transport. It is an emerging technology that is, for the most part, being deployed only by small-medium businesses with offices in multi-tenant buildings.

Mobile IP provides mobile business professionals with follow-me networking capabilities that let them communicate with customers, partners, and colleagues as transparently away from the office as they do while at the office. A worker using Mobile IP appears to others as if he is working from the desktop of his primary workplace. It is an emerging technology that is not yet widely deployed among small-medium businesses.

Content delivery networks are designed to improve the efficiency of delivering streaming and static multimedia information content to workers. They do this by distributing applications and data to servers located throughout a company to reduce the traffic loads and strain on network infrastructures and speed up network response times. Because of their complexity and the number of components they entail, content networks currently are used primarily by larger enterprises.

IPv6 is intended to remedy the eventual shortage of IPv4 addresses. With IPv6, not only is the IP address space increased by orders of magnitude, but operating features that are add-ons to the current system are integrated as part of IPv6's inherent feature set. It is still being defined in standards groups, and it is being deployed very slowly. Adoption is clustered mostly in niche market segments such as academia and the military. The migration from IPv4 to IPv6 will be gradual. It is likely to extend throughout the coming decade or so. Most small-medium businesses should not adopt IPv6 in the near term.

Small-medium businesses should carefully weigh their aversion to risk, IT resource capabilities, and budgets against the positive business value to be gained when evaluating whether to adopt emerging network technologies.

CHAPTER 10

MANAGED NETWORK SERVICES

Small-medium business success often depends on the right person's having the right information at the right time. The Internet helps companies achieve this objective by connecting them to one another, as well as to partners and customers for information exchange, regardless of location. Every business, no matter what its size, should be able to have an IT infrastructure and run Internet-enabled applications that suit its organizational needs and contribute to its growth. Doing so requires keeping up with network technologies and maintaining sufficient resources to provide efficient business process support. That can be a challenge, because IT staffs and budgets are often limited.

One possible solution to this challenge is to work with a managed service provider (MSP). This option is rapidly gaining favor among small-medium business leaders. The intent is for an MSP to help businesses employ network services that they might not be able to adopt or manage on their own.

MSPs let companies outsource their entire IT function or only aspects of network management that the company does not want to handle in-house. The right service provider can support the networking needs (and, by extension, the business needs) of small-medium companies by providing scalable solutions, reliable performance, and comprehensive network security.

Managed Network Services

Managed network services are contractual, subscription-based services delivered by providers, such as value-added resellers (VARs), interexchange carriers (IXCs), incumbent local exchange carriers (ILECs), competitive local exchange carriers (CLECs), and large systems integrators. The services these providers offer customers generally fall within two broad categories, as shown in Figure 10-1:

- **Professional services**—Advisory services, including network assessment, consulting, network design, software and hardware installation, configuration, systems integration, testing and debugging, and management (fault management, performance management, change management, and so on).

- **Operational support services**—Tactical day-to-day hardware, software, and wide-area services facilities maintenance.

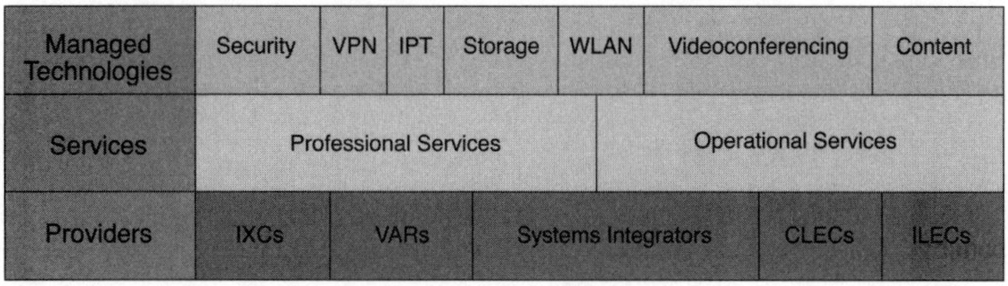

Managed Technologies	Security	VPN	IPT	Storage	WLAN	Videoconferencing	Content
Services	Professional Services				Operational Services		
Providers	IXCs	VARs		Systems Integrators		CLECs	ILECs

Figure 10-1   *Managed Service Providers and Services*

The networking technologies most often provided as part of a managed services package include the following:

- Security (including managed firewalls and comprehensive, defense-in-depth network solutions)
- Virtual private networks (VPNs)
- Internet protocol telephony (IP telephony or IPT)
- Storage and disaster recovery
- Wireless LANs (WLANs)
- Videoconferencing
- Content hosting

Typically, managed services are handled as shared services, with the small-medium business's IT group providing and supporting the company's core network foundation (LAN infrastructure) and business applications. The service provider handles the management of advanced network solutions, including responsibility for certain customer premises equipment (CPE) and connectivity services on an outsourced basis, as shown in Figure 10-2. In some cases, small-medium companies prefer that the entire networking function be outsourced. In those instances, the MSP installs and manages the underlying LAN infrastructure, as well as any advanced services that are to run with it (such as VPNs, security, IPT, and others).

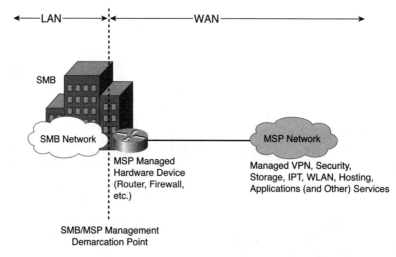

Figure 10-2 *Managed Service Provider and Subscriber Demarcation*

Advantages and Disadvantages of MSPs

LANs, WANs, and the Internet continue to grow not only in functionality and business value, but also in complexity. New networking products are introduced continually, and the old products often do not go away. Keeping up with all these technology changes is difficult. Recruiting, training, and retaining enough qualified staff to deal with it all is time-consuming and expensive.

Many small-medium organizations have decided that it is not worth even trying to keep up, so they have turned to MSPs. MSPs have more resources and support systems at their disposal to stay on top of network advances. And they are often trained and certified by equipment vendors in the latest network product features, operations, and support techniques.

The trend toward companies outsourcing portions of their networks to MSPs is accelerating. It is expected to grow steadily as providers increase their managed services portfolios and as businesses experience the benefits of using such services firsthand.

There are upsides and downsides to using an MSP. The following are some of the key benefits, and possible drawbacks, to weigh when considering working with an MSP.

Here are some advantages of using MSPs:

- **Lower total costs of network ownership for subscribers**—Capital expenditures are assumed by the service provider and are spread across all subscribers as one portion of a recurring service fee. The service provider also is responsible for hiring and training technical staff to ensure that they have the expertise needed to manage services.

- **End-to-end integrated network systems**—This eliminates the complexity of companies having to work directly with multiple equipment vendors to build their own systems. This is a real plus as networks grow in scale.

- **Fixed-cost budgeting by subscribers**—Companies have the flexibility to choose from tiered service bundles that fit their budget. They pay only for what they use.

- **Rapid deployment**—MSPs can deploy network services more rapidly with the resources at their disposal.

- **24/7/365**—MSPs provide 24/7/365 dedicated service and support.

- **Core business focus**—Outsourcing allows a company's IT staff to focus their efforts on improving the efficiency of core business processes and on developing new applications to do so, rather than on managing the network.

- **Current network technologies**—The MSP assumes the burden of anticipating and managing the obsolescence of network technologies. Therefore, subscribers' network services are kept current with the latest and best equipment and features.

Here are some disadvantages of using MSPs:

- **Lack of control**—Companies lose a certain amount of control over their networks.

- **Quality control**—Some MSPs are better than others. A contingency plan should be prepared in case a particular MSP does not work out.

- **Stability**—Subscribers should verify that a potential service provider is financially stable. This is critical, because network operations affect company operations, reputation, and success. Small-medium business continuity, responsive customer care, and company growth are tied inextricably to network reliability, availability, and performance. If an MSP goes out of business, it can bring the operations of a subscribing company to a standstill.

Service Level Agreements

When a company's network or portions of it are outsourced to service providers, it is important to ensure that they are managed well. Service Level Agreements (SLAs) help provide a guarantee for that. SLAs are contracts between a service provider and a small-medium business that set the standards and metrics for network performance (data rate, availability, reliability, and so on) and security that are acceptable and affordable to a subscribing company. The SLAs also specify how the subscriber will be compensated if the service provider does not live up to those criteria. SLAs are an important tool for achieving effective use of outsourced resources. They are used to reach a common level of understanding of network service expectations with a service provider.

SLAs should obligate a service provider to immediately correct any problems that arise with a network to ensure uninterrupted company operations. Small-medium business leaders should check the fine print in an SLA and clarify how the MSP defines various contract terms to understand their implications. For instance, a service provider's scheduled outages might not count as an outage under the terms of an SLA. Scheduled or not, a company should be assured that its network will be up and running.

An SLA typically specifies repayment to a business if the service provider fails to deliver on the level of service agreed to in the SLA. The form of repayment is usually in the form of a credit for network service time or cash-back credits on subscription fees. The credit can be automatic or not. An automatic credit is a regular, agreed-on report that automatically issues the credit when appropriate. Automatic credit is common in the satellite industry and is becoming the standard with larger, more stable service providers. A by-request credit usually sets an agreed-on timeframe during which a subscriber must identify any network downtime, report it, and request the credit.

Even though SLAs typically offer subscriber credits for failure to deliver on promised service levels, nobody really wants to collect the credit. The credit will not recover lost revenues or repair customer dissatisfaction caused by a network failure.

Choosing a service provider to manage a small-medium business's network or applications is a big step, but it can bring measurable benefits to those who choose well.

A well-constructed SLA can play a significant role in the success of outsourcing network resources to a service provider. Businesses should approach a prospective service provider with clearly articulated statements of the company's needs, an awareness of industry standards for designing service guarantees, and the know-how to evaluate a service provider's SLA terms. In this way they can avoid many of the pitfalls and enjoy the tremendous benefits of outsourcing critical network services.

Adoption Considerations

One of the first considerations is whether working with an MSP makes sense for your company. Answering the following questions can help determine that:

- What is the size of the small-medium company's IT staff? Is it a sufficient number to handle the Internet business solutions and network services the company wants to run now? In the next 6 to 12 months?

- Is the IT staff experienced in working with the technologies to be adopted? If not, is the company willing to invest the time and money necessary to bring staff up to speed?

- Does the small-medium business operate in multiple locations? Will IT staff be added to support each location?

- How fast is the company/network growing? Is there sufficient budget to add more network administrative staff to build and support network systems?

If the conclusion is that an MSP is worth exploring, you should ask additional questions. It is important to determine whether a specific service provider offers the kinds of managed network services that makes it desirable to partner with. Visit the service provider's facilities, and be sure to get answers to the following questions:

- Does the service provider (SP) understand the company business model and how network services will affect the company's success? Can the SP clearly articulate the business benefits or value propositions of the managed services it offers in a way that applies specifically to a small-medium company?

- Can the SP provide customer referrals or testimonials from other, similar types of businesses?

- Is the SP financially stable?

- What is the SP's attitude toward SLAs? Will this be a partnership in which the SP offers procedures for fixing problems? Or will it be an adversarial, finger-pointing experience?

- Does the SP offer full-service capabilities (professional services and operations services)?

- Does the SP's SLA guarantee network services if it must operate under cooperative agreements with another SP in another region?

- What security features (physical and network service) are provided? What policies does the SP have about who has access to managed network facilities (at the SP's location and at your small-medium business's premises)?

- What are the SP's backup and recovery procedures?

- Does the SP provide 24/7/365 support and monitoring of all components?

- What is its guaranteed response time for support?

- Does the SP seem knowledgeable about network product alternatives for addressing the subscribing company's needs?

- Does the SP offer a choice of vendors' products, or has it standardized on a single vendor for each technology? If it uses a single vendor, why did it choose that vendor?

- What types of technical certifications do the SP's managed services staff hold? What proportion of them are trained and certified?

- When adding a new service to the company network, how does the SP maintain current network services for uptime?

- Is the SLA adaptable as the company's network requirements evolve?

- Is the SLA measurable?

- Does the SLA provide the following?

  - Built-in tools for tracking and measuring SLA performance data

  - Performance criteria commitments

  - A secure, web-based interface to access data and confirm that the provider is in compliance with the SLA

  - Business metrics such as mean time to provision (MTTP) and mean time to repair (MTTR)

  - Confidential reporting on performance and how often if so?

- Does the SLA cover all network components?

- Is the SLA enforceable? How?

- Do penalties such as time/monetary credits for downtime apply?

- Are the penalties automatic or on-request? Are they enough to motivate the provider?

- Do multiple SLAs cover different network components? In most cases, different network technologies require different SLA terms. Small-medium businesses should ensure that the SLA is defined in accordance with a subscribing business's operational needs.

- Can the SP integrate the services and products it offers with a company's existing network and applications for seamless operations?

- Does the SP offer financing options?

Summary

It is becoming increasingly challenging for small-medium companies to keep up with continual technology changes and to hire and retain sufficient, qualified IT staff to manage growing networks.

MSPs let companies outsource all or parts of an IT group's networking functions. These MSPs typically leave the core IT functions of managing the company LAN infrastructure and business applications to company IT staff. MSPs provide consultative services and handle network management responsibilities for advanced technologies. The greatest advantage of an MSP is that it often lowers subscribers' total costs of network ownership.

The technologies most frequently delivered as managed services include security, VPNs, IP telephony, storage and disaster recovery, WLANs, videoconferencing, and content hosting.

A critical consideration when working with an MSP is to ensure that an SLA is put in place and that it guarantees measurable performance. The SLA should specify reparations to the subscribing company if something goes wrong.

CHAPTER 11

VERTICAL-
INDUSTRY
CASE
STUDIES

The best computer networks allow small-medium businesses to achieve their organizational objectives while streamlining business processes, cutting costs, improving productivity, and creating agility and growth. In fact, the ideal network is one that supports users in their work but is virtually invisible to them. The adage that it should be seen and not heard applies. A well-designed network should also be easy for IT staff to manage and scale without significant resource overhead.

Different vertical industry sectors require different network technologies and designs, reflecting their unique industry practices and priorities. Small-medium business leaders often claim they find it helpful to examine the network implementations of others in similar industries. They say it sparks ideas for their own companies as they move into the often uncharted personal experience territory of matching enabling technologies to business processes for value creation.

To that end, this chapter includes a representative cross-section of small-medium business network case studies, organized by industry segment. It is by no means comprehensive. However, it does provide a sampling of commonly installed technologies and computer networking approaches in leading verticals. Business technology advisors such as value-added resellers (VARs), systems integrators, consultants, service providers, and network equipment vendors should be able to provide additional case studies of their own. The examples they provide should help small-medium business decision-makers gauge the advisor's experience with networks that match their own needs, as well as the advisor's ability to recommend an appropriate roadmap for implementation.

Education: University

Objectives

Enhance students' educational experiences and professors' teaching and research experiences. Recruit and retain the best students and faculty to uphold the institution's reputation.

Organization Profile

- Undergraduate, graduate, doctoral, and professional higher-education programs

- 1800 students enrolled

Challenges

- Differentiate the university from other higher-education institutions.

- Enable the mobility/portability of students' and professors' computing devices for real-time collaboration, locally and remotely, to support learning and research.

- Provide customized content to students and faculty.

- Offer high-speed Internet access.

- Ensure network security.

- Ensure enough IP addresses for all users.

- Maintain or lower IT costs in the wake of government and private funding decreases.

Original Technology Solution

- 10/100 wired Ethernet LAN for student access to the Internet and campus libraries and for e-mail exchange

- Conventional proprietary PBX system

New Technology Solution

- **Upgraded Gigabit Ethernet (1000 Mbps)**—Wired LAN infrastructure with intelligent switches and routers.

- **Wireless LAN (Wi-Fi WLAN)**—Rolled out in phases: First, the main campus and a handful of professors and students (at one school on a remote campus), then three more schools, then all remaining buildings and dormitories.

- **Wireless security**—802.1, with Extensible Authentication Protocol (EAP).

- **In progress**—Evaluating adopting WLAN-enabled handheld computers for use by security guards to check bar-coded doors and ensure physical security of the campus.

- **Dedicated T1 (1.544 Mbps) wide area connection**—For Internet access. Evaluating the merits of a near-term migration to either multiple T1s or a single T3 line to improve network responsiveness.

- **Intranet and university web portal**—For access by students, professors, and administrators.

- **Network printing**—For faculty and students.

- **Storage-area network (SAN)**—For content management and archiving.

- **VPN (virtual private network)**—For secure remote access by faculty and students.

- **Security system**—Firewall with intrusion detection and anti-virus and worm software.

- **Currently evaluating IP telephony (IPT)**—For use in administrative buildings, classrooms, faculty offices, and dormitories.

  - A pilot is under way in one of the colleges on the main campus.

Impact of the New Solution

- The university now functions as a service provider (a profit center), offering its customers (students and faculty) new applications such as online course registration, student retrieval of lecture notes and graphics in classrooms (for simultaneous use with professors), access from dormitories (for archived notes review), streaming video web conferencing (for distance learning between campus locations), high-speed Internet access, web authoring, forms publishing (for administrative processes), improved web communications via multimedia e-mail, mailing lists, directories to departmental area and university resources, chat rooms and discussion groups, training resources (on computer applications), and so on.

- In its service provider capacity, the university configures and distributes all the PCs used by students and administrative departments. Students purchase preconfigured PCs that are network-ready.

- More flexible access to information is provided to faculty and students on and off campus, including public spaces not previously served by the wired network infrastructure.

- Funding has increased as a result of the university's ability to conduct more collaborative research projects with corporate sponsors.

- The availability of web conferencing capabilities has decreased faculty travel expenses.

- Remote access and web-based e-learning capabilities have allowed the university to introduce a new, revenue-generating Internet University program for working adults who take advanced education courses and work toward completing their degrees online.

Relevant Chapters

- Chapter 3, "Local Area, Metropolitan Area, and Wide Area Networks"
- Chapter 4, "Network Foundation Technologies—Switching and Routing"
- Chapter 5, "Network Security Basics"
- Chapter 6, "Intranets, Extranets, and Virtual Private Networks (VPNs)"
- Chapter 7, "Wireless LANs (WLANs)"
- Chapter 8, "IP Telephony and Multimedia Communications"
- Chapter 9, "Emerging Technologies" (the "Storage Networking" section)

Financial Services: Community Bank

Objectives

Improve employee productivity, customer services, and business-to-business communications.

Company Profile

- Independent community bank with a diverse financial services portfolio
- Seven branch locations
- Conducts mortgage business with 200 banks

Challenges

- Deliver personalized business-to-consumer services with the support of larger organizations such as other financial, retail, and services companies.
- Expand geographically.
- Enable multichannel sales and service.
- Enable bank employees to become trusted advisors to customers.
- Improve business resilience.

Original Technology Solution

- Hub-based, wired Ethernet LAN infrastructure
- Automated teller machines (ATMs)
- Fax machines
- Key telephone system at each branch
- PC terminals at teller stations

New Technology Solution

- **Upgraded, Fast Ethernet (100 Mbps)** — Wired LAN infrastructure with intelligent switches and routers.

- **IP telephony (IPT) with unified messaging** — Phased implementation: First installed in new branches to reduce toll call charges, and then extended to all branches over the course of a year.

- **Extranet** — For downloads of interest-rate information posted on Fanny Mae and Freddy Mac and current mortgage rates offered by affiliates.

- **Virtual private network (VPN)** — For remote access from branches.

- **Security system** — Firewall with intrusion detection and protection, third-party anti-virus software, and biometric system for computer access.

- **E-learning system** — To train employees on new financial products and how to position them to customers, and also on how to evolve from purely transactional to more strategic roles. Content is developed by a third party.

- **Storage Area Networking solution** — For offsite and centralized main branch data storage of information that must be readily accessible by branches.

- **Web-based applications** — For customer self-service (including web portal-based: checking account balance management, funds transfer, stock tracking, and so on) and to streamline internal operations and improve productivity (Internet access, e-mail, and voice mail across Ethernet).

Impact of the New Solution

- The IPT system reduced toll call charges by 33 percent, improved customer responsiveness (through more versatile messaging and database applications), and provided more flexible telephone system management (including greater ease in moving employees between branches).

- Cross-selling of products increased as a result of better education using the e-learning system. Those who completed training successfully sold twice the number of products and services as those who did not.

- Training was conducted online at less cost than previous instructor-led courses, which also required business travel expenses and time away from the office.

- Platform officers and tellers experienced greater simplicity in dealing with customers.

Relevant Chapters

- Chapter 3, "Local Area, Metropolitan Area, and Wide Area Networks"
- Chapter 4, "Network Foundation Technologies—Switching and Routing"
- Chapter 5, "Network Security Basics"
- Chapter 6, "Intranets, Extranets, and Virtual Private Networks (VPNs)"
- Chapter 8, "IP Telephony and Multimedia Communications"
- Chapter 9, "Emerging Technologies" (the "Storage Networking" section)

Financial Services: Insurance Company

Objectives

Launch new products faster, improve workforce training on newly available products, and reduce training costs (to employees and customers).

Company Profile

- 300 employees
- 15 regional offices
- Distributed workforce of agents, managers, administrative staff, claims adjusters, and so on

Challenges

- Keep remote workers from becoming isolated from company information while having the flexibility to work at home.

- Improve the speed with which company news and information are disseminated to employees.

- Eliminate the weeks of training and travel costs incurred when new products are introduced.

Original Technology Solution

- Fast Ethernet (100 Mbps) wired LAN infrastructure
- Dialup remote access

New Technology Solution

- **Upgraded Gigabit Ethernet (1000 Mbps)**—Wired LAN infrastructure with intelligent switches and routers.

- **T1 (1.544 Mbps) dedicated leased line**—For shared wide area and Internet access.

- **DSL (digital subscriber line)**—Broadband remote access for teleworkers.

- **IP telephony with unified messaging and interoffice calling**—To reduce toll calls and enable follow-me voice system services to field agents.

- **PC-based web audio and videoconferencing**—For improved information sharing among workers, customers, and affiliated businesses and professionals.

  - **For customers/prospects**—Introduced online seminars and other informational webcasts.

  - **For employees**—Rolled out as a vehicle used initially for monthly updates by executive management.

- **E-learning and streaming video webcasting system**—Used to deliver self-paced online training to employees.

- **Web communications (e-mail, fax over IP, voice mail over Ethernet, and instant messaging [IM])**—Used to communicate between agents and affiliates.

Impact of the New Solution

- **Increased revenues by 40 percent**—A result of faster product introductions.

- **Better collaboration**—Through more extensive use of intra- and intercompany web communications, product development cycles have been streamlined and accelerated by 30 days.

- **Increased productivity**—Web communications and e-learning systems have kept workers focused on the most efficient ways to conduct their work, thereby saving 35 minutes per employee per day.

- **Reduced costs**—A result of less employee business travel and lower long-distance telephone toll charges.

- **Improved worker retention**—The flexibility to telework, combined with convenient access to additional training to acquire new skills, have resulted in 10 percent less turnover.

Relevant Chapters

- Chapter 3, "Local Area, Metropolitan Area, and Wide Area Networks"
- Chapter 4, "Network Foundation Technologies—Switching and Routing"
- Chapter 8, "IP Telephony and Multimedia Communications"

Government: County Government

Objectives

Increase efficiency, attract and retain businesses and residents, and provide improved high-quality, convenient online services to citizens.

Organization Profile

- Fast-growing county
- 38 government buildings
- 3300 employees
- Home to two universities

Challenges

- Migrate a data-only network to handle integrated data, voice, and video support.
- Introduce the ability to support e-commerce transactions.
- Provide new services within the constraints of a fixed county budget.
  - Extend the portfolio of government services that citizens are enthusiastic about.

Original Technology Solution

- 10/100 wired Ethernet LAN infrastructure
- T1 (1.544 Mbps) Internet access
- Website with internal web server

New Technology Solution

- **Upgraded wired LAN infrastructure to Gigabit Ethernet (GigE)**—For faster performance and the ability to support converged data, voice, and video.

- **Secure Wi-Fi wireless LAN (WLAN)**—For network access in courtrooms and for use in the county's mobile medical clinics (deployed in areas requiring health services that are too small to warrant full-time medical offices).

- **IP telephony system and IP phones**—With unified messaging, quality of service (QoS), fax over IP, IP videoconferencing, and broadcast (IP TV) capabilities.

- **Virtual private network (VPN)**—For secure remote access by mobile workers and teleworkers.

- **VLAN**—To maintain privacy, confidentiality, and isolation between private (county) and public (citizen-accessible) network systems.

- **Firewall security**—With intrusion detection and third-party anti-virus software.

- **IP video surveillance**—For physical security and monitoring of government buildings.

- **Storage Area Network (SAN)**—The county is currently evaluating the addition of a SAN to back up increasingly large volumes of data both on-site and off-site (away from government buildings).

Impact of the New Solution

- All employees are now connected to the network.

- The new infrastructure supports more scalable shared Internet access, intranet website access, e-mail, and online fax communications by workers.

- Back-office processes were streamlined using web-based applications (including e-procurement).

- The county online system now supports new web-based services such as the following:

  - An online bid and request for proposal (RFP) system

  - Property and judicial records searches

  - Criminal and parole notices

  - Online tax statement reviews

  - Driver's license renewals

  - Job searches

  - Campsite reservations

Relevant Chapters

- Chapter 3, "Local Area, Metropolitan Area, and Wide Area Networks"

- Chapter 4, "Network Foundation Technologies—Switching and Routing"

- Chapter 5, "Network Security Basics"

- Chapter 6, "Intranets, Extranets, and Virtual Private Networks (VPNs)"

- Chapter 7, "Wireless LANs (WLANs)"

- Chapter 8, "IP Telephony and Multimedia Communications"

- Chapter 9, "Emerging Technologies" (the "Storage Networking" section)

Government: Police/Public Safety Department

Objectives

Provide access to information by police and public safety officers while in the field for mobile crime monitoring and appropriate response (to prevent or solve crimes). Offer field personnel access to the same information that is available to those at headquarters.

Organization Profile

- 48 police officers
- 4 detectives
- 6 community service officers
- 11 dispatchers (3 part-time)
- 21 administrative and management staff
- 26 patrol vehicles
- 15 support vehicles (unmarked cars, motorcycles, radar speed trailers, and so on)

Challenges

- Improve officer, detective, and administrative/management staff productivity.
- Enable real-time decision-making.
- Improve officer safety.
- Allow access to critical resources by related regional agencies.
- Improve the department's operational efficiency.

Original Technology Solution

- Paper incident reports were entered into the computer system manually.
- Two-way radios would tie up the dispatchers for up to 10 minutes while they retrieved license plate and driver's license records for field officers.
- Many dispatchers worked an average of 10 hours per week of overtime for the force to maintain sufficient staffing levels.
- Text-based instant messaging.
- Conventional proprietary PBX system.
- Crime suspects were brought to the station from the field for database checks, fingerprinting, and mug shots.

New Technology Solution

- **Fast Ethernet (100 Mbps)**—Wired LAN infrastructure. Intelligent switches with inline power and routers.

- **Gigabit Ethernet-capable (1000 Mbps) infrastructure**—To enable smooth upgrade migration to the next level of performance if multimedia application usage spikes dramatically.

- **Wireless LAN (Wi-Fi WLAN)**—For mobility within the station, in patrol vehicles, to provide broadband connectivity between department and local government buildings, and to eliminate recurring costs of leased lines.

  - **Wireless-enabled computers and access points in squad cars**—Support real-time database queries and media-rich content transfers while in the field. Photos, mug shots, arrest records, and so on are sent for review by officers before they approach a suspect to decide whether backup is required.

  - **Mobile routers in squad cars**—To gather information while mobile and on the road.

- **Digital cameras and scanners**—For sending mug shots and fingerprints back to headquarters from the field.

- **Broadband streaming video**—IP video surveillance provides remote visibility of in-progress crime scenes to officers in squad cars and those at headquarters.

Impact of the New Solution

- **Acted as a force multiplier at a time when officers were asked to do more with less budget**—Limited resources were refocused on mission-critical operations.

- **Streamlined back-end support for the field force**—Improved access to information reduced dispatcher overtime.

- **Improved productivity**—Officers don't have to return to headquarters to access databases. This saves an average 20-minute/one-way trip plus 1 hour to retrieve the desired information. Networked and mobile systems enable more cross-municipality information sharing.

- **Improved officer effectiveness**—With the broadband video surveillance system operational, a handful of senior officers can serve as virtual backups to more junior officers on car stops, and so on.

- **Lowered costs**—Floor space requirements in cruisers for installing and maintaining video recording equipment were reduced. Less equipment is needed because video is transmitted over the network and is archived on a storage server. This also offers greater indexing flexibility.

- **Software updates are transmitted over the network to mobile computers in cruisers**—Before the broadband WLAN was installed, the cruisers were taken off the street or the mobile terminals were removed from the cruisers for upgrades. This resulted in lost policing time.

Relevant Chapters

- Chapter 3, "Local Area, Metropolitan Area, and Wide Area Networks"
- Chapter 4, "Network Foundation Technologies—Switching and Routing"
- Chapter 7, "Wireless LANs (WLANs)"

Healthcare

Objectives

Mobility, flexibility, and greater freedom for professional staff in providing patient care. Lower operating costs.

Organization Profile

- Nonprofit healthcare provider system comprised of hospitals, physicians' offices, clinics, and labs
- 225 employees
- **Level I**—Teaching hospital
- **Level II**—Trauma center (with a 24/7 trauma team)

Challenges

- Ensure 24/7 reliability, availability, flexibility, and scalability of healthcare information systems.
  - Regularly move lots of staff around within short timeframes while maintaining operational uptime.
  - Remain operational during renovations.
- Ensure security of information systems for patient confidentiality.
- Provide a clear ROI for new technology systems and system upgrades.

Original Technology Solution

- 10/100 wired Ethernet LAN
- Picture archiving and communications system (PACS)
- Proprietary PBX system

New Technology Solution

- **Upgraded to a Gigabit Ethernet (1000 Mbps) wired LAN infrastructure**—Including intelligent switches with inline power and QoS and access routers.
- **IP telephony system and IP phones**—With unified messaging and third-party XML healthcare productivity applications.
- **Secure wireless LAN (Wi-Fi WLAN) infrastructure cross-campus**—To supplement the wired LAN and provide mobility.
- **Wireless-enabled laptops and handheld computers**—For doctors and other caregivers to use at the point of care.
- **Two dedicated T1 lines (1.544 Mbps)**—For shared wide area and Internet access.
- **Digital sebscriber line (DSL)**—For remote access by medical and administrative staff.
- **Virtual private network (VPN)**—For secure remote access.
- **Firewall**—With intrusion protection and detection.

Impact of the New Solution

- **Streamlined organizational efficiencies**—Here are three representative examples:

  - The Emergency Department registrar now has a mobile terminal and moves along with caregivers and patients to gather registration information as patients are being treated.

  - In-patient charts are now maintained online to improve access by multiple caregivers and to prevent misplacement of care records.

  - Prescription orders are sent directly to the pharmacy via IP phones, increasing the speed of order fulfillment and the accuracy of orders (there are no handwriting issues to resolve).

- **The legacy PBX system was replaced**—High recurring lease charges were eliminated. Long-distance toll charges and ongoing administrative costs of moves, adds, and changes were reduced.

- **The WLAN improved staff mobility, information portability, and patient care**—It gives the staff greater flexibility in meeting with patients, reviewing their medical record files or films (including the radiology images from the PACS), and treating them immediately without being tied down to dedicated nursing or radiology stations.

- **Broadband remote connectivity**—Lets physicians conduct remote diagnostics and review patient records (providing 24/7 care) without having to travel from their homes or private offices to the health system campus.

- **Faster online database responsiveness because of the higher bandwidth of the new infrastructure**—Allows the delivery of more-immediate, better-informed diagnostics and care (in patient rooms and in trauma and emergency centers).

- **Network administrators report better control over the network**—With the new intelligent infrastructure installed, they can deploy new applications and services more rapidly, monitor network performance to the device level for reliability, and ensure that information resources are available on a prioritized basis as needed.

Relevant Chapters

- Chapter 3, "Local Area, Metropolitan Area, and Wide Area Networks"
- Chapter 4, "Network Foundation Technologies—Switching and Routing"
- Chapter 5, "Network Security Basics"
- Chapter 6, "Intranets, Extranets, and Virtual Private Networks (VPNs)"
- Chapter 7, "Wireless LANs (WLANs)"
- Chapter 8, "IP Telephony and Multimedia Communications"

Manufacturing Company

Objectives

Enhance business operations such as supply chain management, engineering design, training, and customer care. Increase productivity gains by easing the flow of information and decision-making across department, division, and partner boundaries.

Company Profile

- 935 employees
- Four 35,000-square-foot manufacturing facilities
- Products sold through 300 dealers
- $260 million in revenues
- Services include design, prototyping, and volume manufacturing

Challenges

- Reduce the number of inventory shortages and write-downs.
- Connect manufacturing to distribution centers to better match production output with customer demand.
- Go beyond supply chain management and coordination to improve product development, salesforce automation, channel collaboration, and service and support.
- Improve process efficiencies and give customers greater visibility into manufacturing systems.
- Deliver 24/7 operations with no outages.
- Create a single IT platform that provides high performance, comprehensive security, and flexible scalability.
- Integrate separate accounting, purchasing, inventory, and shipping systems.
- Ensure adherence to government regulations.
- Add new e-business applications, such as e-procurement, e-learning, workforce optimization, and web communications.
- Improve employee productivity.
- Lower costs of operations.

Original Technology Solution

- Outdated proprietary PBX system
- Hub-based Ethernet LAN in the back office only
- Modem pool for analog dialup remote access

New Technology Solution

- **Upgraded to industrial grade Gigabit Ethernet (1000 Mbps) wired LAN infrastructure, including intelligent switches and routers** — Integrates shop floor systems, back office, and front office operations and adheres to safety regulations.

- **Secure WLAN (Wi-Fi WLAN)** — Wireless infrastructure plus handheld computers and laptops with embedded wireless adapters for mobile information access within the manufacturing facility.

- **IP telephony (IPT) system** — Integrates voice and data with unified messaging and third-party XML productivity applications (workforce time management, directories, machine downtime tracking, parts ordering, documentation ordering, project calendars, and so on).

- **Web-based IP videoconferencing** — To conduct meetings and selected sales calls, maintain business relationships when it is not feasible to travel, and so on.

- **Web services** — Including customer extranet (for customers to go online to order parts, check equipment availability, check price quotes, apply for credit, and so on).

- **Dedicated T1 (1.544 Mbps) WAN connection** — To the Internet and key partners.

- **Virtual private network (VPN)** — For secure remote access by the sales force, managers, and supervisors.

- **Firewall** — With an intrusion detection/protection system and third-party anti-virus software for security.

Impact of the New Solution

- **Change management was improved** — Control processes were streamlined (with online work-order schedules, bills of materials, inventory updates, and purchase order information) for faster time to market.

    - Process engineering changes are now handled in 40 percent less time.

- **Real-time inventory reporting was initiated**—Profitability was improved as a result of reduced inventory costs.
  - Internet-connected PCs are used to monitor raw-material supplies, perform quality-control checks, and track subcontracted processes.
- **Manufacturing equipment was linked to the network**—Work in progress can be monitored readily for more effective project tracking.
  - Supervisors now monitor production line status in real time and fix problems immediately.
- **Product development is more collaborative**—Time to market improved by 15 percent.
  - Approvals of prototypes were reduced from 20 days to 1 day.
- **Order entry manpower costs decreased**—This decreased by $40,000 within the first year of the new solution's introduction.
- **Customer satisfaction improved**—This is a result of the new self-service web portal. Customers like the flexibility of being able to quickly check for answers to questions without having to call or send an e-mail to technical support and then wait for a reply.
  - Customers regularly use the extranet site to check on their projects and shipment status, decreasing calls to customer support and the field force by 12 percent.
  - Customers worldwide now easily interact with sales representatives via videoconferencing to request quotes and initiate new orders.
  - Customers participate in e-learning, so usage of new web-based training courses is up 20 percent. Third parties are contracted to develop content.
  - Urgent critical account calls are handled on an expedited basis. Engineers working away from their desks now receive such calls immediately on the IP softphones installed on their laptops. Automated attendant software is used to screen and prioritize calls and is programmed as to how to handle them.

- **Administrative overhead costs were reduced by 60 percent**—This was the result of linking manufacturing planning to financial operations systems. As an example, one person can now handle accounts payable, versus the four that previously were required.

- **PBX lease charges were eliminated**—The old PBX system was retired. Attractive financing options for the new IPT solution, offered by the network vendor, paid off the remainder of the PBX lease for the customer.

- **IP telephony generated cost savings on toll calls between plants and partners**—It eliminated the need for a dedicated network administrator to handle moves, adds, and changes, as was required by the previous PBX system.

  - Third-party XML applications for IP phones contributed to worker productivity improvements, shaving 10.5 hours per week off previous manual processes per employee.

  - Currently, the adoption of additional XML applications is under evaluation.

Relevant Chapters

- Chapter 3, "Local Area, Metropolitan Area, and Wide Area Networks"
- Chapter 4, "Network Foundation Technologies—Switching and Routing"
- Chapter 5, "Network Security Basics"
- Chapter 6, "Intranets, Extranets, and Virtual Private Networks (VPNs)"
- Chapter 7, "Wireless LANs (WLANs)"
- Chapter 8, "IP Telephony and Multimedia Communications"

Professional Services: General Contractor

Objectives

Enable employees to work more productively and be more responsive to clients whether at the office or on a job site.

Company Profile

- Specialists in industrial construction
- 200 employees, including architects and consultants

Challenges

- Complete projects on time and within budget.
- Monitor technician efficiency to improve project delivery.
- Make decisions faster.
- Maintain reliable, constant communications to deal with continually changing conditions at construction sites, including disputes that arise and need to be resolved quickly.
- Keep workers' compensation, safety, and insurance records up-to-date.
- Replace mostly manual (paper-based) business processes for handling architectural planning, design, project management, and so on with electronic alternatives.
- Integrate existing applications and application-related data into a new solution.

Original Technology Solution

- 64 kbps Frame Relay service for WAN and Internet connectivity.

  - Internet access is possible only from workers' offices. E-mails and job site data were printed out and carried to meetings.

- Conventional proprietary PBX system.

- Labor-intensive fax communications.

- A third-party (ISP) e-mail system was used between employees, subcontractors, vendors, and clients.

- A PC-based job-tracking application managed job site and contractor information.

- A PC-based supply chain management application coordinated materials delivery from various suppliers.

New Technology Solution

- **Fast Ethernet (100 Mbps) wired LAN infrastructure**—Intelligent switches with inline power, quality of service (QoS) features, and access routers to support integrated data, voice, and wireless applications were deployed.

- **Shared WAN and Internet access bandwidth were expanded**—An upgraded 1.544-Mbps Frame Relay service was provisioned.

- **Wireless LAN (Wi-Fi WLAN)**—Wireless network infrastructure, wireless laptops, and handheld computers were added for mobility.

  - Network access was extended to meeting rooms and open office spaces as well as to job sites.

- **IP telephony**—For unified messaging, time-records management (third-party XML application), materials management (third-party XML application), data mining, and mobility.

  - Softphone software was installed on laptops and some handheld computers to emulate IP phone features but provide mobility.

- **Virtual private network (VPN)**—For secure remote access by employees and partners from job sites and clients' offices.

- **Security system**—Firewall, intrusion detection system, and third-party anti-virus software application.

Impact of the New Solution

- The old PBX system was removed, eliminating recurring lease costs.

- The new IP telephony (IPT) system allows workers to log on to any phone in the office to access their personal calling features and use software-based IPT directories. They can look up client and partner phone numbers on their laptops and dial by name. IPT also lets workers maintain a single extension number whether they are in or out of the office, making them easier to reach.

  - Unified messaging enhances employees' ability to manage messages received throughout the workday, saving workers approximately 40 minutes per day.

- The single converged voice and data infrastructure has resulted in reduced network administration costs and lower total costs of ownership for the network.

- Ready access to supply chain and job site information during meetings by architects, designers, and project managers was improved by using the WLAN.

  - Decision-making time was reduced by 50 percent.

  - Dispute resolutions were handled 66 percent faster.

  - Productivity improved. Workers connected to network resources increased their productivity by 50 percent.

- The WLAN also increased the flexibility of training room setup for trainers and extended hands-on training to locations other than meeting rooms at the main office.

- Client responsiveness and satisfaction increased as a result of the improved mobility of professional staff and their ready access to information while mobile.

- The company has gained market share points relative to competitors.

Relevant Chapters

- Chapter 3, "Local Area, Metropolitan Area, and Wide Area Networks"
- Chapter 4, "Network Foundation Technologies—Switching and Routing"
- Chapter 5, "Network Security Basics"
- Chapter 6, "Intranets, Extranets, and Virtual Private Networks (VPNs)"
- Chapter 7, "Wireless LANs (WLANs)"
- Chapter 8, "IP Telephony and Multimedia Communications"

Professional Services: Graphic Design Firm

Objectives

Increase employee productivity, improve communications with business partners, and facilitate better customer service.

Company Profile

- 75 employees
- Regional customer base (serves one region of the country)
- Sales representatives frequently work one-on-one with customers
- $5 million in revenues

Challenges

- Ensure ease of collaboration with a wide range of constantly changing business partners: printers, advertising agencies, film production companies, and so on.
- Meet aggressive scheduling deadlines.

- Exchange large multimedia files at high speeds.
- Centralize customer intelligence and records that do away with separate customer files maintained by each salesperson, which are vulnerable to loss.

Original Technology Solution

- Courier and overnight delivery services to deliver layouts to and from clients and business partners
- Hardcopy files
- 10/100 wired Ethernet LAN infrastructure
- Dialup analog access by salespeople to the headquarters network

New Technology Solution

- **Upgraded Gigabit Ethernet (1000 Mbps) wired LAN infrastructure with intelligent switches**—To ensure high performance of real-time multimedia communications.
- **DSL-enabled WAN access routers**—For teleworker remote access to the company's new intranet and partner and client access to the company's new extranet websites.
- **Virtual private network (VPN) for secure information exchange across the WAN**—For employee intranet access and for information exchange with external partners.
- **Network security**—Firewall appliance with intrusion detection, worm protection, and third-party anti-virus software.
- **IP-based videoconferencing and a wireless LAN (Wi-Fi WLAN)**—Under consideration to enable web-based meetings between creative staff, contractors, and clients (videoconferencing), and for mobility enablement at the office and in public-access hot spots (WLAN).

Impact of the New Solution

- **Courier costs**—Reduced by 75 percent.

- **Project turnaround times**—An average of five days was shaved off project delivery.

- **Client satisfaction improved**—Customers can now log in to the company extranet to track project status, view deliverables, and comment on works in progress. This makes it possible to interact with designers in real time to collaborate on project development and ensure fewer revisions to complete a final deliverable.

  - **Customer issues are resolved faster**—Some through client self-service via the company website and some through the ability to exchange information in real-time with customer service staff and/or design staff.

- **Mobile workers can now connect to the company network remotely, securely, and at high speeds**—To remain productive while traveling or working at home.

- **More deals are closed more quickly and with fewer sales calls**—Salespeople can demonstrate the firm's capabilities to potential clients remotely via the web using virtual private network (VPN) and broadband access. This reduces the cost of sales.

- **Sales efficiency improved**—Salespeople now can better monitor customer orders, customer payment history, new product information, review consolidated sales figures, identify bid opportunities from pipeline data, and gather competitor intelligence more efficiently online.

Relevant Chapters

- Chapter 3, "Local Area, Metropolitan Area, and Wide Area Networks"
- Chapter 4, "Network Foundation Technologies—Switching and Routing"
- Chapter 5, "Network Security Basics"
- Chapter 6, "Intranets, Extranets, and Virtual Private Networks (VPNs)"
- Chapter 7, "Wireless LANs (WLANs)"

Professional Services: Law Firm

Objectives

Improve professional staff productivity and agility, increase billable hours, and provide more responsive services to clients.

Company Profile

- 100-year-old business
- 73 attorneys, 19 of whom are partners
- Practices include intellectual property and technology, trusts and estates, criminal law, labor and employment, and international business.
- Member of a collaborative network of more than 12,000 attorneys in 150 jurisdictions.

Challenges

- Reduce long-distance charges between offices.
- Create a single, integrated network that is resilient and that supports more features and third-party software applications.
- Reduce administration costs that are skyrocketing with the traditional PBX phone system and from maintaining a separate data communications network.
- Provide access to more than just voice mail to attorneys who are at court, at client offices, or working at home.
- Integrate call accounting software with the phone system for more efficient billing records and to eliminate manual entry of records (and the accompanying performance hits to the firm's computer systems at month's end).

Original Technology Solution

- Aging proprietary PBX
- Wired 10/100 Ethernet LAN infrastructure
- Fax machines
- Hardcopy files
- Analog dialup for remote access

New Technology Solution

- **Upgraded to a Gigabit Ethernet (1000 Mbps) wired LAN infrastructure with intelligent switches and routers**—to support high performance with new applications.

- **IP telephony system with unified messaging and third-party XML applications**—productivity improvement (including internal and external directories, time allocation and call tracking with interfaces to leading call accounting programs, court and deposition schedules, news alerts to regulations, law library index, and so on).

  - IP softphones were installed on attorneys' and paralegals' laptops and handheld computers for mobile access to IPT system services and the systems' follow-me phone number capability.

- **Secure wireless LAN (Wi-Fi WLAN) infrastructure in the office**—including wireless-enabled laptops and handheld computers for ease of information access while mobile at the office, at home, in coffee shops (and other public hot spots) and at court.

- **IP videoconferencing**—is used for selected depositions, virtual court appearances (in some pro bono cases), and consultations with attorneys in the collaboration network.

- **Intranet with web services**—including a self-service web-based audio and videoconference call setup process that automatically sends e-mail alerts to call participants to notify them of call logistics.

- **VPN**—for secure remote access.

- **Network security**—by means of firewalls, with intrusion detection system (IDS) capabilities.

- **Storage Area Network (SAN)**—system to reduce paperwork and improve attorney access to and archiving of client records is under consideration.

Impact of the New Solution

- **Productivity improved by 35 minutes per day per lawyer and paralegal**—A result of implementing wireless mobility and IPT messaging, database applications, and call accounting capabilities.

- **Lower operational costs**—The legacy PBX system was removed and associated lease costs were eliminated. Long-distance toll charges were virtually eliminated, and phone system moves, adds, and changes (MACs) were completed in about half the time. MACs were handled by an administrative assistant instead of the trained, dedicated network administrator who was needed for the PBX system.

- **Attorney responsiveness to clients improved**—A result of the IPT and IP videoconferencing systems' flexibility, mobility, and availability.

Relevant Chapters

- Chapter 3, "Local Area, Metropolitan Area, and Wide Area Networks"
- Chapter 4, "Network Foundation Technologies—Switching and Routing"
- Chapter 5, "Network Security Basics"
- Chapter 6, "Intranets, Extranets, and Virtual Private Networks (VPNs)"
- Chapter 7, "Wireless LANs (WLANs)"
- Chapter 8, "IP Telephony and Multimedia Communications"
- Chapter 9, "Emerging Technologies" (the "Storage Networking" section)

Professional Services: Real-Estate Business

Objectives

Centralize operations, eliminate or reduce paperwork, maintain up-to-date property and client information, reduce administrative overhead, and move quickly for first-mover advantage and responsiveness to customers.

Company Profile

- Regional real-estate and mortgage brokerage firm
- 180 employees
- 9 offices throughout the region
- $31 million in annual revenues

Challenges

- Reduce paperwork in a paper-intensive business, including the thousands of listings active at any time.
- Give remote agents access to the same types of information, at the same time, as agents at the office (versus the usual 48-hour or more wait for information to be distributed).
- Allow agents to share office space *hoteling* effectively during staggered work schedules.
- Ensure secure and confidential access to and exchange of information.

Original Technology Solution

- Hub-based, wired LAN
- ISDN remote access by agents
- E-mail system
- Hard-copy faxes and printouts

New Technology Solution

- **Upgraded Fast Ethernet (100 Mbps) wired LAN infrastructure using intelligent switches and routers**—Gigabit Ethernet-ready for future scalability to support increasing multimedia applications.
- **Company intranet and web portal**—With links to partners such as mortgage bankers, architects, general contractors, staging companies and interior designers, inspectors, plumbers, electricians, painters, landscapers, and so on.

- **High-speed, dedicated T1 WAN service**—For shared Internet access by employees.

- **Digital subscriber line (DSL)**—For remote access by agents.

- **Virtual private network (VPN)**—For secure remote access by agents.

- **Firewall with intrusion detection capabilities**—For security.

- **Virtual LAN (VLAN)**—To maintain separate network system operations for residential and commercial properties groups.

- **Third-party software applications**—To connect to the multiple listing service (MLS).

- **Wireless LAN (Wi-Fi WLAN) and Frame Relay WAN**—To connect remote offices. Currently in a trial phase. The goal is to eliminate $40,000 a year in dedicated line charges at each office.

- **IP telephony system**—Also currently under consideration for adoption to ensure more responsive and effective communications between agents and clients.

  - Services being evaluated for use with the IPT system include unified messaging, follow-me IP phone number capability, interactive voice response (IVR), coupled with voice recognition for tailored information delivery, softphone software for laptops and handheld computers, and third-party XML applications for real-estate businesses.

  - The firm has constructed a business case that anticipates reducing customer service and telephony-related costs by 12 to 15 percent in the first 9 months with the IPT system in place.

Impact of the New Solution

- **Immediacy of listings**—New property listings are entered into a central database that is immediately available to all agents via the firm's intranet.

- **More dual-agency**—After 48 hours, listings are posted to the firm's public website. By controlling the holding period, the odds of the firm serving as seller and buyer of listed properties have improved.

  - The firm now represents the buyer and seller in at least 50 percent of all transactions (15 percent higher than the industry average).

- **More efficient selling**—Online access to the MLS has streamlined selling across agencies.

- **Improved sales growth** —Within 6 months of the new network's deployment, the firm closed escrow on 26 percent more properties than in the previous year (compared to an overall 12 percent across all other agencies in the same region).

- **Lower administrative costs**—With more than 85 percent of internal processes transitioned to the online system, administrative overhead and paperwork were reduced, and costs were cut.

- **Fewer manual processes**—Office managers no longer have to calculate agent commissions or track agent performance manually. This has resulted in a savings of 50 hours per month that was previously needed to generate the same information.

- **Remote access cost savings**—DSL remote access resulted in $700 per month in cost savings versus the old ISDN system.

Relevant Chapters

- Chapter 3, "Local Area, Metropolitan Area, and Wide Area Networks"
- Chapter 4, "Network Foundation Technologies—Switching and Routing"
- Chapter 5, "Network Security Basics"
- Chapter 6, "Intranets, Extranets, and Virtual Private Networks (VPNs)"
- Chapter 7, "Wireless LANs (WLANs)"
- Chapter 8, "IP Telephony and Multimedia Communications"

Retail Shop

Objectives

Boost the local shop's profile nationally, increase sales and profits, and grow the business. Offer e-commerce capabilities typical of a larger company while adhering to a small-business budget.

Company Profile

- 15 employees
- Local, single-shop operation
- $2 million annual sales revenues

Challenges

- Increase the customer base for the business without the cost of opening new stores and purchasing more inventory.
- Grow beyond the local geographic area.
- Make online shoppers feel as though they are actually in the store interacting with sales clerks.
- Raise sales levels that have hit a plateau.

Original Technology Solution

- 56 Kbps analog dialup Internet access
- Traditional point-of-sale (PoS) cash registers
- Hardcopy advertising in the yellow pages and other local publications

New Technology Solution

- **DSL service and access router**—For faster Internet access by employees.
  - Currently weighing cost-benefit trade-offs of an upgrade to a T1 (1.544 Mbps) dedicated leased line.
- **Fast Ethernet wired LAN (100 Mbps) infrastructure**—Includes intelligent switches and routers for high-speed information exchange among employees and for shared web and Internet access.
- **E-commerce web storefront application and database interfaces**— Hosted by multiple hosting sites to ensure resilience and higher-bandwidth access by customers.

- **Webcams to display and demonstrate products in real-time via streaming video**—Controlled by sales clerks while interacting with online customers or controlled by customers via browser when they are "just looking around" the store.

- **IP video surveillance installed in the store for the shop's physical security**—Transmits images to the website for real-time monitoring and offsite archived video records that are less vulnerable than closed-circuit TV videocassettes.

- **PoS credit card verification system**—PCs now act as point of sale cash registers and terminals for faster verification as well as customer intelligence database integration.

- **Firewall appliance and third-party anti-virus software**—Helps block external hacker attacks.

- **Online e-procurement system with vendors**—Expedites orders, aggregates orders for more substantial discounts, and controls the price paid per product.

- **Web-based e-learning tutorials on new products**—Used by staff and customers.

- **Online newsletter used for e-Learning**—Customers opt in to be on the e-mail list.

Impact of the New Solution

- **National presence**—The store's market expanded from citywide to nationwide.

- **Expanded customer base**—News and product information are now sent to more than 1700 customers nationwide. This is up from the prior off-the-street local walk-in business only.

- **Higher sales**—Revenues increased 40 percent in one year to $2 million.

- **Higher proportion of online sales**—E-sales represented 70 percent of the company's revenues within 1.5 years of the new solution's implementation. The web storefront is open 24/7 and is accessible from anywhere.

- **Higher profits**—Sales volumes increased significantly and allowed shop owners to negotiate higher discounts with suppliers. This boosted profits an additional 16 percent.

- **Lower inventory costs**—Inventory carrying costs have been reduced with the online procurement system for just-in-time (JIT) restocking capabilities coupled with drop-shipping directly to customers from vendor warehouses.

- **Improved customer intelligence**—90 percent of marketing is now conducted via the web. The most visited links on the website are tracked, as are customers' web purchases.

  - Increased use of the Internet for customer intelligence has influenced inventory choices and contributed to a higher overall ROI for the business.

  - Online discount coupons and promotions are targeted to shoppers based on their previous purchases.

- **Business growth**—As a result of its growth, the shop is currently in the process of physically doubling its space and adding more employees.

Relevant Chapters

- Chapter 3, "Local Area, Metropolitan Area, and Wide Area Networks"
- Chapter 4, "Network Foundation Technologies—Switching and Routing"
- Chapter 5, "Network Security Basics"
- Chapter 6, "Intranets, Extranets, and Virtual Private Networks (VPNs)"

Travel and Hospitality: Hotel

Objectives

Deliver a superior, personalized guest experience through world-class service and leading technologies. Give mobile business professionals convenient access to their corporate network resources while on the road. Boost customer loyalty.

Company Profile

- Boutique hotel with locations in five cities
- 235 guest rooms per hotel
- Fitness center, spa, executive suites
- Meeting spaces and a boardroom are available for guest use.

Challenges

- Create innovative, differentiated, and competitive branding to attract guests, especially business travelers.
- Personalize guest experiences.
- Expand to 20 additional properties.
- Introduce secure, high-speed WAN and Internet connectivity services for guests and internal operations.
- Provide easily accessible information about amenities (dining, events, attractions, shopping, and so on) in the area surrounding the hotel.
- Train employees to ensure that they and guests know how to use the hotel's network technologies.
- Provide various touchpoints for guests to interact with the hotel brand.

Original Technology Solution

- ISDN WAN Internet access for the hotel
- Analog dialup remote access to the Internet and company intranets from guest rooms
- Conventional proprietary PBX system
- Wired 10/100 Ethernet LAN (for internal staff use only)

New Technology Solution

- **Upgraded Gigabit Ethernet (1000 Mbps) wired LAN infrastructure**—Includes intelligent switches and routers to support the WLAN, IP telephony, and other hotel-related software applications the hotel is installing.

- **Virtual LAN (VLAN)**—Separates the internal hotel network system from the guest-accessible network.

- **Wireless LAN (Wi-Fi WLAN) hotspot access in public spaces**—Lobby, coffee shop, informal restaurant, meeting facilities.
  - Staff are currently evaluating extending the WLAN for guest room access.
  - Wireless curbside guest check-in by hotel attendants is available.

- **Dedicated T1 WAN and Internet access service and associated access routers**—To increase Internet access response times for staff and guests, to guarantee network availability/reliability, and to improve network security.

- **High-speed Ethernet Internet access in guest rooms**—Installed using existing telephone wiring.

- **Network printing**—Available from guest rooms (with output printed to the 24/7 business center or to the front desk for delivery to guests).

- **IP telephony system**—IP phones and unified messaging systems are in guest rooms and back offices.
  - Third-party lodging XML productivity applications are utilized (room service, engineering, housekeeping, sales and conference services, and so on).

- **Web-based hotel information portal and eConcierge self-service for guests**—Allows guests to book meeting rooms, make dining and spa reservations, purchase tickets for events and entertainment, and so on.

- **In-room IP-based video-on-demand (VoD) entertainment system**—For pay-per-view, digitally downloadable movies with VCR functionality and interactive games (an amenity for guests and a profit generator for the hotel).

- **Extranet**—For information sharing and e-procurement processes with hotel suppliers.

- **Virtual private network (VPN)**—Has intrusion detection and protection for secure networking.

- **Firewall**—Provides intrusion protection and detection features and third-party anti-virus software.

- **e-marketing**—An opt-in direct-marketing newsletter is sent to previous guests, highlighting new services, area amenities, discounts and promotions, and so on.

Impact of the New Solution

- **Improved efficiencies**—Employee communications are streamlined.

- **Customer-focused personalization**—Improved business amenities and personalized guest services resulted in traveling business professionals spending more time in their rooms and ordering more hotel services (such as room service, laundry, massages, and so on).

Relevant Chapters

- Chapter 3, "Local Area, Metropolitan Area, and Wide Area Networks"
- Chapter 4, "Network Foundation Technologies—Switching and Routing"
- Chapter 5, "Network Security Basics"
- Chapter 6, "Intranets, Extranets, and Virtual Private Networks (VPNs)"
- Chapter 7, "Wireless LANs (WLANs)"
- Chapter 8, "IP Telephony and Multimedia Communications"

Wholesale Business

Objectives

Diversify and grow the business, harvest more value from every customer contact, increase revenues, and improve employee productivity.

Company Profile

- Fish and seafood wholesaler, a supplier to 100 restaurants, retail operations, and nursing homes
- Purchases mostly from distributors and processors
- 20-year-old family business
- 17 business locations nationwide

Challenges

- Provide personalized customer care.
- Offer a high-quality, consistent, extensive product supply.
- Deliver fast, reliable service at competitive prices.
- Collect timely customer intelligence to provide to sales and customer-service staff.

Original Technology Solution

- Hub-connected PCs for back-office operations
- PC-based inventory database
- Hardcopy files
- Refrigerated warehouse and trucks
- Conventional proprietary PBX

New Technology Solution

- **Fast Ethernet (100 Mbps) wired LAN infrastructure with intelligent switches (to replace the hubs) and routers**—For a more scalable, reliable, and high-speed infrastructure to handle advanced network technologies, services, and business applications.

- **iSCSI storage area network (SAN)**—To handle the increasing volume of information that must be retained for regulatory purposes.

- **IP telephony with unified messaging and an IP contact center**—A customer care solution that links customer service representatives with online customer account information.

- **Fax over IP (FoIP)**—To convert paper-based fax systems to electronic systems that integrate with web services and the unified messaging system.

- **Company intranet**—For news, online training tools, directories, product specifications, customer information, supplier information, competitor information, marketing programs, and so on.

  - Web-based customer care solution with account information, order histories, credit records, order status, product information, and so on to improve customer responsiveness.

- **Extranet**—With personalized websites for larger customers.

- **vitual private network (VPN)**—For secure remote access by salespeople.

- **Firewall**—With intrusion detection, worm protection, and third-party anti-virus software.

Impact of the New Solution

- **New cross-selling opportunities**—Because of more readily available customer information.

- **Increased customer satisfaction**—Customers can now quickly check the customer extranet for their order status.

- **Orders placed via the web generate automatic confirmation notices to customers**—This has improved customers' perceptions of how their orders are handled.

- **Broadened sales channel**—Customers can now connect with the wholesaler via the phone or web or in person. The company expanded the possible touchpoints between itself and its customers.

- **More targeted marketing campaigns**—Web-enabled customer intelligence-gathering improved marketing effectiveness and lowered costs.

  - Salespeople are better prepared for sales calls. Real-time order and account history data are accessed directly from the company intranet.

  - Direct marketing promotions are now based on previous purchase orders, and web-only discount promotions are frequently generated (stimulating customers to visit the company website regularly).

- **Reduced costs and improved employee productivity**—The online customer care system has helped sales and service employees handle more cases in less time.

  - The company is currently exploring financing options that will let it remove its old PBX system, pay off its remaining lease charges, and expand its IPT system's services capabilities.

Relevant Chapters

- Chapter 3, "Local Area, Metropolitan Area, and Wide Area Networks"
- Chapter 4, "Network Foundation Technologies—Switching and Routing"
- Chapter 5, "Network Security Basics"
- Chapter 6, "Intranets, Extranets, and Virtual Private Networks (VPNs)"
- Chapter 8, "IP Telephony and Multimedia Communications"
- Chapter 9, "Emerging Technologies" (the "Storage Networking" section)

Summary

Small-medium companies in different industry sectors use computer networking technologies in their own unique ways, but generalizations can be made. Size doesn't matter, but the desire to grow the business and streamline processes does. Those who strive to increase customer satisfaction, boost employee productivity and convenience, enable business agility, and realize total cost of ownership savings are the ones who tend to view IT as a business value creator and networking systems as vital for enabling successful operations.

The most prevalent network investments being made by small-medium businesses are to upgrade their LAN and WAN infrastructures to ensure that they provide a robust-enough foundation to support other advanced technologies and applications. Comprehensive network security systems are one of the highest-priority investments, as are advanced technologies such as wireless LANs and IP telephony systems. There appears to be an accelerating trend toward the adoption and evaluation of storage area networking systems across various vertical markets as well. For the most part, business leaders report that their network systems are paying back measurable returns on investment, beginning within 6 months and going up to 18 months from the time of systems installation. Often, this depends on the type of technology, the amount of training that goes into ensuring it is used properly, and the sensitivity of the business to the state of the economy.

APPENDIX A

ABBREVIATION LIST

3DES	Triple Data Encryption Standard
AAA	authentication, authorization, and accounting
ACL	access control list
ADSL	Asymmetric Digital Subscriber Line
AES	Advanced Encryption Standard
ANSI	American National Standards Institute
AP	access point
ARPA	Advanced Research Projects Agency
ASP	application service provider
ATM	Asynchronous Transfer Mode
ATM	automated teller machine (in banking)
AUP	acceptable use policy
BDM	business decision-maker
BRI	Basic Rate Interface
BSS	Basic Service Set
CAPEX	capital expenditure
Cat 5	Category 5 cabling
CDN	content delivery network
Centrex	central office exchange service
CEO	chief executive officer
CFO	chief financial officer
CIO	chief information officer
CIR	committed information rate
CLEC	competitive local exchange carrier
CoS	Class of Service
CPE	customer premises equipment
CRM	customer relationship management
CSMA/CD	carrier sense multiple access/with collision detection
CSP	content service provider
CTO	chief technology officer
DAS	direct attached storage
DDoS	distributed denial of service
DES	Data Encryption Standard
DHCP	Dynamic Host Configuration Protocol
DiffServ	differentiated service
DNS	Domain Name Services

DoS	denial of service
DSL	Digital Subscriber Line
DSSS	Direct Sequence Spread Spectrum
DTMF	Dial-Tone Multi-Frequency
E1	2.048 Mbps Leased Line (in Europe)
E3	34 Mbps Leased Line (in Europe)
EAP	Extensible Authentication Protocol
EMI	electromagnetic interference
EMS	Ethernet Multipoint Service
ERP	enterprise resource planning
ERS	Ethernet Relay Service
ESS	Extended Service Set
EWS	Ethernet Wire Service
FA	foreign agent
FCC	Federal Communications Commission
FCIP	Fibre Channel over IP
FDDI	Fiber Distributed Data Interface
FHSS	Frequency Hopping Spread Spectrum
FoIP	Fax over IP
FR	Frame Relay
FTP	File Transfer Protocol
FTTC	Fiber to the curb
g.SHDSL	Symmetric High Bit Rate Digital Subscriber Line (ITU designation)
GB	gigabytes
GbE	Gigabit Ethernet
Gbps	gigabits per second
GHz	gigahertz
GigE	Gigabit Ethernet
GRE	Generic Route Encapsulation
GUI	graphical user interface
HA	home agent
HIPAA	Health Insurance Portability and Accountability Act
HQ	headquarters
HR	human resources

HTML	Hypertext Markup Language
HTTP	Hypertext Transfer Protocol
IDS	intrusion detection system
IEEE	Institute for Electrical and Electronic Engineers
IETF	Internet Engineering Task Force
ILEC	incumbent local exchange carrier
IM	instant messaging
IP	Internet Protocol
IPng	IP Next Generation
IPP	Internet Printing Protocol
IPS	intrusion protection system
IPSec	Internet Protcol Security
IPT	Internet Protocol Telephony
IPv4	Internet Protocol version 4
IPv6	Internet Protocol version 6
IPX	Internetwork Packet Exchange
IR	Infrared
IS	Information System
iSCSI	Internet SCSI
ISDN	Integrated Services Digital Network
ISM	industrial, scientific, and medical
ISO	International Standards Organization
ISP	Internet service provider
IT	information technology
ITU	International Telecommunications Union
IV	initialization vector
IXC	interexchange carrier
JBOD	Just a Bunch of Disks
JIT	just in time
kbps	kilobits per second
KTS	Key Telephone System
L2	Layer 2
L2TP	Layer 2 Tunneling Protocol
L3	Layer 3
LAN	local area network

LCD	liquid crystal display
LDAP	Lightweight Directory Access Protocol
LED	light emitting diode
MAC	Media Access Control (in context of addressing)
MACs	moves, adds, and changes
MAN	metropolitan area network
MB	megabytes
Mbps	megabits per second
MEF	Metro Ethernet Forum
MIC	message integrity check
MLS	multiple listing service (in real-estate)
MPLS	Multiprotocol Label Switching
MSO	multiple service operator
MSP	managed service provider
MTTP	mean time to provision
MTTR	mean time to repair
NAS	network attached storage
NAT	Network Address Translation
NIC	network interface card
OFDM	Orthogonal Frequency Division Multiplexing
OPEX	operating expenditure
OS	operating system
OSI	Open Systems Interconnection
PACS	Picture Archiving and Communications System (in healthcare)
PAN	personal area network
PBX	private branch exchange
PC	personal computer
PCMCIA	Personal Computer Memory Card International Association
PDA	personal digital assistant (handheld computer)
PDIO	planning, design, implementation, and operation/optimization
PKI	public key infrastructure
PMS	property management system (in lodging and hospitality)

POP	point of presence
POTS	plain old telephone service
PPP	Point-to-Point Protocol
PPTP	Point-to-Point Tunneling Protocol
PRI	Primary Rate Interface
PSK	preshared key
PSTN	public switched telephone network
PVC	permanent virtual circuits
QoS	quality of service
RADIUS	Remote Access Dial-In User Service
RC4	Ron's Code 4 or Rivest Cipher 4
RF	radio frequency
RFC	request for comment
RFP	request for proposal
RIP	Routing Information Protocol
ROI	return on investment
RTP	Real-time Transfer Protocol
SAN	storage-area network
SCM	Supply Chain Management
SCSI	Small Computer Systems Interface
SDSL	Symmetric Digital Subscriber Line
SFA	salesforce automation
SIP	Session Initiation Protocol
SLA	service-level agreement
SMDS	Switched Multimegabit Data Service
SMTP	Simple Mail Transfer Protocol
SNMP	Simple Network Management Protocol
SONET	Synchronous Optical Network
SP	service provider
SPI	Security Parameters Index
SSID	Service Set Identifier
SSL	Secure Sockets Layer
T1	1.544 Mbps leased line
T3	45 Mbps leased line
TB	terabytes

TCO	total cost of ownership
TCP/IP	Transmission Control Protocol/Internet Protocol
TDM	technical decision-maker
TDM	time division multiplexing
TFTP	Trivial File Transfer Protocol
TG	Task Group (an IEEE working group)
TKIP	Temporal Key Integrity Protocol
TLS	transparent LAN service
TV	television
UDP	User Datagram Protocol
UPS	uninterruptible power supply
URL	uniform resource locator
USA PATRIOT	United and Strengthening America by Providing Appropriate Tools Required to Intercept and Obstruct Terrorism Act
UTP	unshielded twisted pair
VAR	value-added reseller
VDSL	Very High Bit Rate Digital Subscriber Line
VLAN	virtual LAN
VoD	video on demand
VoIP	voice over IP
VOMIT	voice over misconfigured Internet telephones
VoWLAN	voice over wireless LAN
VPN	virtual private network
WAN	wide area network
WebDAV	Web-based Distributed Authoring and Versioning
WECA	Wireless Ethernet Compatibility Alliance
WEP	Wired Equivalent Privacy
Wi-Fi	wireless fidelity
WLAN	wireless LAN
WPA	Wi-Fi Protected Access
W-VLAN	wireless virtual LAN
XML	Extensible Markup Language

APPENDIX B

REFERENCES

A.T. Kearney. *The Road to Business Value*. Chicago, IL: A.T. Kearney, 2003.

Aber, Robyn. "A Comprehensive Approach to Security," *Business Communications Review*, May 2003.

Aber, Robyn. "Connecting Remote Users," *Entrepreneur.com*, 14 October 2002.

Aber, Robyn. "Equip Your Business for Broadband," *Entrepreneur.com*, 19 August, 2002.

Aber, Robyn. "Internet, Intranets, Extranets: What's What," *Entrepreneur.com*, 13 January, 2003.

Aber, Robyn. "Selecting the Right Wireless LAN Protocol," *Entrepreneur.com*, 1 December, 2002.

Aber, Robyn. "Switching to an IP Telephony System," *Entrepreneur.com*, 10 February, 2003.

Aber, Robyn. "Using Technology to Achieve Your Goals," *Entrepreneur.com*, 12 May, 2003.

Aber, Robyn. "Why You Need Broadband," *Entrepreneur.com*, 15 July, 2002.

Alexander, Bruce and Snow, Stephen. "Preparing for Wireless LANs," *Packet*, Second Quarter 2002.

Anderson, R. and Outlaw, J. "SMB Leaders to Focus on Collaboration and Interoperability," *GartnerGroup Research Note*, 4 December, 2002.

Anthes, Gary H. "Internet Protocol Version 6," *ComputerWorld*, 20 January, 2003.

Apicella, Mario. "Pure IP SANs Are Here," *ComputerWorld*, 15 July, 2003.

Barry, David. "Metro Ethernet: More for Less," *Packet*, First Quarter 2003.

Barua, Anitesh, et al. "Measures for E-Business Value Assessment," *IT Pro*, January/February 2001.

Boggs, Raymond L. and Valovic, Tom. "Hosted VoIP Service Providers: Innovation in the SMB Market," *IDC Report*, May 2003.

Brick, Frank. "Are You Ready to Outsource Your Storage?" *NewsFactor Network*, 30 July 2003.

Brown, Scott, et al. *Net Impact 2003: Driving Networked Business Productivity.* San Francisco: The Momentum Research Group, 2003.

Browning, Jim, et al. "Midsize Business: Infrastructure Investment Plans and Priorities, North America 2002: User Wants and Needs," *GartnerGroup Report*, 7 October, 2002.

Captain, Timothy. "Wireless Networking Now," *Ultimate Mobility*, Winter 2002.

Chan, Helen, et al. "SMB Communication Services Survey 2002: Overview," *The Yankee Group Report*, August 2002.

Chen, Man. "Ethernet Moves Into the Metro," *SPIE's OEMagazine*, August 2002.

Clare, Gary. "The New Three Cs of E-Business," *Line56: E-Business Outlook 2003*, 10 September, 2002.

Clark, Tom. "Get the Most From Your Storage Investment," *.netmagazine*, May 2003.

Druce, Cedric. "Enterprise View of Ethernet WAN Service," Cisco White Paper, 2003.

Dulaney, K. "Wireless LAN Vendor Magic Quadrant Update," *GartnerGroup Research Note*, 15 July, 2002.

Farrell, Diana, et al. "Getting IT Spending Right This Time," *The McKinsey Quarterly*, Number 2, 2003.

Flynn, Christin. "An Examination of the Productivity Impact of IP Telephony," *The Yankee Group – Communications Network Infrastructure*, February 2003.

Gabler, J. and Adams, J. "The Business Value of IT: Justification Hierarchy," *GartnerGroup Research Note*, 7 August, 2000.

Gallo, Michael A. and Hancock, William M. *Networking Explained,* Second Edition. Boston: Digital Press, 2002.

Gandhi, Prashant and Klessig, Bob. "Metro Ethernet WAN Services and Architectures," *IEC Annual Review of Communications*, June 2003.

Gownder, JP. "Carriers Tout Managed VPN Services for SMBs," *The Yankee Group Report*, April 2003.

Green, Heather, et al. "Wi-Fi Means Business," *BusinessWeek*, 28 April 2003.

Halpern, Jason. "SAFE: IP Telephony Security in Depth," Cisco White Paper, 20 July 2002.

Hayward, S. "2003 Key Issues: E-Workplace Systems and Technology," *GartnerGroup Report*, 3 February, 2003.

Hayward, S., et al. "Hype Cycle for E-Workplace Technologies, 2003," *GartnerGroup Report*, 6 June, 2003.

Herman, Jim. "New Ways to Create Business Value," *Business Communications Review*, August 2002.

Huston, Geoff. "Opinion: The Mythology of IP Version 6," *IP Journal*, June 2003.

Johnson, Johna Till. "Managed Services: What's Next?" *NetworkWorld*, 4 August, 2003.

Kavanagh, Kelly and Couture, Adam. "Security Services Outsourcing, 2003: User Wants and Needs," *GartnerGroup Report*, 11 April, 2003.

Klein, Daniel. "Hosted IP Telephony Will Help Providers Reduce Churn and Build Customer Loyalty," *The Yankee Group – Communications Network Infrastructure*, March 2003.

Krammer, Mika and Clark, William. "Wireless LANs Add Value to SMB Applications," *GartnerGroup Strategy, Trends, Tactics*, 20 February, 2003.

Krammer, Mika. "IS Departments Must Grow with SMBs," *GartnerGroup Strategy, Trends, Tactics*, January 31, 2003.

Krammer, Mika. "SMB IT Services Buying Trends and Preferences, 2003," *GartnerGroup Market Analysis*, 16 September, 2003.

Landoline, Ken. "Intrusion Detection and Prevention: Status and Strategies," Robert Frances Group, 26 February, 2003.

Landoline, Ken. "Mitigating Voice Telephony Security and Fraud Risks," Robert Frances Group, 2003.

Lauricella, Mike. "Broadband: Delivering Value and Increasing Business Productivity," *The Yankee Group Report*, July 2002.

Luzine, Chris. "Some Industries Receptive to Managed 802.11 Services," *ISP Planet*, 3 July, 2003.

McGrath, George and Schneider, Anthony. "Measuring Intranet Return on Investment," *Complete Intranet Resource*, June/July 1997.

"Metro Ethernet Services," Metro Ethernet Forum White Paper, 2003.

Metz, Chris. "Moving Toward an IPv6 Future," *IEEE Internet Computing*, May/June 2003.

Mohapatra, Prasant, et al. " QoS in Mobile Ad Hoc Networks," *IEEE Wireless Communications*, June 2003.

Molta, Dave. "Wireless Hotspots Heat Up," *Network Computing*, 15 May, 2003.

Mullaney, Timothy J., et al. *"The E-Biz Surprise,"* *Business Week,* 12 May 2003.

Parry, Ed. "Be the CFO of IT," *CIO*, 18 September, 2003.

Phifer, Lisa. "Understanding Wireless LAN Vulnerabilities," *Business Communications Review*, September 2002.

Pisello, Tom. "IT Value Chain Management for CIOs and IT Executives," Alinean White Paper, May 2003.

Pisello, Tom. "Spenders and Savers," *Network World*, 4 August, 2003.

Poe, Jonathan. "Operations Excellence: CIOs Tone Up," *CIO*, 15 October, 2003.

Raider, Rhonda. "Office on the Go," *Packet*, Second Quarter 2003.

Rasco, Jose A. "Engine of Growth: Productivity," *Optimize*, September 2002.

Rolfe, Andy. "802.11g Wireless LAN Products Will Appeal Most to Small Businesses," *GartnerGroup FirstTake*, 16 June, 2003.

Roshan, Pejman. "A Comprehensive Review of 802.11 Wireless LAN Security," Cisco White Paper, August 2002.

Scardina, L., et al. "The Business Services Value Chain," *GartnerGroup Research Note*, 25 September, 2003.

Schwartz, Jeffrey. "Top CIO Technology Spending Plans," *VAR Business*, 9 December, 2002.

Shapland, Ed. "Making Wireless LANs Work for You," *Business Communications Review*, August 2002.

Stehman, John. "What's Missing in WLAN Network Management?," *RFG IT Agenda*, 13 March, 2003.

Stehman, John. "What's Really New in Wireless Local Area Network (WLAN) Security?" Robert Frances Group, 28 February, 2003.

Strechay, Rob. "Beyond the SAN Islands," *Business Communications Review*, August 2003.

Stuart, Anne and Maxwell, Jill Hecht. "Inside Story," *Inc.*, April 2002.

Tanner, Dan. "iSCSI SANS Are Approaching Market Readiness," *AberdeenGroup Perspective*, 18 October, 2002.

Tulloch, Mitch and Tulloch, Ingrid. *Encyclopedia of Networking*, Second Edition. Redmond, Washington: Microsoft Press, 2002.

Wexler, Joanie. "Telephony Winds Shift Towards IP," *Packet*, First Quarter 2002.

Wexler, Joanie. "Wireless Takes Off," *Packet*, Third Quarter 2003.

Whiting, Rick. "Extranets Go the Extra Mile," *InformationWeek.com*, 20 May, 2002.

Woodcock, James and Unden, Lisa. *SMB User Demand for Public Network Data Services: Focus Report*. GartnerGroup, 16 December 2002.

Index

Numerics

A

X-Z

DISCUSS
NETWORKING PRODUCTS AND TECHNOLOGIES WITH CISCO EXPERTS AND NETWORKING PROFESSIONALS WORLDWIDE

VISIT NETWORKING PROFESSIONALS
A CISCO ONLINE COMMUNITY
WWW.CISCO.COM/GO/DISCUSS

CISCO SYSTEMS

THIS IS THE POWER OF THE NETWORK. now.

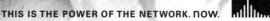